B-26
MARAUDER
at War

B-26 MARAUDER at War

Roger A. Freeman

with Trevor J. Allen
and
Bernard Mallon

LONDON
IAN ALLAN LTD

First published 1978

ISBN 0 7110 0823 X

Design by Robert C Wilcockson

© Roger A. Freeman 1978

Published by Ian Allan Ltd, Shepperton, Surrey,
and printed in the United Kingdom by
Ian Allan Printing Ltd

Contents

Introduction

Of all the warplanes of World War II none underwent such an extreme change of fortunes as the Martin B-26 Marauder. Appearing in 1940 it was the most advanced bomber in its class – unfortunately too advanced for all but the best pilots and mechanics. A spate of fatal accidents led to rumours of the Marauder being unsafe to fly, a cry taken up by the Press and politicians and exaggerated out of all proportion. Additionally, the way it was first committed to operations led to a series of catastrophes, culminating in the annihilation of one mission force. Yet, following a change of tactics, the Marauder produced the lowest loss per sortie ratio of any Allied bomber and its crews achieved a remarkably high standard of bombing accuracy. But further development of the design was stifled through the antipathy of some US Government and military authorities, influenced by its early troubles. Even so, Marauders were the most numerous of Allied medium bomber types during the final year of hostilities in Europe. Paradoxically, their final fate was to help restore the very industry they were used to destroy.

With such a complex and extraordinary story to relate, the feelings and views of those who flew and serviced this remarkable bomber have been sought, while the narrative touches on technical matters – some hitherto unpublished – detailed specifications and technical data are not included to avoid repetition from standard reference works.

The great Jimmy Doolittle summed up the Marauder from a pilot's viewpoint as an unforgiving aircraft. Others will agree it did not suffer fools gladly, yet understood and respected had much to commend it. The type demanded considerable attention from mechanics, but even those who worked on other aircraft exhibit a first loyalty to the Marauder. For the spectator it was a fascinating aircraft and a contender for the title of best looking bomber of its day. As a contributor to this book remarks, the Marauder 'came and went fast and hard' on runways – the writer can vouch that it was an untiring thrill to watch those (then) incredibly speedy landings.

Dedham, England   Roger A. Freeman
December 1977

Acknowledgements

As with my previous books in this series the object has been to explore new areas of the subject, discover the answers to questions previously unanswered and correct faulty accounts, so that the reader can be presented with a fair study and even the avid enthusiast will find fresh facts. To achieve this I have been dependent on the generosity of many people who provided material and information.

Two leading authorities on the Marauder, Bernard Mallon and Trevor Allen, have made a study of this aeroplane for the best part of 20 years and have amassed a collection of material which they made available. Bernard Mallon's interest is in the technical aspects of the aircraft, its design and development; Trevor Allen had been absorbed in the Marauder's combat use, the record of individual aircraft and the operating units. Bernard contributed the first chapter as well as providing a number of research papers and always responding to my endless questions. Trevor made available his extensive photographic collection and many documents while constantly commenting and advising on progress. I am indebted to both gentlemen for their unfailing support.

The major proportion of those assisting were B-26 Marauder veterans: Karl Berry, Roy Burlingame, William Erwin, Jack Havener, George Howard, W. S. G. Maydwell, Tom Jenkinson, Denny McFarland and Robert Mims are sincerely thanked for the personal stories they contributed and Ashley Woolridge for furnishing considerable material. Also William B. Monroe for allowing me to adapt the Edgar Pewitt account of Bridge Busting. Other veterans whose help is no less appreciated are: Franklin Allen, General Samuel Anderson, Harry Bacon, David Backhouse, George Beaman, William Billig, A'Delbert Bowen, Lyman Cokely, William Craddock, Joe Cunningham, Frank Davitt, Richard Denison, James Doolittle, George Doran, Robert Dorsey, Lloyd Ellefson, John Ewbank, Mickey Flynn, Roy Frankenfield, Don Fry, George Fugate, Jack Garvey, Walt Gaylor, Don Gibson, Ira Guldin, William Hega, Richard Harrell, Walter Harper, Howard Jackson, Oscar Johnson, John W. Johnston, David M. Jones, Floyd Kaler, Walter Krell, Louis Kundrath, Robert Layhe, Richard LeBoy, Gerard Lecaroz, Adolph Leirer, Millard Lewis, William Locke, Roger Lovelace, Earl Luikens, James Macia, Walter Maiersperger, John McBride, Richard Meldon, William Miller, George Moscovis, Harold Oyster, Robert Paulsen, Ed Payne, Claude Penfold, Joseph Perrin, Jack Roberts, Larry Reineke, Alva Ryan, Elmer Schrantz, Roland Scott, James Seidell, Jay Sherlock, Allen Sherman, James Shipler, Verne Shrewsbury, Richard H. Smith, Jack Skipper, Cass Sochocki, John Sorrelle, John Statts, Herbert Thatcher, Richard Travis, Tommy Tucker, Ben West, Sam Wherry, Sam Wilkinson, Stan Wisniewski, and David Wurst. Roger Ward, a Martin veteran, was also most helpful. My thanks to all.

Special mention must be made of Harold and Esther Oyster without whom the story of the MTO Marauders could not have been presented so accurately. Esther came to the author's rescue on a number of occasions and ranks as his most helpful correspondent. The photographic expertise of Ian MacTaggart has results on many pages of this book and his research in US archives on my behalf earns sincere gratitude. Alan and Peter Crouchman, spending hours locating material on the 387th Group (their special interest) are also deserving of special thanks.

Many other friends and associates have helped in various ways: Malcolm Bates, Dana Bell, Steve Birdsall, Robert Cavanagh, Serge Blandin, Peter Doll, Lt Col Arie de Jong, John Foreman, Garry Fry, Werner Girbig, George Pennick, Kenn Rust, B. A. Stait, Carl Vincent and Gerrit Zwanenburg. Their kindness is greatly appreciated.

Helpful to Bernard Mallon were Michael DePhillipo, Chris Kilgus and William 'Ken' Ebel, Peyton Magruder, Cliff Leisy, Vernon Outman, Cliff Roberts, Willem Van Zelm and O. E. 'Pat' Tibbs of the Martin Company.

The Imperial War Museum and Public Records Office in London provided facilities for research, as did the National Archives in Washington and Maxwell AFB, Alabama. The Air Force Museum at Dayton were, as always, particularly helpful. The USAF Photographic Depository in Arlington gave their services most willingly. Finally, special thanks to Major General John Huston and his Office of Air Force History for arranging research at the above US establishments.

On the production side I wish to thank Ken Ranson and John W. Archer for proof reading, Norman Ottaway for drawings, Jean Freeman for a prodigious amount of typing, and my good friend Bruce Robertson for much advice and editorial assistance.

Design and Development

Right: Undeniably a streamlined beauty. The first B-26 exhibits a very high standard of finish as it is prepared for ground handling tests./*Martin*

Below right: First take-off. Ken Ebel flies 40-1361 from the Martin Field runway on 25 November 1940. Co-pilot was Bob Fenimore and flight-engineer Al Melewski./*Martin*

Glenn L. Martin was an American aviation pioneer who built aeroplanes in the infancy of that business and often met his payrolls and paid for material with prize money won at flying exhibitions. His Baltimore, Maryland-based company produced the first indigenous bomber design for the US Army when, towards the end of World War I, that service half-heartedly conceded some expediency in the ability to scatter high explosive from the air. But thereafter selling aeroplanes became difficult as the government turned back to an isolationist policy. There were too, other manufacturers in the field, some of whom once worked for Martin, vying for the few orders going. Nevertheless, Martin managed to hold his own by producing the first all-metal monoplane bomber and exporting aircraft, notably to China.

As the thirties progressed, it became apparent that war could involve the United States. With Congress voting considerable funds for defence, the Army Air Corps urgently sought the large numbers of modern aircraft it had been denied. The initiation of new designs was by the War Department issuing to industry a 'Circular Proposal', specifying mission and performance and inviting tenders; in effect, a competition with manufacturers bidding for the contract. In March 1939 Circular Proposal 39-640 called for a medium bomber with truly impressive potential and all-round superiority over European designs. Of prime importance were requirements for high top speed (300mph) and heavy bomb load. This Proposal was prompted by news from Europe about the capabilities of the Luftwaffe; particularly the detailed news and views brought back by Charles Lindbergh.

Speed was particularly stressed. William E. 'Ken' Ebel, Martin's chief engineer and test pilot, received this message personally when he flew to Wright Field (from whence the Proposal emanated) for a conference with Air Corps officers, after the firm's preliminary design group failed to agree.

When Martin submitted their bid on 5 July 1939, it consisted of 15 separate proposals for their Model 179, varying mainly in engine type and supercharger arrangements. Five of the alternatives proposed the Wright R-2600, six the Pratt and Whitney R-2800, and four the Wright R-3350, still in the early development stages. Significantly, four proposals were based on a wing of 650sq ft, which was finally adopted later after much contention. Martin's proposed No 6 won the competition; this called for the P&W R-2800 with 1-stage, 2-speed supercharger, and a 600sq ft wing. Following the fashion of the time this design had a twin tail configuration. Wind tunnel work showed that a single tail was as effective as any other configuration. A notable aspect was a profuse (for the era) use of electrical and hydraulic systems; a sophistication that complicated its maintenance. Among the innovations was the use of high strength clear plastic mouldings, large alloy castings and emergency air brakes; it was also the first US Army Air Corps bomber featuring a power-operated gun turret and self-sealing fuel tanks.

The R-2800 engine and Curtiss electrically-operated propeller was first introduced into service on the Martin 179. The structure was ideal for a warplane. The Model 179 featured a strong monocoque type fuselage, Alclad covered. Spot-welding was used wherever possible on internal work, and the skin was flush riveted. A unique 'baking' process was used to remove wrinkles from exterior surfaces after they were incorporated. Such care

8

improved the finish and thereby the speed of the aircraft, while the stressed skin contributed to the inherent strength of the structure.

The Air Corps wanted 385 medium bombers, and Martin had won the competition with 140 more points out of 1,000 than their nearest rival, North American. But the firm was heavily committed producing Maryland and Baltimore bombers for the British and French. Glenn Martin would not further commit his company for such a large additional number of units. The orders, therefore, were split between Martin (201 B-26s, the Army designation for the Martin 179 Marauder) and North American, (184 B-25 Mitchells).

Martin was a rather typical aircraft company of that era, with the exception of Glenn himself, who was an old-time flyer but no engineer and extremely autocratic and arbitrary. Assisting him were several men who had helped to train the Chinese to fly modern planes against the Japanese in the early 1930s. On the engineering side besides Ken Ebel, were G. T. Willey, Executive Engineer and later Vice President and General Manager of the Nebraska plant, Ivan Driggs, Clifford Roberts, Peyton Magruder, Clifford Leisy, Larry Wade, Carl Hartgard, Fred Jewett, James Murray, George Trimble; all of whom participated in the Marauder design.

The deteriorating international situation was evident in the War Department's decision to order the B-26 'off the drawing board', unlike the B-25 which was a development of an existing prototype. In more leisurely pre-war days, a single hand-built aircraft would have undergone exhaustive testing before being committed to production. The B-26 was the first of many to go into production without a prototype. Ironically, shortly before taking up the first B-26 on its maiden flight, on 25 November 1940, Ken Ebel made a quick (and secret) trip to the North American plant in California to gain experience with the tricycle-wheeled Mitchell – a type he had not flown before – North American having completed their first B-25 shortly before Martin completed their first B-26. The first flight of the Martin and subsequent testing flights were relatively uneventful; although once Ken Ebel had a nose-wheel strut failure. The Marauders began to flow into Army Air Corps units in early 1941, and almost immediately were grounded because of a rash of nose-wheel strut failures. This trouble was traced to improper heat-treatment of a component by a sub-contractor, although a contributory cause was the nose-heaviness that resulted when the dorsal turret, guns, ammunition, and other equipment was not installed, as was often the case in delivery flights. Other teething problems developing were with the hydraulics through insufficient-

ly trained maintenance personnel and cracking exhaust sleeves (a Pratt & Whitney fault). More serious was loss of propeller control which could, and did, cause accidents, especially on take-off; this was quickly rectified when battery trolleys were provided. When systems were operated on the ground, routine during training, the internal batteries became depleted and were liable to failure at more critical times. The first of the really modern aeroplanes, the B-26 had many electrically-operated systems.

Further trouble began when those handling the aircraft were no longer professional pilots, but men and youths who a few months previous had been civilians. As experienced pilots said, you had to stay on top of the ship. The B-26 was 'as manoeuvrable as a P-38 fighter', but it required the same attention.

By mid-1941, Martin were designing larger main and tailplane surfaces to improve landing and take-off characteristics, this wing to be placed on the first 'automotive' model, the B-26C to be built at the new Martin-Nebraska plant, and introduced on the Baltimore line with the B-26B-10 model. The Air Corps term 'automotive' referred to consortium production of Marauder parts by Chrysler, Hudson and Goodyear, for assembly by Martin-Nebraska. The government

Below: Part of the initial order, B-26s under construction early in 1941. The fuselage was composed of three sections, the forward units clearly show the step-down in the bombardiers' compartment over the nose wheel housing. Upper turret wells were fashioned on all early Marauders and a removable plate installed until power turrets became available late in 1941./*Martin*

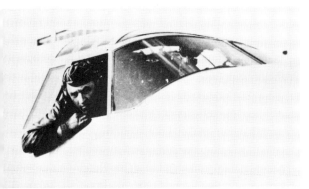

was attempting to duplicate the Boeing/Vega-Douglas group B-17 production, but the B-26 consortium did not enjoy similar success, due primarily to the inexperience of the new partners in aircraft production, and compounded by management difficulties at Martin-Nebraska at the outset.

The first 'big wing' B-26s were delivered by the Nebraska plant in October 1942, followed a few months later by the Baltimore plant. The larger wing, coupled with the inevitable increase of armour and ammunition, actually increased the wing loading instead of decreasing it, thereby aggravating the shortcomings of the original model.

The National Advisory Committee for Aeronautics (NACA, forerunner of NASA, the space agency) having earlier done wind tunnel work on the design was in a position in 1941 to make suggestions for improving landing performance. Among these were wing slots, drooped ailerons, closing landing gear doors during flight; also it was calculated that full-span flaps would lower the landing speed to 82mph. Air tests were performed by Sam Shannon of Martin in a programme to determine which of the suggested modifications might improve take-off performance. In these tests, a standard B-26 would be flown in the morning, then the change would be made (drooped ailerons, different flaps, etc) one at a time, and the aircraft would be flown again in the afternoon. In this way it was hoped to obtain comparative results from each modification.

Surprisingly, Shannon discovered that the modifications made little difference but, from flying experience gained during the tests, he was able to take-off after around a 1,800ft run with the aircraft in its original configuration – an improvement of some 800-1,000ft. Handling experience was a factor that was to crop up again; lessons having to be learned anew each time. At about the time of Shannon's tests, some Air Force instructors were sent to Martin for further training. O. E. 'Pat' Tibbs, chief test pilot in charge of the project

Top left: The diminutive Ken Ebel was an outstanding aeronautical engineer. He was 41 when he made the first flight in the B-26./*Martin*

Centre left above: After undergoing prototype testing, the first B-26, 40-1361, served at Laughlin Field, Del Rio, Texas as a transition trainer. It led a charmed life, finally being retired through old age and scrapped in February 1945. Appropriately nicknamed *Gran' Pappy* the aircraft was tended by (l. to r.) S/Sgt Herbert J. Jolly, S/Sgt William W. Green, and Cpl Joe Denowicz./*USAF*

Centre left below: Although this B-26 (40-1542, serving with the B-26 Pilot Transition School at Laughlin Field in 1942) exhibits a sizeable amount of wing, the bulbous fuselage and large noisy engines tended to be the dominating features and led to the Marauder being called the 'bumble bee' – amongst other less kind sobriquets./*USAF*

Below: The 28th B-26B became the prototype for the heavily armed ground attack Marauder with standardised .50-cal armament. The Bell power turret was first installed on this aircraft, as were improved flank positions and a battery of five fixed forward-firing .50s. Subsequently this 12-gun configuration was introduced on the B-26B-10-MA and B-26C-5-MO – as well as provision for four 20mm cannon on the lower fuselage!/*Martin*

with some 5,000 flying hours to his credit, was shocked to discover that these men had only flown around a *total* of 350 hours. This, in an aircraft that 'behaved more like a pursuit than a bomber' but was far heavier and less forgiving, was asking for trouble.

As early as September 1942, the Chief of the Air Service Command at Wright Field reported that the B-26 had gradually tended to grow out of its class, pointing out that 2,100lb had been added with no increase in power, so that its cruising speed had dropped from 250 to 200mph at the same settings, and the positive angle of attack necessary for flight had increased, adding to the decrease in cruising speed. His recommendations included the removal of various equipment and some ammunition, repositioning the waist gunner and eliminating the ventral tunnel gun (both outcomes of combat experience and field modifications in the Pacific), sealing the rear bomb-bay, changing the front bomb-bay doors to the roll-up type of the B-24 and moving the dorsal turret to the radio compartment also as in the B-24. Some of the weight reducing measures were taken; the rear bomb-bay was sealed off and was never used in the ETO. The design of the front bomb-bay doors was not changed, possibly due to the large engineering effort that would have been required.

The removal of the dorsal turret to the radio compartment was accomplished on only one aircraft, 41-34680, *Gypsy Rose* (named after a famous strip-tease dancer, Gypsy Rose Lee), the XB-26E. The XB-26E designation is not official – the 'E' suffix was used originally to signify an aircraft modified in to the configuration which, when accepted, became the F model. The lightening of this aeroplane by 'stripping' non-essential items suggested its name.

Another Air Service Command recommendation had more success. This approached the weight-reducing problem by eliminating the co-pilot's position. Fifty-seven aircraft were allocated to this project, with 49 additionally available as spares. Apparently only 64 aircraft were actually stripped in this manner, since vociferous complaints from the theatre of operations led to all the single pilot aircraft being reconverted to standard 2-pilot configuration or scrapped. The weight saved by the removal of the co-pilot's seat, controls, etc, was about 3,000lb, but in the words of the commander of the only formation to use such aircraft, 'weight was never a handicap in this aircraft if properly flown'. In USAAF combat operations the B-26 was considered a handful for one pilot – the recommendation for co-pilot removal had come from a home-based group. In an 'attack' aircraft, the single pilot idea may have been successful. Along these lines, one Marauder was modified by Martin with two guns in each wing, four attached to the fuselage, and a 37mm cannon in the 'solid' nose. O. E. 'Pat' Tibbs, testing this modification remembers with awe the 'cloud burst' churned up in the ocean as he dived at a range target with all guns firing. The packet guns on the fuselage, originally a field conversion in Australia, were the only fixed guns retained.

The last major attempt to improve the performance of the B-26 was the most successful, but it started out poorly. Some Air Force procurement personnel believed that Martin was trying to 'pull a fast one' for some undefined purpose, and that this would result in slower production and increased costs. What Martin did was to increase the incidence of the wing on one B-26 by 3½ degrees, and have comparative tests flown. Difficulty arose because the modification having been made by a verbal agreement between Glenn Martin himself and General Arnold was without the knowledge or approval of the appropriate Air Force department. After it had been established that General Arnold had condoned the modifications, and Martin had given assurances that the 'twisted wing' change would not interfere with production, the incidence change was allowed – but none of the other proposed changes were permitted. (A plan to achieve the increased incidence into existing planes by canting the fuselage was projected, but discarded when the magnitude of the job was appreciated).

A pilot with a year's combat experience in Marauders who flew the modified ship in September of 1943, unbeknown to the procurement authorities at the time, was very enthusiastic about the handling and visibility, stating that some of the crews lost overseas

Below: The last Marauder model, the B-26G, was characterised by the upward tilt of the engines, very evident in this photograph, taken late in 1944, of a Replacement Training Unit (RTU) aircraft from MacDill. /USAAF

The antipathy of Material Air Command towards the Marauder is said to have played a major part in many from later production being delivered as target-towers under the designation AT-23 and, later, TB-26./*USAAF*

Below: B-26G, 44-68254, the last of the 5,266 Marauders built, making its test flight on 18 April 1945 from Martin Field, Middle River, where the first B-26 had taken to the air four years and nearly five months before./*Martin*

and in the States would have been alive if earlier B-26s had had these features. The repositioned wing aircraft also featured sharp-nosed ailerons and a short-chord rudder.

The wing modification was to be the Marauder's last major change and was incorporated in, and was the main reason for, the F and G models. While the top speed was slightly lowered, visibility and handling improved. A further proposal, that never passed the planning stage, was an escort fighter version. But it soon became apparent that such a modification of the B-26 would fail for the same reasons that the B-40, an escort version of Fortress, failed.

When the B-26F model deliveries ensued from the Baltimore factory in early 1944, many of the older models, still in the States, were converted for advanced training as AT-23s.

The decision had been made by mid-1943 to close down production of the Marauder at the Nebraska plant, so that another source for the B-29 Superfortress could be established. The final B-26C rolled out of the Omaha plant in April 1944, the last of over 1,200 Marauders built there under the firm hand of Joseph T. Hartson, sent out by Glenn Martin to straighten out a confused production situation early in the plant's history. Under Hartson, production picked up, to be interrupted only briefly at one time by a Marauder on a test flight crashing through the roof on to the production line.

The last Baltimore-built Marauder, appropriately called *Tail End Charlie,* but also named '30', the newspaperman's shorthand signifying end of the story, left the factory in April 1945. At the controls for its test flight before being accepted by the Air Force was Pat Tibbs, but sitting in the right-hand seat was Ken Ebel, who flew the plane for 30 minutes of the 2½ hour production test flight. Thus Ken Ebel, who had failed advanced training in the Air Corps for 'flying deficiencies' (being too conservative) achieved a rare distinction in flying the first and the last of a famous combat aircraft type.

Bernard Mallon

Debut Down Under

In the vernacular of the time, the Martin B-26 was a 'hot ship'. It was the fastest bomber flying – as speedy as a fighter and even handled like one – yet able to carry the same bomb load as a Flying Fortress. So went the word around the bases of the then rapidly expanding US Army Air Corps; hearsay fuelled by the pronouncements of senior officers in the know and publicity from the Glenn Martin company. During the early weeks of 1941 the B-26 was prime topic of conversation among men of the 22nd Bombardment Group at Langley Field, Virginia, for they had been chosen to receive the first from the production line. Langley, 120 miles from the Martin plant at Baltimore, was well situated for Company engineers to keep an eye on developments, particularly as the B-26 was going straight into service without any test programme. Technical problems were considered inevitable for such an advanced design, featuring several innovations, new engines and the first fully-feathering propellers.

The first production B-26 stayed with Martin, the next two went to the 22nd at Langley late in February. Compared with the Douglas B-18 that the Group currently flew, the B-26 was sensational. For the pilots making the transition during the following weeks, it was more a large jump than a step. The B-18 was an adaption of the successful, docile, commercial Douglas DC-2 airliner that became airborne in 460 yards and drifted in on a landing approach at 90mph. In contrast the B-26 demanded full attention. With a wing loading 2½ times greater than the B-18's it needed over twice the take-off run and, because it came close to stalling at 120mph, had to be brought in for landing at 140mph. In short, the old and the new bomber were so different that a new piloting technique was necessary.

Experienced pilots soon mastered the Martin, but for the average Army pilot of the day it was a tricky transition, particularly on landing – and it was here that trouble first started. Touch-down with a tricycle undercarriage required a slight nose-up attitude, so that the main wheels made ground contact

Below: Nose wheel strut failure was an all too frequent occurrence with the early B-26s received by 22nd BG. This one, 40-1362, the second built, cracked up landing at Patterson Field. Only the first seven B-26s were delivered in natural metal finish./*AFM*

Above: Martin power turrets were not available from production until late 1941. One of the first aircraft so fitted was 40-1503 seen flying over Ohio on 28 November 1941. The last 22nd BG B-26 received its turret the day before the move west./*USAF*

Left: Modified side hatch with additional observation windows. Note ladder attached for entry through camera hatch. This 33rd BS aircraft was wrecked when a tyre blew while landing at Laliki, New Guinea, 2 November 1942. In the background Lt Aleron Larson's *Sourpuss*, 40-1532, is being refuelled./*Australian Official*

Top: Preparing to taxi out at 7-mile 'drome, Port Moresby, during the summer of 1942, 40-1437, assigned to Group Headquarters, was one of two B-26s destroyed in a Jap bombing raid on this airstrip, 17 August 1942./*USAAF*

Above: Major Walter Greer (on tail) inspects the newly devised unit flash applied to his aircraft by M/Sgt Fuller (right). Greer was the pilot of this B-26 in June 1942 when Lt Commander (later President) Lyndon B. Johnson flew a combat mission as an observer./*W. Miller*

first, and then the nosewheel could be eased onto the runway. But in many landings pilots could not prevent the front of the aircraft slamming down with the resulting collapse of the front leg, causing the B-26 to career along with its nose ploughing the ground. The incidence of this type of failure rose and in April the thirty-odd B-26s flying were grounded. There had been no turrets or tail guns fitted on the aircraft delivered from the factory, servicing tools totalling some 900lb being placed in the rear fuselage in lieu of the missing armament. At Langley, or Patterson Field, Ohio, where an accelerated service test was being run on the B-26, the service

tools were innocently removed, upsetting the centre of gravity. Ballast of 900lb rectified the balance until turrets were fitted late in the year. Additionally nosewheel castings were strengthened and the Martins took to the air again – only to be grounded once more in July because engine exhaust sleeves kept cracking. The hydraulic systems which actuated undercarriage, bomb doors and some controls on the aircraft were complicated in design and required frequent bleeding. These too brought failures that once again restricted flying in following months while modifications were carried out to prevent leaks. Trouble was also experienced with the propeller pitch mechanism. Failure here, such as on take-off, could prove disastrous. Further propeller difficulties led to a major investigation that found the principal source of the trouble was a lack of knowledge on the correct operation and maintenance of the 12-volt electrical system. In part this was occasioned by the absence of detailed service manuals. Not until the end of the summer did the 22nd receive its full complement of B-26s and a start made to equip the second group, the 38th at Jackson Field, Mississippi and a third, the 42nd, at Boise, Idaho.

That the Marauder had more than its share of teething troubles was only to be expected considering the circumstances of its initiation. As one Martin engineer reflected: 'When the bugs are worked out of a single prototype not many people get to hear. When you have 200 prototypes – for that's what happened with the B-26 – everyone's gonna hear!' The situation was aggravated by the performance computations given in the pilot's manual not being calculated on its actual service weight.

On 7 December 1941 when the United

States was precipitated into war, there was an imminent possibility that the Japanese might raid the eastern seaboard. The 22nd Bomb Group, one of the few medium bomber organisations considered fully trained, was moved next day to Muroc, California, to fly coastal patrols. The transfer was not completed without tragedy. After a refuelling stop the aircraft piloted by the CO, Lt Col Mark Lewis, suffered an engine failure and crashed, killing the crew, causing the Group's first fatalities. The accident was attributed, in part, to the fitting of a wrong type of sparking plug.

The sojourn in California was brief, for the serious threat to Australia from the rapid Japanese advances in the South-west Pacific area (SWPA), demanded immediate action to reinforce the meagre forces in that continent. The 22nd was ordered across the Pacific in February 1942. The ground personnel sailed to Australia, and the aircrews to Hawaii where 56 Marauders arrived by sea, not having sufficient range to fly the 2,000-odd miles to these islands from California. While the aircraft were being re-assembled, a stage-by-stage flight over the Pacific was planned as Mission X. Calculations showed that if a B-26 grossing 32,000lb flew at 1,000ft and cruised at 185mph, fuel consumption would run at 116 US gallons per hour. This gave an endurance of 10 hours and a 1,400 mile range, sufficient to reach each island refuelling point. Future practice would be to furnish units going to combat zones with new aircraft before leaving the United States, but in this case there was neither sufficient time nor enough new B-26As available and the bombers that the 22nd received in Hawaii were mostly those it had flown at Langley. One was the first Marauder received by the Group, the third production model, which successfully negotiated the 4,500 miles to Brisbane under the care of Lt Louis Ford and crew.

Of 51 B-26s setting out from Hawaii, 48 arrived in Australia, including two delayed by major repairs. Two were lost in ditchings near Palmyra Island on the first leg from Hawaii. A weather front was travelling swiftly over Palmyra when the Marauders arrived and they were asked to stand-off until the storm had passed. The delay left many aircraft low on fuel and by the time the last two were called in to land they had exhausted their reserves and were forced to ditch, with fatal results for all but two of the fourteen occupants. The Marauders had been in the air 9 2/3 hours. The third B-26 lost apparently flew into the sea while trying to penetrate heavy rain off New Caledonia; only wreckage was found. Another B-26 was badly damaged on landing in Australia; it overran an airfield

near Brisbane and crashed into a house, causing no hurt to its crew but some distress to a surprised housewife.

Not only was the 22nd the first B-26 group sent into a combat theatre, but also the first complete air group of men and aircraft to reach Australia from the USA. Upon arrival the organisation found itself having to contend with shortages of equipment. Several co-pilots were transferred to depleted US bomber units driven from Java: in their place a number of RAAF pilots were received who had to be trained in the intricacies of flying the Marauder. The general disruption was probably a factor in a spate of flying accidents that occurred during this period.

After the flight echelon was reunited with the ground party, the Group moved to the Townsville area of Northern Queensland to prepare for combat. The first tactical problem of its employment was range. The enemy, ensconced in the East Indies to the west, and in the great part of New Guinea, was extending his empire into the island chains to the north-east of Australia, menacing the whole northern part of the continent. The immediate threat was through New Guinea and the Solomon Islands.

Bombing installations and shipping at Rabaul in New Britain, where the enemy had established a base, offered an immediate means of disrupting Japanese preparations for continuing their invasions. Unfortunately few B-17 or B-24 long-range bombers were on hand and the immediate solution was to employ the newly-arrived Marauders, by reducing bomb load, adding extra fuel and staging through airstrips around Port Moresby in New Guinea where the Allies still maintained a foothold. The round trip from Townsville in Northern Australia to Rabaul involved 2,600 miles and imposed a great strain on both crews and aircraft. The first mission, by nine B-26s, was flown on 5 April 1942. Marauder 40-1442, sustaining damage to an engine had to be ditched on the return flight; one man was killed, the rest rescued.

Sixteen times during April and May 1942 the 22nd set out for Rabaul with 2,000lb bomb loads, and 1,212 gallons of fuel including 250 in a rear bomb-bay tank. The 600 mile flight to Moresby was usually timed so that the bombers arrived late in the day and were at less risk of being caught in a Japanese air raid. Refuelled during the night, the Marauders would leave next day, usually at dawn, flying 50 miles along the New Guinea coast through the Kavisi Pass in the Owen Stanley mountains and then over water 500 miles to Rabaul. Bombing was carried out from 8,000 to 10,000ft and during the 16 missions six vessels were claimed sunk in the harbour. Destruction was also wrought on

storage buildings and at two nearby airfields. The cost was four B-26s shot down and a few crash-landings back in New Guinea. The Marauder appeared to stand up to battle damage quite well and gave a good account of itself in combat with enemy fighters, a factor that greatly contributed to crew morale. But while the Marauder was undoubtedly 'a tough cookie', Japanese anti-aircraft weapons were not fully effective. Their .27 machine gun bullets would not penetrate armour and did not have the velocity to cause major structural damage unless fire was concentrated. The 20mm cannon used in the Zero fighters had weak velocity and impact fusing in the early months of the war, which resulted in the shells often bursting without penetration, causing only skin damage. Japanese ammunition, although well made, was vul-

nerable to the effects of the high humidity of the tropics, causing a high incidence of dud rounds. Japanese interceptors also had difficulty in closing with Marauders because of the bomber's high speed when lightly loaded, an advantage American crews quickly learned to exploit. After delivering their bomb loads escape could be made by diving down to sea level at 350mph and racing for home at full throttle, a tactic the Zeros were hard put to follow. At low level too, the top turret and tail gunners were well situated to fire on any attacker who could not then approach the unprotected undersides of the Marauder. In any case, if an enemy fighter did not destroy or disable a B-26 with a first pass, it was unlikely to overhaul the bomber in a chase.

By late May 1942 the job of bombing Rabaul was taken over by night flying heavy

bombers. Not only were the Japanese improving their defences against daylight attacks, but the range at which the B-26s were operating was proving too great with little reserves of fuel for the emergencies that often arose. While the B-26s had not suffered prohibitive losses, battle damaged aircraft had little chance of returning safely over such distances. The frequent weather fronts, the peaks of the Owen Stanley mountains rising to 13,000ft and cloud flying made an inhospitable environment for twin-engined bombers operating near the limit of their endurance. While continuing to stage through Port Moresby airstrips, the 22nd Group was diverted to attacks on enemy airfields and other installations in New Guinea that were more within the Marauders' range. While tactics were varied, it was usual to plan an escape route over the sea, diving away after bombing at high speed.

Shortly before the 22nd made its last trip to Rabaul, Lt Col Dwight Devine took command of the Group. His introduction to combat in the B-26 was during a mission to the enemy's air base at Lae on 9 June. A fighter attack caused extensive damage to the Group's first and oldest B-26 in which Devine was acting as co-pilot. With hydraulics out of action this Marauder had to be brought in on her keel at Moresby, but although extensively damaged this prized veteran was flown again.

At forward bases, where technical facilities were primitive or lacking, the B-26 was considered a maintenance headache. The complicated hydraulic and electrical systems needed constant vigilance. Devine's engineering officers instituted a system of inspection that far exceeded anything required by maintenance manuals. Problems were identified and

action taken to prevent or minimise their recurrence. The result of this policy became evident as 1942 wore on, for accidents attributable to malfunction – frequent during the first weeks in Australia – now became few and far between. Another problem that was acknowledged – and had been evinced in the USA – was that no two B-26s seemed to have the same flying characteristics. This was particularly so with directional control, where each rudder movement gave different responses. The degree of overbalance was so extreme in some aircraft that they would fly in a crabbed attitude, and continued to do so even when the rudder pedals had been returned to their original position! Where a pilot was familiar with the individual quirks of a particular machine he was in a far better position to maintain control in an emergency, so whenever possible pilot and co-pilot would fly the same Marauder.

To these actions can also be attributed a rapid decline in operational losses. Crew morale was good because of a belief that their bomber gave them a better chance of survival than either the B-25 Mitchell or the A-20 Havoc doing similar work in the theatre. Indeed, there was ample evidence that the Marauder could absorb heavy damage to the fuselage and fly on – one came back to Moresby with nine 20mm hits from cockpit to tail. Hits on the wing were more lethal, but this applied equally to the other American medium and light bombers.

All US units reaching Australia during the early months of hostilities were affected by the absence of spare parts and tools. Groups and their back-up servicing organisations had to improvise on the spot. Spares for the B-26s came from bombers that were too badly damaged for economical repair. The contin-

Right: Modified for special low-level operations, this B-26 has a large camera behind an aperture in the nose plexiglass, package guns for strafing, and a D/F antennae housing (aft of cockpit). /*J. Galagher*

Below: Viewed from the cockpit of a following 'Silver Fleet' B-26, *Little Audrey* unloads 250lb fragmentation bombs from both front and rear bomb-bays. The rear bay was only used for light loads./*J. Shipler*

gencies of combat also fostered a host of modifications. Little air-to-air gunnery training had been undertaken in the US and combat soon revealed that the top turret guns frequently jammed due to faltering power in the electric motor boosting ammunition feed. This was overcome by removing the motor altogether, for it was found that, providing the ammunition belts had no more than a 20in lift to the breach the gun would operate satisfactorily. The two .30 rifle calibre machine guns were found lacking in punch, and were gradually replaced with appropriated .50s. One was for use through the two low side hatches in the rear fuselage. There was a poor outlook from these hatches,

so they were enlarged and a scanning window added above each opening. To take a .50 machine gun in the nose, steel bands had to be added to support the weapon and prevent the plexiglass being shattered by recoil vibration. The manner of this installation varied, but all had restricted fields of fire and obstructed the bombardier. Their value was even dubious on those occasions when Zeros were able to make frontal passes, the provision of bullet-proof glass for the protection of pilots and the bombardier would have been more beneficial. Tail gunners had 25-round magazines on their weapons which often meant changing magazines while under attack. 'Requisitioning' 100-round magazines from B-17 Fortresses solved this. When later tactics sometimes involved low level bombing and strafing, a varying number of fixed forward firing .50s were installed in a few Marauders.

A major cause of abortive sorties was electric failure. The 12-volt system was found wanting and became a constant worry on missions, not least because the power turret became inoperative once a generator failed. One of the Marauder's advanced features was the electrical bomb release system which was bedevilled by the moisture-laded atmosphere of the SWPA, so that release solenoids on the stainless steel bomb shackles often failed to function. This was overcome by removing the shackles immediately after return from an operation and packing them in oily rags in old ammunition boxes until required again. A major problem was encountered with the hydraulically actuated bomb doors, which would come open or remain open if there was fluid loss in flight. Not only did the open doors cut down airspeed drastically, but they made belly-landings more dangerous. Eventually the bomb hoist was adapted for cranking a cable so that the doors could be wound up if hydraulics failed.

While Devine and the 22nd were establishing the worth of the B-26, Air Force commanders in the Pacific had come to a decision that in order to simplify logistics in the vast area of hostilities they would concentrate on only one medium bomber, the B-25. The Mitchell was thus selected for standardisation, having proved far more flexible in operations and with better range than the Marauder. There was no dispute over the B-26's superior speed and ability to take punishment, but its lower sortie rate than the Mitchell reflected its more complex maintenance problems. Although the B-26 could carry a larger bomb load, the long take-off run when heavily loaded made it unsuitable for operations from the compacted soil and mat runways hacked from the New Guinea jungle and Australian bush. War loads also had to be severely restricted to obtain long range.

So in the summer of 1942 Washington decreed that no more B-26s would go to the Pacific and that units already there would gradually convert to the B-25. The move was far from popular with the Marauder men, although when the time came not many would question the Mitchell's better handling qualities but few said they felt as safe.

There had been but a trickle of replacement Marauders for the 22nd, but there were never more than 60 B-26s in Australia at any one time. By the end of 1942 losses, accidents and general wear and tear had reduced this number to a point where the 22nd was hard put to launch a dozen bombers. Early in January 1943, when only 32 B-26s remained in the theatre, the Group was taken off operations. Their record looked imposing, for of 229 interceptions by enemy fighters in 52 missions, 94 had been claimed destroyed. Of 20 B-26s lost during the course of these missions, six were attributed to fighter action and the rest to ground fire while another five bombers had crash-landed at base.

The Marauders were flown to the air depot at Garbutt near Townsville for overhaul and other assignments while the 22nd prepared to reform as a Mitchell group. The demand for Mitchells by other units was such that one squadron of the 22nd volunteered to go back into action with the best of the surviving Marauders. Thus the 19th Bomb Squadron received some of the old B-26s plus a few B-26Bs gathered from elsewhere and returned to combat in July 1943. Everything had been done to improve the performance/load carrying ratio of the Marauders, even to the extent of removing camouflage paint. The shiny Marauders became known as the 'Silver Fleet' for at this date camouflage was still mandatory on other USAAF aircraft. The rest of the 22nd did not join the 19th Squadron until October and in January the whole group withdrew to convert to B-24 Liberators and meet the demands for long range bombing operations. The 'Silver Fleet' flew its last mission on 9 January 1944 and the following month the Marauders were struck off the SWPA inventory.

Old timers in the 22nd would wistfully recall the B-26 as 'the best damn airplane the air force ever had'; the uninitiated were less enthusiastic. The 5th Air Force (to which the Group was assigned) could not indulge such loyalties; the plain facts were that the B-25 did more work with less back-up effort than the B-26 and in the kind of air war being waged in the SWPA its sorties were more telling.

Nevertheless, the 22nd had acted as trouble shooter on the first B-26s, highlighting weaknesses and developing modifications that were embodied in improvements on the production lines. Operational experience and tactics also influenced training programmes for B-26 units going to Europe. Unfortunately, what had worked Down-Under didn't fit the bill for the Big League.

Above: Our Gal en route to target, astrodome in place – it could be swung up into position during flight. One of the original 22nd Group complement, that arrived in Australia in March 1942, this B-26 was scrapped two years later after completing some fifty combat missions./*A. Leirer*

It Never Bounced

Roy Burlingame

I joined the 19th Bomb Squadron at Langley Field in August 1941 and was assigned to the Operations Office. At the time all the B-26s assigned to the Group were parked in the grassy area behind the main hangars, almost all without props, and few people knew just what the hell kind of airplanes they were. Some had doubted that it really was an airplane. It certainly bore little resemblance to anything flying at that time – and I'm being only partly humorous, or humorous in part, when I say this. A few years later they wouldn't have seemed at all odd; a prop-less B-26 looked just like a post-war jet.

I soon learned that the new four-bladed props were in short supply and when a new '26 was delivered from the factory the props were then removed, hoisted on a dolly and towed back to the Baltimore plant behind a car. Neither was it long before I was made well aware that the B-26 was as revolutionary to fly as it looked. This was the time following the Air Corps acceptance tests on the type which took place at Patterson Field. One of the personal accounts I remember was that of an early co-pilot marvelling at the fact they did 305 indicated over the measured mile. Another man, Claude McCredie, a bombardier, clearly recalled the day they went through the fence at Patterson Field on one of those take-offs that just didn't take off. His biggest worry, he said, was the heavy auto traffic on the highway outside the field, 'way past the end of the runway. The movement across the Pacific and subsequent operations from Australia and New Guinea allowed me many opportunities to observe the missile-like comings and goings of this remarkable airplane.

A B-26 coming in for a landing was for me a never-boring experience. I stood by the runways many times and not once did I ever see one coming down that I wasn't positive the pilot had changed his mind and was trying to take-off again. Nothing in the Air Corps ever came in so fast and so goddam hard. I always marvelled at the strength of those main struts, for the B-26 never, never bounced. And, as happened more than once, the tyres sometimes exploded on impact and you just knew that was a *really* hard landing. Once I even survived a landing standing between the pilot and co-pilot's seats. For a moment I thought I was going out the windshield and would beat the aircraft to the end

of the strip. But the expression of controlled terror on the pilot's face told me I must never again accept a landing so casually. The usual position of every crewman on the approach was hunched tightly against a bulkhead with a parachute pack to ease the expected impact against your head. On every subsequent landing I was usually first in position. God couldn't have prised me loose.

One airplane landed at Iron Ridge, blew all the tyres and went streaking down the runway with scarcely a waver. At the end of the runway, 'way past the usual stopping point, the airplane was resting on what looked like factory-made magnesium skids, the lower part of the tyres and wheels having melted down to the hubs – and very smooth they were, too!

Many aircraft were lost on ground accidents that had little or nothing to do with combat. True, some of those with combat damage did engage in hairy landings and subsequent crack-ups. For instance, there was the fantastically good airmanship of Lt Barry Burnside, co-pilot on Captain Baumgartner's B-26, which was one example of how unpredictable the B-26 could be. They were over Rabaul when a Jap 20mm came in through the lower left of the cockpit, knocked a piece out of Baumgartner's heel, passed through the control pedestal, out the right side of the aircraft and through the prop governor of the starboard engine, all without exploding. Baumgartner was helped into the rear of the ship, and sometime later came back into the cockpit. There he found Burnside had been flying on trim tabs only, the 20mm having locked up the auto-pilot and the controls were frozen solid. The starboard engine was cause for concern as well, alternatively revving up and falling off in a capricious fashion.

Now there was a predicament for two experienced B-26 pilots. Just to stay aloft required no mean ability, but they began to prepare for a landing. There were other wounded aboard, so they intended to land instead of ordering everybody out. On their first approach – this is using trim tabs for control – they overshot and pouring on what passed for full power went round again. Baumgartner saw they were fully committed; too low for anyone to jump and with the engines about ready to poop out, no chance of another circuit if they didn't make it on the second. They came in again, trimming as best they could, but at the last moment it was obvious the nose was not going to come up. They both grabbed their control wheel and proved a theory: sufficient pull on even locked controls could overcome the auto-pilot. And everybody walked or hobbled away from that one.

The Marauder was a tremendous load carrier. One pilot claimed you could pour cement into it filling every space and it would still get off the ground. On one trip from Iron Ridge to Townsville for supplies they filled a B-26 with a tremendous quantity of fresh vegetables and a supply of long lengths of water piping. They had to make a very long take-off run before they could break loose, and then had a hard time gaining altitude. The pilot's big worry was that even if they hit moderately hard, he was bound to be skewered like an olive on one or more lengths of pipe.

Then there was the one on a transit flight that carried a quantity of bombs, full crew and ground crew with tools, and a Navy torpedo slung under the fuselage. You *never* landed with ordnance yet in this case two landings, two take-offs – and a blown tyre on the second landing. No crash; no one hurt. Another miracle. Lt Moy took a fully bomb loaded B-26 off at Garbutt at night, found he had trouble, made a wide circuit of the field and approached for a landing. I was standing close to the edge of the runway when it became apparent he was going to return. There was quite a crowd of us to see a bomb-laden B-26 land in the dark. By the time he got on the ground I had, seemingly without conscious effort, drifted through all the by-standers and was pressed against the brick wall of the administration building. Given a few more seconds I think I could have proceeded through that, sort of like osmosis. Man, I was some kind of scared, like everyone else. But no one was going to make any obvious break for safety.

A lot of this wasn't as foolhardy as it seems. The B-26s were in short supply all the time we were in Australia and New Guinea and pilots tried their damnedest to get troubled ships back on the ground in one piece. Some of these men were legends. There was Walt Krell who looked more like a movie star playing the serious bomber pilot than anyone I've seen in the movies. He was one of the earliest and most excellent B-26 pilots. Walt Maiersperger was another and got involved in several hairy incidents. At one time in New Guinea he flew a test on a repaired aircraft and the control pedestal burst into flame. He claims his engineer practically dismantled the damn thing, found the short, made repairs, and put it all back together in approximately the time it required

to change a fuse in much less complicated components. Those boys could move fast when they had to.

The number of times an airplane was repaired when it would normally have been junked was downright amazing. There was no other way if the Group was to keep in combat. The third B-26 off the line, 01363, was a wreck when the Group Commander brought it in for a wheels-up at Moresby. Jacked-up, temporarily repaired for flight back to Garbutt Field, the bent bomb-bay doors had to be hammered shut and then roped to lock them. This one was later scrapped.

Number 01532 *Sourpuss* was a heartbreaker. It had just been returned to Iron Ridge after overhaul. On the taxi strip progress was interrupted by a B-24 coming up. They carefully pushed the B-26 into a nearby revetment and set the brakes. While we were all watching the B-24 crew preparing to move past, we noted a sort of high, brief squeak from we knew not where. And when the B-24 was gone, the B-26 crew chief noticed his airplane had drifted back and quietly destroyed its tail section against one of the telephone poles which were intended to support camouflage nets overhead. Around this time 01403 had brake failure while taxying and piled up into an obstruction off the side of the strip. The tail section was taken and spliced onto *Sourpuss*.

One of the longest lived of the real early B-26s we had was the number eight ship off the line, 01368. It finally crashed in a cloud of dust on take-off 8 September 1943 at Dobodura, New Guinea. The co-pilot pulled the landing gear too soon, the airplane skidded along the runway and broke in half. No fire. The turret gunner scrambled out of the back and burst through the bomb bay door on his way up front to offer help. He damn near lost his mind when he found himself standing in the middle of the runway unable, for a moment, to find the rest of the airplane. After a few minor injuries were treated it made a hilarious story. Although the co-pilot didn't laugh!

Tin Fish

Following the Pearl Harbor debacle and other reverses in the Pacific, US naval and military forces in the area sought means of arresting the ascendancy of Japanese sea power. The air-launched torpedo was considered. In Europe, it was noted, both Britain and Germany had adopted twin-engined aircraft as far ranging torpedo bombers. The US Navy had no suitable aircraft so, despite sensitive relations between the two Services, they co-operated in a scheme to employ Army Air Corps bombers for torpedo work.

The Marauder was an obvious choice and Martin engineers and US Navy experts adapted it for the task. Its substantial keel former along the bottom of the fuselage provided a suitable mounting point for the cradle, and in flight the aircraft behaved reasonably well with the 2,000lb missile slung externally. Clearance between the ground and the torpedo, when the Marauder's nose was raised during take-off, was only some four inches so a tyre failure could be disastrous. Provision for torpedo carrying was subsequently built into all new B-26s; although the Navy looked upon this as the Army poaching on its preserves it had, as related, no aircraft of similar performance to adapt.

In December 1942 a four-plane detachment of 22nd Group B-26s under Lt Franklin S. Allen underwent a crash course on torpedoes at the North Island US Navy base, San Diego. Racks and release equipment for carrying and launching torpedoes were made available in Hawaii for B-26s en route to the SWPA. The 22nd Group was hurried through and received most torpedo kits in Australia. The following B-26 force was the first to be fully equipped to use the weapon.

The grounding orders and modifications necessary on early B-26s delayed equipment of a second group, the 38th, until the autumn of 1941. As a result crews were still only partly trained when this group and the 22nd were ordered to Australia and Java in January 1942. Nevertheless all personnel except aircrews and chief mechanics sailed that month, leaving the flight echelon to continue training. The 22nd's aircraft had been shipped to Hawaii by sea but it was planned to install extra tanks in those of the 38th and fly them the 3,000-odd miles from San Francisco to Oahu.

To be prepared for the flight the first contingent of the 38th's aircraft were moved from Jackson Field, Mississippi, to Patterso..

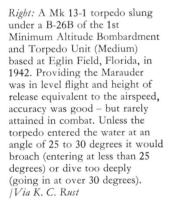

Right: A Mk 13-1 torpedo slung under a B-26B of the 1st Minimum Altitude Bombardment and Torpedo Unit (Medium) based at Eglin Field, Florida, in 1942. Providing the Marauder was in level flight and height of release equivalent to the airspeed, accuracy was good – but rarely attained in combat. Unless the torpedo entered the water at an angle of 25 to 30 degrees it would broach (entering at less than 25 degrees) or dive too deeply (going in at over 30 degrees). */Via K. C. Rust*

Field, Ohio, then a satellite test station of Wright Field. Computations gave a requirement of 1,906 US gallons necessary for the long over-water flight; this was nearly a thousand gallons more than the Marauder's built-in wing fuel cells capacity and so extra tankage had to be installed in the bomb-bay. The gross loading with this extra fuel, plus servicing equipment, was in excess of 35,400 lb-3,000lb over the stipulated maximum. In trials at this gross weight Marauders needed a mile run to become airborne from Patterson's grass surface.

At this time American Intelligence, having broken Japanese radio codes, were aware that preparations were in hand for the invasion of Midway and the Aleutian Islands. Air reinforcements were needed and the squadrons of the 38th preparing to move as soon as trials were complete, were suddenly ordered off 'at once'. The Group had been receiving new B-26B models to take overseas. These featured an improved tail gun emplacement, and a 24-volt electrical system replacing the troublesome 12-volt one; against this an extra ton in weight over the original B-26 was a definite liability.

The first flight of four Marauders successfully completed the 2,091 mile flight from Hamilton Army Air Base, California to Hickham Field, Hawaii on 22 May 1942. At Hickham were the two B-26s of the 22nd Group that had been delayed in their flight to Australia; in the current emergency they had been impressed into local defence. These and two of the 38th's B-26Bs immediately serviceable, were sent up to Midway armed with torpedoes ready to meet the approaching Japanese fleet. On 4 June this flight, in company with six Navy Grumman TBFs, attacked enemy carriers in the face of concentrated fighter and anti-aircraft defences. Of the Marauders only two, badly shot-up, survived; the leading B-26, *Suzy Q,* piloted by Captain James F. Collins, and Lt James P. Muri's 40-1391, the thirteenth B-26 built – but neither flew again. While American forces won this decisive naval battle in the Pacific, the Marauders' contribution was of little consequence as all torpedoes missed. Despite the courage of the crews, none had experience or training in delivering these devices.

The remaining aircraft of the 38th Group's initial movement arrived in Hawaii safely but too late to participate in the battle. The two squadrons involved, the 69th and 70th Bomb Squadrons, practising torpedo drops before moving on across the Pacific island chain towards Australia. The two other squadrons of the Group remained in the US for the decision had been taken to send no more B-26 units to the war with Japan.

Among hurried actions to meet the threatened landings in the Aleutians was the movement of the 406th Squadron to Alaska from north western USA. This unit came originally from the third Marauder group, the 42nd, which had been equipped at Gowen Field, Boise, Idaho in the weeks prior to hostilities and then despatched to bases in Washington and Oregon, from whence its aircraft patrolled the north-western seaboard of the country. The B-26 squadrons of the

Below: Ground crew preparing a torpedo for loading at Cold Bay, Aleutians./*National Archives*

Above: The thirteenth B-26, 40-1373, fitted with a torpedo at Adak, Aleutians, while serving with the 73rd BS in November 1942. Torpedo weight was taken by cables from shackles inside the bomb-bay./*National Archives*

42nd were gradually dispersed, the 77th going to Elmendorf, Alaska, immediately after the Pearl Harbor attack and later joining the 28th Composite Group. In February 1942 it supplied some crews and aircraft for the conversion of another squadron of that organisation, the 73rd, while taking some ponderous Douglas B-18s in exchange.

The Aleutians were well known for their inhospitable environment with chill mists and low clouds. Here new airstrips were cut out of the tundra on some of the islands and B-26s of the 77th Squadron, armed with torpedoes for the first time, moved in from Alaska to meet the crisis. The steel mat strips on spongy surfaces were hazardous enough for the operation of docile aircraft; with the unforgiving B-26 it demanded unfaltering pilot judgement and presented the most precarious landing grounds this type ever had to operate from. Searching for the Japanese invasion fleet, the Marauders were hindered by bad weather and only three aircraft released torpedoes, all of which missed although at the time crews claimed some success.

The three B-26 squadrons continued to serve with the 28th Group, periodically raiding the Japanese occupied islands at the western end of the Aleutian chain for several months until their aircraft were replaced by B-25 Mitchells. The original mother group, the 42nd, received other squadrons and re-equipped with B-25s before eventually moving into the Pacific island war. Similarly the other two squadrons of the 38th Group, withheld in the USA, had their Marauders replaced by Mitchells before going to the South-West Pacific.

As for the 69th and 70th Squadrons, their trans-Pacific flight terminated in Fiji where the torpedo-carrying Marauders remained to counter any further Japanese advance. With this danger past, detachments went to Guadalcanal for bombing forays but for the most part contact with the enemy was limited. More aircraft were lost through flying into weather fronts, or in local crashes, than to enemy action. With no replacements, a force of four Marauders often constituted maximum effort. Finally, when these squadrons too received the doughty Mitchell, the best of the surviving Marauders went to Australia as replacements for the 22nd Group.

As far as is known none of the few torpedoes launched at enemy shipping by Marauders ever found their target, due primarily to a lack of crew training in the technique of making attack runs. The Midway action had shown that the B-26 was too large and too slow to escape the considerable anti-aircraft firepower of a warship while the smaller more manoeuvrable Navy aircraft were less vulnerable and had greater effectiveness. Additionally, the US Navy had by late 1942 introduced a twin-engine Lockheed patrol bomber that could handle a torpedo thus cancelling the requirement for the Army interest. Operational trials with 'Tin Fish' were also carried out by B-26 units in Australia and North Africa, but the weapon was quickly abandoned in preference for the so-called skip bombing of ships.

The time lag between tactical decisions affecting equipment and being implemented on production is well illustrated in this case, for a year after torpedo carrying had been abandoned, Marauders were still leaving the factory with provision for carrying this weapon.

Top right: Mammy Yokum, 40-1372, became a training aircraft at MacDill following service with the 73rd BS in the Aleutians. The scoreboard of Japanese shipping was optimistic./*USAAF*

Centre Right: The bitter Alaskan winter provided few days suitable flying. Bump under rear fuselage of this 73rd BS aircraft is the rubber skid fitted to early B-26s for protecting fuselage skin in the event of the tail dropping too low./*Public Archives of Canada*

Below: Queenie, one of 70th BS's B-26Bs operating from Guadalcanal in January 1943. /*AFM*

SNAFU in North Africa

By the summer of 1942 the Army Air Forces had tentatively decided not to send any more B-26s to the Pacific theatre. Despite the good showing in combat by those in Australia, the B-25 Mitchell had proved to be more adaptable in that exacting environment. With the early decision by the Allies that their European enemy should be defeated first, the establishment of a large American air force in the United Kingdom was a prerequisite to any major offensive. The high standard of airfield surfaces and support facilities in England appeared more suited to sustaining the tricky Marauder.

The three original B-26 groups had either been despatched overseas or partly dispersed, so that some re-organisation of the training programme was necessary to produce a smooth and steady flow of new combat units. With the possibility of a 'Second Front' being opened in Europe to bring relief to the Russians, the matter became even more pressing as medium bombers were an essential element of tactical air support for invading armies. To organise and control operations of new B-26 units, when they reached the UK, the 4th Bomb Wing was established in June 1942 under the command of Brigadier General James H. Doolittle, leader of the recent raid on Tokyo. On the same date the 3rd Bomb Wing had been established to carry out a similar function for B-25 units destined for England.

The training of medium bomber crews was conducted mainly in the south-eastern United States. Later in June the personnel of two B-25 groups were parted from their aircraft and moved to Barksdale Field, Louisiana and MacDill Field, Florida, stations which then became the main centres of B-26 crew training. Both groups formed a new group by splitting their establishment of experienced men and building to full strength with graduates from flying and maintenance schools. They also absorbed the remnants of the B-26 trained 38th and 42nd Groups. At Barksdale, the 17th Bomb Group, oldest medium bomber group in the Army Air Forces, with squadrons that had seen action in World War I, raised the 319th Group; while at MacDill the 21st Group – itself stemming from a division of the 17th – built the 320th. It was the 17th that had provided nearly all the airmen that took part in the sensational carrier-launched raid by B-25 Mitchells on Tokyo the previous April and many survivors rejoining their parent group found themselves transferred to the nucleus of the 319th. Training began in a motley collection of early B-26 models with Martin and Pratt & Whitney representatives in watchful attendance at both stations. The reputation of the 'hot ships' brought a cautious approach to piloting: for the former B-25 men conversion was not difficult, but for those recently graduated from flying school it proved

Below: Jabbo's Skyking resposing in a hedgerow having failed to stop on the wet grass at Warmwell, Dorset. Lt William Craddock (Jabbo) and crew were the sole survivors from the flight that strayed over France. Stars and Stripes painted on the fin was an additional nationality marking in case the North African populace were unfamiliar with the US white star./*V. Galloway*

Bottom: Hornet's Nest; first Marauder to reach Europe. Used in the UK for evaluating the type's potential in low-level attack./*USAAF*

particularly daunting as some had no twin-engine experience. The hazard feared by pilots of loss of power on take-off happened all too frequently. An increase in B-26 accidents caused the USAAF to set up a Board of Inquiry – the second that year.

At the end of July 1942 the Allies decided to invade French North Africa, an operation mounted partly through Britain and partly direct from the United States. Three groups of medium bombers previously earmarked for Britain, the 319th, 320th and a B-25 group, were committed to the air support. On 1 August these groups were alerted for overseas movement. In the next few days there was an influx of pilots and other personnel straight from advanced training schools, many of whom had never seen a B-26 before. In this hurried situation, the accident record of the Marauder burgeoned. Engine and propeller malfunctions were blamed for these crashes but the troubles were compounded by the inexperience of pilots making the transition from docile flying school trainers to this demanding bomber. Their rawness was demonstrated on several occasions. During one take-off Lt Ashley Woolridge raised a hand to move his sun visor which the co-pilot misinterpreted as a signal to raise the undercarriage – the B-26 sank onto the runway. The 319th reaped particular misfortune after moving to a Barksdale satellite, Harding Field, for while there five Marauders crashed with 21 fatalities – two through a collision when one aircraft apparently stalled during formation flying.

At MacDill and nearby Drane Field – to which the 320th had moved – the situation was worse. In a period of 30 days 15 B-26s were written off in accidents often incurring fatalities. In most cases the crashes occurred after an engine or a propeller failed and led to the 21st Group reporting that the B-26 could not be landed safely on one engine. The 320th was as concerned as its mentor, with some trainee pilots refusing to fly the aircraft. To counter this lack of confidence, senior Wright Field test pilots were sent down to the B-26 training fields early in September to demonstrate that flying and landing on one engine was not a difficult feat, while technicians from the same station gave instruction on correct propeller feathering procedures. Much of the trouble with the Curtiss Electric propellers was traced to improper servicing and adjustment by inadequately briefed mechanics. Modifications were also introduced to make the mechanism more reliable.

While the Marauder had a number of weaknesses that could precipitate disaster, once the technique of flying the aircraft had been mastered and its particular idiosyncrasies understood, the performance of the aircraft

put it in the front rank of bomber types. Unfortunately, the problems of the Marauder proved more susceptible to gossip than its virtues and the ill repute that it was accorded was out of all proportion to the truth. There was no denying that the Marauder accident rate was high; during 1942 there were 165 incidents per 100,000 hours flown as against 104 for the Mitchell. In other words, for every two B-25s wrecked there were three B-26s. By the same token for every three B-26s crashing there were four A-20 Havocs and five P-38 Lightnings, yet no such criticism was levelled at the latter types, nor were they maligned as 'Widow Maker' and other such epithets.

At Barksdale in mid-July the 17th Group had given substance to another new group, the 335th, which took over the role of its parent as a training unit so that in August the 17th could be added to the B-26 force being prepared for movement to the United Kingdom. The intention was for the three groups to operate while in England to gain experience before the North African invasion was launched. To this end it was decided that the 4th Wing organisation should move to England as soon as possible, to prepare for the arrival of the first combat units and to study British techniques for medium bombers.

Above: Situation Normal, All.... and Situation Unchanged Still ......, meanings of the respective names on Cpt Donald G. Smith's and Lt David Floeter's aircraft at Attlebridge, November 1942. These B-26Bs were some of the first fitted with special air filters (evidenced by the cowling bulges) and without the large propeller spinners. Note tube for collecting and discharging spent cases from fixed nose gun./*G. Doran*

Right: 2/Lt Clarence Wall's aircraft down on a Dutch beach. It is claimed that the Germans repaired the Marauder at Gilze/Rijen and had it flying in December 1942./*Via S. Clay*

Below: Major General Doolittle explains the local war situation to 17th BG aircrew at Maison Blanche. A few days later *Thunder* was wrecked when Lt Delmer Essmyer had to crash-land it with battle damage on return from the Group's first mission./*USAAF*

Meanwhile, the three combat groups were being made ready to follow. All personnel of the 319th and 320th, and part of the 17th that were to travel by sea, sailed from New York in September. Earlier that month pilots had begun to collect new B-26Bs from Martin at Omaha to fly them to Baer Field, at Fort Wayne, Indiana, where final processing and preparation for overseas movement of the three groups was taking place. There was a concentrated effort to get the 57 aircraft of the 319th ready to depart, but equipment shortages among other problems caused delay. During the processing, Martin engineers finally discovered the reason for the hitherto unexplained intermittent loss of engine power; the sticking of moving parts in carburettors.

The 319th finally began its journey to Britain, a squadron at a time, on 21 September, by which time most pilots had put in 100 hours flying B-26s and were reasonably competent. The run of bad luck – which had seen yet another crew lost while at Baer – was not over. Only two hours out on the first leg of the journey a crew was killed in a crash after encountering bad weather. Another aircraft got out of control in these conditions and although recovery was made, the wings were found to be badly wrinkled after landing. Part of the trouble was the gross overloading of 36,500lb which probably precipitated the fatal accidents. At 2,500lb over the specified maximum, handling qualities were impaired. At Presque Isle, Maine and Goose Bay, Labrador, two gunners, all guns, specialised servicing equipment and other items were removed to reduce weight, the discarded men and equipment following by air transport. At Presque Isle, the point of departure from the USA, a Marauder jumped the chocks while the engines were being run up and before it could be shut down a wing tip had smashed that of a nearby companion.

The first squadron to move, the 438th, preceded the next, the 437th, by three days,

In the event, the 3rd Wing was given this mission for both B-25s and B-26s and was transferred to the 8th Air Force in England early in September. Colonel Charles T. Phillips, who had taken command of the 4th Wing (he had previously been in charge of Barksdale), now moved to the 3rd Wing.

The RAF was introducing Mitchells in the UK, but there were no service Marauders so Phillips decided to take up his appointment by flying one over the North Atlantic ferry route. With him in B-26B 41-17750 went Major Grover C. Brown, an experienced Barksdale B-26 pilot and technical authority on the Marauder. On 15 September Phillips and Brown brought the Marauder into the 8th Air Force depot at Honington, near 3rd Wing's location at Elveden Hall, Suffolk, having proved the route for ferrying B-26s from Maine through Newfoundland, Greenland, Iceland to Scotland.

sufficient for it largely to escape the early onset of wintry weather and allowing a fairly untroubled crossing, apart from a short delay in Greenland. On leaving Goose Bay the 437th encountered a cloud layer that was too high to fly above while below snow and sleet produced ice on control surfaces making conditions too perilous to continue the flight. Two days later, on the next attempt, clouds extended to 14,000ft, near the limit of the B-26s ceiling. After some alarming experiences all aircraft reached Greenland, but one had to belly-land. Although further delayed, this squadron eventually staged in Iceland and was the first to reach Scotland.

The weather had deteriorated further by the time the third squadron, the 439th, arrived at Goose Bay. They too lightened their aircraft before setting off for Greenland. One Marauder miraculously survived a spin while flying on instruments, the pilots returning it to Goose Bay where they discovered both fuselage and tail warped, rendering the aircraft unsafe. The leg from Greenland to Iceland proved even more treacherous, for two of the bombers disappeared without trace and only six eventually reached Scotland. The last squadron, and all but two of the residue of the other squadrons, did get to Greenland but an attempt to gain Iceland in atrocious weather resulted in another loss. Thereafter further flights were halted and the 17 Marauders at Bluie West, Greenland, returned to the USA as opportunity permitted; later most crossed the Atlantic to Africa via the South Atlantic.

The first aircraft of the 319th Group reached Scotland on 3 October but not all that reached Scotland were to complete the final stage of the journey. B-26 41-17790, captained by Lt Clarence C. Wall, over-flew both Scotland and England after leaving Iceland. Above an overcast, and drawn by a false homing signal emanating from an enemy source, the Marauder headed out over the North Sea towards continental Europe. Lost in clouds, the pilot's predicament worsened when a failure of a fuel transfer pump brought flight on one engine. With less than five minutes' fuel left, a coastline was seen and Wall elected to belly-land on the beach. With the appearance of German troops the crew learned they were in enemy occupied territory – Noord Beveland, a Dutch island. The local German Command first reported the aircraft as a Boston. When the Luftwaffe arrived on the scene they were amazed to find a little-damaged example of a Marauder – a type never before encountered.

The last of the 34 Marauders to complete the transit flight arrived at Horsham St Faith and its satellite Attlebridge near Norwich on 24 October, too late to give the 319th combat initiation from England, the invasion of North Africa being set for early November. Indeed, the main body of ground personnel left to embark before the last B-26s had arrived at Norfolk airfields. The 3rd Bomb Wing, expressly set up to handle medium bombardment in the 8th Air Force, played no part in the 319th's brief training – which was mostly concerned with the standardised operational procedures.

Crew inexperience in bad weather flying showed up on 5 November when six Marauders were despatched on a transit flight to Chivenor in south-west England, preparatory to moving to North Africa. Encountering heavy cloud the bombers became separated; one landed on Middle Wallop and suffered a collapsed undercarriage on this small grass field. A second was wrecked in a crash-landing at Attlebridge, the crew being unhurt. A week later another transit flight, this time to St Eval in Cornwall, was even more disastrous. Ten B-26s encountered an extensive weather front giving low cloud and rain soon after take-off. Two aircraft managed to return safely to Attlebridge and three others made emergency landings at other airfields, one burning out the brakes, another blowing both main tyres and the third damaging a wing. Seeking an airfield another B-26 bellied in while trying to land at Gravely in poor visibility, the crew surviving. Captain Donald Smith, an ex-Tokyo Raider, was not so fortunate; hitting a hill at Hunnington, west of Hereford, he perished with his crew. The remaining flight of three Marauders, one carrying the Group CO, Lt Col Alvord Rutherford, and another Captain Frank Tuttle, a squadron commander, climbed above the overcast. After two hours flying it was evident that they were way off course and lost. Lt William Craddock piloting the third aircraft became concerned when his radio operator advised that they were over the Cherbourg Peninsula! Reaching a broken layer of cloud, the leader led the flight in descent, finally breaking out at 1,500 feet. They were over a coastline – seemingly hostile as shells burst around them. For some reason Rutherford and Tuttle turned inland, but Craddock broke away to seaward and escaped. His companions went missing and German records show both were shot down and all crew members killed. In failing light and poor visibility Craddock regained the English coast. With little fuel remaining he landed at Warmwell, a small grass surfaced fighter base. Unable to stop on the wet turf the Marauder overran and ended up on its nose.

Despite this catastrophe that had seen 18 men killed or missing (including the group CO and two other senior pilots), four aircraft destroyed and four damaged, the 319th's movement to North Africa went ahead and two days later, on 14 November, the first Marauders reached the former French airfield of Tafaraoui in Algeria. By the 21st seventeen had arrived, completing the 1,500 mile overwater run from England to their destination near Oran in 9½ hours. To avoid detection by enemy radar much of the flight had been at 500 feet, imperilling safety as extra equipment and 1,300 gallons of fuel carried raised the total weight to 38,000lb, a state of exceptional over-load.

The misfortunes of the 319th, that had gradually whittled away the original USA fly-away force from 57 to 17 aircraft had, understandably, lowered morale and caused some conjecture among the fliers that they were burdened with an aircraft that was gradually eliminating them. The black reputation of the Marauder had even reached the British; an RAF officer told one 319th pilot he didn't envy him his job in flying the aircraft but admired his courage!

The Allied armies had encountered stiffening resistance in the push towards their major objective, Tunis. A hurried counter attack by German forces necessitated attacks on harbours and airfields by Allied bombers. Although the 319th had little more than single squadron strength and few B-26s serviceable, the 12th Air Force was forced to put the Group into action as the only medium bomber force available. On the 24th the Marauders were moved to Maison Blanche, another former French airfield, some 200 miles to the east and within range of prospective targets. Maison Blanche had a paved runway but the soil taxying and parking areas were churned to mud by the time the 319th arrived. Instead of the hot dry climate expected of North Africa, conditions were cold and wet; living accommodation was in tents and the British camps now seemed like luxury. Lacking specialised equipment removed in Greenland to reduce weight, many tools had to be improvised and spare parts were non-existent. There was little heavy maintenance equipment and to change a wheel it was necessary to build supports under a wing and dig a hole under the tyre. Refuelling was accomplished by a human chain passing five-gallon cans up to the wings or pulling each can up to the wing by rope. It required 960 cans to fill one B-26. Bombs had to be manhandled under the bays. Flight and ground crews often worked together on the aircraft. It was, they said, a case of SNAFU. (Well-known obscene military comment on chaos: Situation Normal All Fucked Up.)

The group was alerted to fly its first strike the day after arrival at the new base but low clouds caused a cancellation. Not until the 28th were conditions favourable enough for the Marauders' debut when nine were despatched to bomb the Tunisian airfield of Kairouan with Sfax harbour as an alternative. Mission leader was Major David M. Jones, another Tokyo veteran, who as senior pilot had taken temporary command of the 319th. A dearth of maps found the briefing team unable to provide the crews any showing the target area in sufficient detail. Even with this handicap Kairouan was located, only to be found deserted, so the Marauders turned south to Sfax. The Group had been trained to bomb at 'low altitude' which was an arbitrary 2,000 feet. Now at a thousand feet each individual bombardier sought a target among the warehouses, storage tanks, rail tracks and quays at Sfax harbour. Most aircraft made two runs, some three, to drop their loads of eight 300lb bombs each. With so long spent in the target area anti-aircraft defences had time to loose off a considerable number of rounds and the Marauders were fortunate to survive. Many were hit and a tail gunner was severely wounded.

Two days later a similar force making for Gabes airfield escorted by eight P-38 Lightnings, found and attacked their target which was well defended by light flak guns. It brought the Group its first fatal combat casualty when Lt Ashley Woolridge's aircraft, last in the formation, took a direct hit on the tail gun position, wounding gunner Sgt Robert L. Christman so severely in the abdomen that he died five days later. Also, the first B-26B, *SUSFU*, brought down in enemy territory when Lt David L. Floeter crash-landed a few miles north of the town. Recounting what happened he said, 'As we left the target my plane was limping badly having been hit many times by flak. My right engine was damaged and I could not keep up with the formation. I had a desperate feeling when I realised that my plane could not carry me and my crew to friendly territory. I turned to Houser (Lt Alan L, the co-pilot) who passed my message to Scogin (Lt Vernon G, the Bombardier) to be on the look-out for a place to land. I couldn't hold my altitude so I began to manoeuvre my ship into a position for a crash-landing on a level place we spotted. The plane slid to a halt and remained intact. All of us crawled out. We were safe but had to cope with the situation of being in enemy territory. We saw one of our P-38 escort circling over us so we decided to wait at the spot in case help should come. Scogin decided to remove the nose glass from our crashed B-26 since one was needed to repair another ship back at base. At about dusk we sighted an A-20 with an escort of two P-38s which came in for a landing some distance from us. We poured gasoline on our plane and set her afire. I hated to see her burn. Soon we were crowded into the rescue ship and on our way home.'

This daring rescue gave a brief fillip to

morale, but the battle damage the 319th aircraft had sustained in two missions gave an indication of the risky nature of these bombing operations. On 2 December the 319th put up 12 B-26s (as it transpired the largest number for any mission it would fly in North Africa) for an attack on El Aouina, Tunis airport, the major enemy air base in the country. Defences proved as effective as at Gabes and while all aircraft returned, some were damaged. One, hit on the nose and unable to lower the wheel, was written off in a crash-landing. Damage to hydraulic lines highlighted the effects of drag caused by bomb-bay doors that could not be closed.

Lt Col Sam Agee had come down from a B-17 group in England to take command and on 4 December flew his first mission – also his introduction to flight in a B-26 – riding in the leading aircraft with Major Jones for a strike on the Axis supply port of Bizerte. Seven aircraft went over the target at 4,000 feet in an effort to get above range of light flak, only to find the Germans had installed quick-firing long reach 88s. Notwithstanding violent evasive action, all but one of the Marauders suffered damage and the leader – as Jones later put it – 'Zigged when I should have zagged'. Then finding his bomber losing power, he had to force-land resulting in the crew, including the new and acting COs, being taken prisoner.

Eight days were to pass before weather and serviceability allowed the Group to attempt another mission, the port of Sousse. Due to freezing conditions and heavy clouds the raid was abandoned, but not before ice forming on flying surfaces caused one Marauder to spin down with loss of all lives. Another stricken aircraft, brought under control at the last minute, bellied into what appeared the only flat field in an area of hills and rocks. As the shaken crew emerged, their bombardier Edgar Pewitt jumped from the wreck, stuck his knife into the ground, fired

a flare and pronounced, 'I take this land in the name of Texas!'.

During December the 319th moved to Telergma situated in the wide Rhumel valley 2,500 feet up in the Algerian mountains. Telergma was supposed to be a dry weather field and while it did dry rapidly when it wasn't raining, it nearly always was, and the mud, if a different consistency to Maison Blanche's, still made life uncomfortable. Early in December, the 12th Air Force managed to obtain the experienced Colonel Charles Phillips to head its Bomber Command. Phillips had brought the first B-26 to Europe and was making preparations in England to receive combat units. One of his first tasks on taking up his duties in Africa was to examine US medium bomber employment, currently incurring heavy punishment for generally poor results. On 15 December Phillips went to see for himself in a raid on El Aouina, flying with Captain Arnold, a squadron CO leading the formation of seven. Keeping down to around 200 feet on target approach the bombers pulled up to between 600 and 1,000 feet to sight and bomb. They found anti-aircraft defences considerably bolstered since the previous visit; naval vessels added to the barrage and the lead aircraft plummetted into Tunis harbour, taking the crew and the XII BC commander to their deaths. Later, on hearing of Phillips' loss in a B-26, one senior AAF officer remarked: 'That ship is cursed.'

Matters were brought to a head three days later when six Marauders set off to Sousse again, briefed to bomb the railway station. Here too, flak defences had multiplied since the first raid. The bomber flown by Lt Gibbs – who the day before had shot down a Ju88 while flying the Group's first anti-shipping mission – received a direct hit and exploded. A second B-26, also hit, crashed in the harbour. The remaining bombers limped back to Telergma, all damaged with between three

Above: The lead flight of the 319th (all 438th BS) setting out from Telergma on 4 December 1942 mission to Bizertte. Leader is 41-17815 flown by Major Jones with Colonel Agee. Far wing aircraft is 41-17795 *Eleanor II* piloted by Lt Meyers and the nearest 41-17803 captained by Lt Crow./*USAAF*

and ten hits from 20mm shells and other missiles.

In the first 21 days the 319th had flown ten missions, lost five complete crews and additionally two men killed and four wounded. Ten aircraft were lost or wrecked and many others were unserviceable for lack of parts or damage. A few B-26s and crews trickled in from England but there were no further replacements and at the current rate of attrition the Group seemed destined for oblivion. The A-20 and B-25 groups in the theatre were also sustaining heavy loss – not that this was any consolation to the 319th. General Doolittle and his staff were compelled to review tactics. All three groups were trained for low-level operations, whereas the lone 15th Bomb Squadron that flew Douglas DB-7s (ex-RAF Bostons) had been operating at around 10,000 feet, suffering less and achieving better bombing. The RAF practised both ultra-low and medium altitude attack with its light and medium bombers, the tactics for the former being speed and surprise. The US mediums used the D-8 bomb-sight which needed altitudes of at least 500 feet and preferably 1,000 feet to be effective. This meant that however low the bombers made their approach, they had to climb for the bombardier to do his work accurately. But a climb at this point immediately exposed the attacker to the ground defences – notably the effective 20mm cannon. Consequently Doolittle ordered that in future land targets would only be attacked from medium altitudes (around 10,000 feet) above the range of light flak. This posed problems because the D-8 was of limited accuracy at this altitude. However, the first B-26s of the 17th Bomb Group were then reaching North Africa and every fourth aircraft had an M-7, the famed Norden sight, which would give far greater accuracy at the proposed higher levels.

The 17th Group had left Baer Field on 16 November, staging through the Caribbean, Brazil and Ascension, with the first elements reaching Accra before December. Range problems then delayed the flight for two weeks while negotiations were carried on with the French West African authorities for passage. Hard on the heels of the 17th came the aircraft of the third B-26 group, the 320th, which left Baer three days after the 17th but was held at Morrison Field, Florida until the 17th cleared the route. The advance elements of the 17th finally reached Telergma on 21 December and were immediately prepared for operations. The Group was largely equipped with the B-26B-2 which had new model engines rated as having an extra 150hp each. The 320th, arriving at Tafaraoui from the 29th, was held in reserve to train for medium altitude operations and also flying

anti-submarine patrols over the approaches to Oran.

The 17th was ordered to fly missions at the medium altitudes decreed by XII BC, building experience while operational. The initiation on 30 December was rough. Six B-26s flying to Gabes were shot at by Me 109 fighters and flak guns. Two B-26s with hydraulic systems damaged had to belly-in on return. Back over the same target next day the 17th lost its first Marauder in battle; another loss was suffered on New Year's Day. On this early showing, medium altitude operations were not reducing losses.

Telergma's compressed soil runway was so soggy by the end of December that the seven serviceable lower-powered B-26Bs of the 319th Group moved south of the mountains to the B-17 base at Biskra, on the edge of the Sahara. In contrast to Telergma, dust was the problem as a brisk wind off the desert seldom abated. In charge was the Group Operations Officer, Captain Randy Holzapple, with a new brief to carry out low-level search and attack missions on Axis shipping plying between Tunisia and Sicily. If no shipping was encountered, then alternative targets were ports, rail bridges and communications in Tunisian coastal areas. Despite Doolittle's order, these alternatives would also have to be attacked at low-level because of the sights carried. The normal D-8 was removed and in place a modified N-6 reflector gunsight, as used in B-26 turrets, was installed behind the cockpit windshield for the co-pilot to use.

Before the 319th could give much attention to this new task it was temporarily thwarted by the enemy. On the night of 3 January 1943 the Luftwaffe bombed Biskra destroying one Marauder and damaging five of the other six. It took a few days to effect repairs and a week later, after little luck with shipping strikes, the detachment returned to Telergma where conditions were much improved. On 21 January the sea sweep tactics at last paid off when Lt Robert Paulsen's crew hit a freighter amidships from 200 feet and reported it sinking. Next day Holzapple led five B-26s over an area south of the Gulf of Tunis, fought off attacks by Me 109s and claimed a freighter sunk. Flak from escorting destroyers crippled two aircraft which had to make crash landings near Bone. In one bombardier Captain Robert E. Miller was fatally wounded by shrapnel; he was the second of the five Tokyo fliers with the Group to be killed. On the morrow Captain Donald Gilbert led a similar sized force over the Gulf of Hammamet and claimed the despatch of two vessels. Formidable convoy escorts made it imprudent to attack after the next two sightings, but north of Tunis on the 29th Gilbert, with only three B-26s, braved the fire put up by a large convoy and claimed

two large cargo vessels left sinking and burning. One Marauder was shot into the sea and another, with a dead bombardier, had to make a wheels-up landing at base. In these attacks on shipping enemy fire was mostly directed at the oncoming aircraft so that the nose section frequently suffered shell splinter hits. In an effort to give the bombardier some protection and reduce casualties, the 319th armament section fashioned a protective steel shield out of armour plate taken from wrecked bombers.

If these missions proved more dangerous than those against land targets they were morale boosters, for at last the 319th appeared to be achieving results. However, attrition and maintenance difficulties reduced the Group's maximum effort to four or five sorties, despite the assignment of six crews and 18 aircraft from the 320th Group in the

latter part of January. The 17th Group had also suffered grievously during the month, losing 12 aircraft and seven crews for mostly dubious bombing results. Early February brought snow and sleet, adding to the discomforts and difficulties at Telergma and restricting operations.

To deny the Axis the use of their main airfield at El Aouina the 319th flew its first briefed strike against a land target for some time on 13 February. Five B-26s that joined eight from the 17th were, however, caught by fighters emerging from cloud and two Marauders from the 319th were shot down – one crash-landing within Allied lines. Faced with this further blow to the dwindling physical existence and morale of the 319th, XII BC withdrew the Group from combat to rest and re-equip. The high rate of attrition, lack of replacements and spares, meant that

Above: Mechanics using a portable compressor to clean engine accessories, the ingress of grit being a constant problem due to strong desert winds. B-26B in the background is *Miss Fortune* of 444th BS, which later served as a trainer with the RAF and the French./*USAAF*

37

for the time being only one B-26 group, the 17th, could be maintained in combat. During 165 sorties the 319th had lost 17 aircraft with 47 men killed or missing. Added to the nine aircraft and eight crews lost en route from America to Africa the record was indeed grim. Perhaps war is more tolerable to the combatants if it is known that someone's plight is worse than your own. Hence, around the 12th Air Force bases rumour held that the 319th had been all but wiped out. A B-17 commander summed it up: 'It wasn't that it had a jinx; it just had the B-26!'

Before the 319th retired to Oujda, Morocco, its B-26B-2s were turned over to the 17th Group. Among the older aircraft retained were two that had flown on the first mission. The most distinguished aircraft, *Eleanor II* 41-17795, had sadly to be scrapped after the Group's penultimate mission, having been on no less than 23 of the 29 missions. On 3 February 'Randy' Holzapple led a sea sweep with *Eleanor II*. Flak from vessels attacked severed hydraulic lines and on return to Telergma only the nose wheel would extend but then could not be raised. Holzapple carefully brought the aircraft in, accomplishing a smooth touch-down with the underside of the tail turret and the nose wheel. The bomber slid to a stop and then tipped over on the left wing. Even so, damage was beyond economical repair. The number of belly landings through battle damage to the vulnerable hydraulic system was disturbing. The strong construction of the Marauder withstood these extremely well, and many aircraft would have been repairable had the necessary tools and facilities been on hand. As it was, these 'belly-landers' were a source of spare parts to keep others flying.

Doolittle was one man who did not acquiesce with the extreme views circulated about the B-26. He had mastered the aircraft in one cross-country flight early the previous year with only a crew chief accompanying him. But then Doolittle was an exceptional pilot. He liked the aircraft but was aware that the unwary had no place in its cockpit. In Africa he usually borrowed a B-26 to reach the airfields in his command and later, in England, regularly flew a stripped-down Marauder on communication flights. Doolittle believed in discovering the facts of a situation for himself and news that he intended flying with the 17th on a mission to Sardinia also acted as a confidence boost for the crews. The objective was an airfield from where the Luftwaffe despatched transports to Tunisia. Doolittle acted as co-pilot for Captain Joe Klein, a squadron CO, in the formation of 15 Marauders despatched. Perhaps the Group was trying a little too hard to impress the Major General with their formation flying,

for on the flight out two aircraft collided and went down. The briefed target could not be located due to broken cloud, so another airfield seen was bombed. Doolittle had a special association with the 17th as he had led the Tokyo mission for which the Group provided crews; there were still a dozen veterans of the raid with the 17th.

At La Hencha, between Gabes and Sfax, were two important bridges which high and medium altitude bombing had failed to destroy. Command was forced to the conclusion that the necessary bombing accuracy would only be obtained from low level and the task was handed to the 17th. To minimise flak, fragmentation bombs were to be dropped on gun emplacements by a formation flying at medium altitude, while eight other Marauders came in low to hit the bridges. The first attempt was abandoned when the fighter escort was intercepted by Me109s. On 1 March they were successful in wrecking the rail bridge but at the cost of two bombers shot down and another written off on landing at base. Approaching the target at 60 feet the two six-plane flights were met by intense small arms and cannon fire. Turbulence and flying debris from bombs dropped by the first flight caused the left wing of *Coughin' Coffin,* the lead in the following flight, to drop and scrape the ground. The pilot, Captain William R. Pritchard, successfully raised the wing while at the same time co-pilot, Lt David Bolten, feathered the left engine which had faltered. With a crash-landing seemingly imminent, Pritchard lowered flaps to prepare to belly-in. But Bolten, having second thoughts, unfeathered the propeller causing the engine to come to life at the critical moment. *Coughin' Coffin* skimming the ground, was so low that when Pritchard realised he had full power again and started to climb, the rear fuselage brushed the surface. After salvoing bombs at the bridge, the hundred-odd mile flight back across enemy territory was completed without further incident.

Although the Allied ground forces had taken the initiative during the spring, poor weather restricted air operations. The 17th's bombing left much to be desired; the best work was with fragmentation bombs against largish areas such as airfields. Anti-shipping patrols were a regular feature during this period, with new tactics of splitting the attacking force between low and medium altitude. The B-26Bs inherited from the 319th were usually used for low attack while aircraft equipped with the Norden or D-8 sights flew at around 8,000 feet where they were better able to spot shipping in good weather and alert the lower formation. Experimental flying with torpedoes was carried out during March, but this weapon was not dropped

Right: Arleen dropped fragmentation bombs on flak emplacements at Gabes during the attempt to destroy bridges on 1 March 1943. This original combat aircraft of 17th BG went on to fly 65 missions before being retired and used for training at Telergma. Passed to the French it was still flying at Dijon in 1945. /*F. Davitt*

Below: 'They sure peppered our ship'. Morning inspection; 3 January 1943. *Fertile Myrtle* with shrapnel holes in wing, fuselage and propeller, resulting from the night bombing of Biskra./*USAF*

operationally. There had also been some training in night flying, with the idea of using the dark to minimise losses. This was abandoned after a fatal crash into a mountain, when it was concluded that the poor airfields and hilly terrain presented too great a hazard. The 17th was also showing signs of battle strain and in early April Doolittle brought the 320th Group east to Montesquieu in eastern Algeria. The first operation was to a Sardinian port on the 22nd and thereafter airfields and harbours on that island became the prerogative of the 320th while the experienced 17th kept chiefly to targets in the rapidly diminishing Axis-held territory in Tunisia. The 320th had, like the other two groups, been prepared for low-level operations while training in the USA. 'Randy' Holzapple and other 319th veterans assisted in re-training the Group for combat at medium altitudes, devising and improving formations to give better defensive cover in case of fighter interception.

When on 13 May 1943 the Allied campaign in North Africa ended, with the last Axis troops driven into the Cape Bon peninsula captured, the record of the Marauder was reviewed. Despite adverse operating conditions, the initial inexperience of crews, difficult maintenance and tricky flight characteristics, the contribution of the Marauder was questioned. The 12th Air Force was asked to prepare comparative operating statistics on the B-25 and B-26. The report, which cast a bad light on the Marauder, was

kept secret so that its findings did not affect morale.

For most of the campaign there had been more B-26s than B-25s in the theatre, yet Mitchells flew 2,689 sorties to 1,587 by Marauders. Proportionally the B-25 had done 80 per cent more work than the B-26 over the period and twice the work during the last three months. The total of B-25s lost was 65 as against 80 B-26s, the loss per sortie rate being 2.4 and 5.00 and abortive sorties 3 and 12 per cent respectively. In combat the claims against the enemy were the same – four enemy fighters for each bomber lost – the true figure, not then known, was approximately two bombers lost for every fighter. Faced with this damning evidence, and that from an analysis of training accidents in the States, plus the fact that it cost half as much again to build a B-26 than a B-25, plans were put in motion to terminate Marauder production in favour of other types.

Despite the general aversion to the B-26 at Headquarters USAAF, lower echelons directly concerned with the bomber had learned to identify the problems and endeavoured to overcome them – foremost in those battered combat units that fought in North Africa. But at the date of the official termination of that campaign, the Marauder was about to make its bombing debut in the European Theatre of Operations. A debut that was shortly to lead to the blackest day of all for this defamed aeroplane.

Below: The nose wheel twists for stowing as this 444th BS B-26B-2-MA clears Tarfaraoui, Algeria. 320th BG made a practice of painting individual aircraft radio call-letters on the fuselage sides of its aircraft. /O. Moritz

Sea Sweep

William Erwin

Telergma was just a field; no concrete, just dirt. When it rained, which it did a great deal of the time, we couldn't fly because the ground was turned to mud. When the sun shone the surface changed to dust just as quickly, the wind spreading a thin layer over everything. On 22 January 1943 it was fine and we flew. I'm never likely to forget that day.

We were called from our quarters in an old cow barn pretty early. The accommodation may have been poor but we slept on hay and that was a vast improvement over the concrete floor we had had to bed down on at our previous base. At briefing we learned the mission was another sea-sweep to catch enemy shipping bringing supplies down from Italy to Africa. As we would be looking for targets of opportunity to skip-bomb briefing was a simplified affair. For a week or two we had practised skip-bombing trying to hit a pile of hardtack biscuit cans, the idea being to skip the bombs into the side of the target by release at high speed and very low altitude. So far we hadn't had a lot of success in combat with this technique.

I got the crew together and went out to the plane. My co-pilot was Webster Brown, who hailed from Washington. He was always complaining he didn't have any clothes so we called him 'Nekkid Brown' – down in Texas we don't speak the King's English too well and it's 'nekkid' not naked. Jim Barr was the bombardier/navigator only his job would chiefly be to man the nose gun and look out for shipping on this mission as the sighting and bomb release was done from the cockpit. Turret gunner and flight engineer was Roy Grinnell from Michigan, and the tail gunner was Vernon Ohland from Spokane, a quiet, pleasant fellow. There was only need for a crew of five on this type of operation.

We took off around 0930hrs and formed elements. Only five B-26s were available, Captain Holzapple leading the first three-plane vic and I the trailing element with 2/Lt Harry Graham flying my wing. Once we had reached the sea we reduced altitude to about 250ft. The area of the search was over the Gulf of Tunis and we were to have fighter escort. I was flying my regular plane, *Lovely*

Below: Bill Erwin's assigned B-26B which he ferried to North Africa. /*W. Erwin*

41

Louise, named for my wife, which I had flown across the Atlantic and used on most of my missions. It had been a lucky plane and we had been a lucky crew; the original complement of the 439th Squadron having been reduced to less than half by combat and accident. Even so, I had confidence in the B-26. I knew it demanded constant attention from a pilot and would kill you if you failed to respect it – and I'd seen many people killed who didn't. At low level it didn't bounce around like many lighter airplanes and was good for this type of mission.

After we had been tracking across the Mediterranean for about an hour, approximately 50 miles north-east of Tunis we sighted a convoy on the horizon. Holzapple immediately gave the wing wobbling signal to attack, turning his element on course for the target. Following him down until less than 50ft above the sea, I advanced the throttles until the plane was indicating 250 mph. The plan was for elements to select separate targets with each B-26 releasing half its load of six 500lb bombs, so that another run could be made if the defenses were light.

They were far from light on this occasion. When we were still a mile away tracers began arcing out towards us from the escorting vessels. The size of the convoy was difficult to gauge as we sped over the wave-tops but I could see two large freighters. The lead element had selected one of these and we went for the other. I didn't know it at the time but when we turned into the attack Graham had mistakenly followed the first element so we were headed in alone on our target. Fear welled up inside at the sight of the defensive fire we knew we had to run through. During the 15 seconds it took to cover the last mile, I kept the plane level at 50 feet, using the rudder pedals to keep headed for the freighter. The B-26 had a slight nose-up flight attitude and the instant the ship was lost to view I stabbed my right thumb on the bomb release button and jerked the wheel back to clear the ship's masts, immediately afterwards dropping *Lovely Louise* down as low as I dare to make our getaway. The dreaded word 'fighters' rang in my earphones. Almost at once I could hear our guns firing and feel cannon shells hitting the plane. We were supposed to have an escort of 12 P-38s only they were nowhere to be seen. 'Fighters, three o'clock.' 'Here come two at five o'clock': Ohland and Grinnell kept calling out one attack after another. There were a whole bunch of Me109s back there and seeing the other four B-26s ahead I realised the fighters were giving us all their attention. I must have been pretty scared as I started calling over the radio for the other planes to slow down: if I'd had time to think about it I'd have realised they

would have been unlikely to comply. Anyway, the radio had been hit so I couldn't raise them. Holzapple's element was right down near the water and hauling away pretty fast so I just shoved everything forward to try to catch up. More cannon shells thudded into *Lovely Louise* making the plane skid one way or the other as pieces were knocked off and the trim lost. A shell exploded against Ohland's tail position spraying his legs with fragments although he continued firing his guns. I could hear Grinnell cursing over the intercom and couldn't figure out what he was talking about. Later I learned that one Me109 flew alongside and lower than us where Grinnell couldn't depress his guns to reach. The B-26 shuddered from another hit and I had to work the trim tabs to stop the plane sliding off to one side. An Me109 passed our wing, pulled up and was shot down by the B-26s ahead of us. I pressed my back more deeply into the armoured seat. A large hole appeared in our right wing and Grinnell called out that we were on fire. Fire, the most feared thing for any flyer; but in the confusion I only wanted to catch up with the other planes where the combined defences would give some measure of protection. Already their tail guns were firing at our pursuers, orange tracers passing over us.

After ten minutes the fighters finally broke off the fight; miraculously we had survived all their attacks. The fire in the right wing root was now sweeping into the bomb bay through a hole in the fuselage. Ohland and Grinnell left their white-hot guns and came forward. Despite having twice taken shell splinters in his left leg and arms Ohland grabbed a fire extinguisher from the navigator's compartment and set about extinguishing the fire in the rear bomb-bay. Jim Barr wanted to come out of the nose, Brown slid his seat back and Barr scrambled out. He was nursing a small flak wound in his arm but went back to help Ohland. I had looked at the airspeed indicator as we were trying to regain the formation and it was hovering between 290 and 300mph. We had to use full power as due to damaged hydraulics the bomb doors remained open causing considerable drag. Climbing to about 500 feet I jettisoned the three remaining bombs in the sea. But my greatest concern was the wing fire and loss of fuel. Thankfully, the whole of the back end of the tank was shot out so the gas just burned away; there was nowhere for the vapours to collect so we were spared an explosion. Speed swept the fire back away from the rest of the wing confining the damage to the trailing edge, but this didn't stop me from expecting the wing to burn through at any moment. We were losing gas at an alarming rate and I was concerned we might have the right engine fail. We kept trans-

Left: Lt William Erwin receiving the DFC from General Cannon for his conduct on 22 January 1943. On his left is Sgt Vernon Ohland who was also decorated. /*W. Erwin*

ferring gas to keep it going. Much to our relief after about half an hour – although it seemed like two days just sitting there watching – the fire eventually burned out. With the heavy damage to the plane I didn't want to make a belly landing with the bomb doors open and only one engine running so we kept transferring fuel from the left tank over to the right engine until it looked like we were going to run out of gas. We were still about 150 miles from base and there was a range of mountains to go over. So I decided we'd better try and set down on the first available place. About 25 miles south-east of Bone we saw a relatively smooth place, a marshy area. I took one pass at it to see if there were any logs or stumps and then really concentrated on preparing to land like I had never done before in my life. You don't get practice in crash landings and as this was going to be my first it just had to be a good one if we were going to walk away unharmed.

As we made our final approach I leaned over and told Webster Brown that as soon as we hit the ground he was to cut off all switches and to pull the emergency cockpit hatch release because of the danger of fire and the normal hatch release might become jammed. I came in fairly fast and keeping the nose up slightly until I felt the tail contact and suddenly we were skidding along. The marsh was softer than it looked from the air and almost immediately mud splashed into the cockpit from the rear. The plane kept skidding along – seemed like it was never going to stop as mud welled up through the

open bomb bay and flooded the fuselage – waist high in places. As we were sliding along, I noticed out of the corner of my eye that Brown was tugging at the emergency release with all his might. This release was a steel bar, perhaps three to four inches long and about one half inch thick. He was a big strong man and as we eventually slowed to a stop, he yelled that the hatch would not open. I looked up at the steel bar and saw he had bent it to about a 45 degree angle. Apparently, Brown's adrenalin gland was operating at maximum capacity because it took superhuman strength to bend that steel bar. The fear of being trapped was real for both of us until I reached up and pulled the normal hatch release. The hatches opened wide without any difficulty. As I was starting to unbuckle my safety belt, Jim Barr came out of nowhere, stepped on my right shoulder, literally vaulting through the hatch and ran off down the left wing. He could have made the Olympic team at that particular moment. I didn't blame him; he'd had about all he wanted that day. We were all anxious to get out of the plane because we didn't know whether it would catch fire again. Ohland was weak from loss of blood and we had to push and tug to get him out of the cockpit top hatch on top of the fuselage. Very unpleasant for him and he groaned when it hurt; but he was a courageous fellow; he didn't complain. We doctored him up, put sulphur powder on his wounds and gave him a shot or morphine before two of us walked a couple of miles and got help from some British troops.

When we went back with an ambulance to pick up Ohland I looked over the plane. It had taken some 20 cannon shell hits and every surface was riddled with bullets or splinter strikes. There was a 3ft wide hole in the fuselage in the area of the bomb bay and close by a couple of 18in wide gaps. A 2ft hole had burned out of the trailing edge behind the main wing tank. The elevators, fin and rudder had several perforations the size of a man's fist. The tail gunner's position was a complete shambles. The nose had evidently taken a near flak hit from the convoy for the plexiglass was smashed. The engines had been hit but not damaged and that was the saving grace; you could lose just about everything except the engines and the B-26 would keep flying.

We were five very shocked young men, wondering how we came out of such a wreck alive. It made quite an impression on me for I have never been so close to death before or since. I had nightmares about it for several months afterwards; something like this you don't forget easily. Neither will I ever forget I'm alive because the B-26 was a tough, tough airplane.

Ijmuiden

The name of a major fishing port on the coast of Holland is synonymous with the bad reputation of the Martin Marauder. Because so little of the true facts were known, the IJmuiden saga has for many years been distorted by speculation. This account sets out to establish what really happened on that infamous occasion.

When the 3rd Bomb Wing was established in England in September 1942 it was ultimately expected to control the operations of 15 medium bomber groups. With no specific directions from Washington, the first tentative proposal for using the B-25s and B-26s in the European Theatre of Operations (ETO) was to attack targets within a 400 mile radius from heights of between 8,500 and 12,000 feet. The operational plan that developed was for 'zero' altitude formation employment which had proved successful in the SWPA.

Determining factors were the D-8 bombsight which was inaccurate above 400 feet for small targets, the 200 to 4,000 feet range of German light flak and the north-west European weather conditioning more low than medium altitude operations. In the absence of precise tactical doctrine, 3rd Wing proceeded to produce its own, following closely the practice of No 2 Group, RAF, which for over two years had been operating light and medium bombers against targets in occupied Europe. In the autumn of 1942 this Group (equivalent to a USAAF Wing) acquired enough Mitchells to equip two squadrons and Major Glenn C. Nye of 3rd Wing Operations spent some time with these units at Foulsham, studying tactics and flying on training missions. As both B-25 and B-26 units were scheduled to arrive in England, Nye specialised in the operational possibilities of the B-25 (the Wing later received a B-25C of its own) while Major

High noon at Marrakech with the snow capped Atlas mountains in the distance. The protruding fixed nose guns on these B-26B-4s made handy clothes hooks. Centre aircraft is 41-18099, *Lorraine*. The nickname was removed prior to Roland Scott and Othel Turner flying the aircraft to IJmuiden on 14 May. Cpt Jack Crane took it on the second raid./*P. Lauppe*

Grover Brown, who had brought the first B-26 to England, carried out a similar study on that type. Attempts were made to obtain reports or manuals on the employment of medium bombers from the USA. As there was little forthcoming in response to this request 3rd Wing found itself developing a doctrine without any benefit of experience in the SWPA or the early days in Africa.

On 1 December 1942, 3rd Wing received the ground contingent of its first combat group, the 322nd. Headquarters and two squadrons were based at Bury St Edmunds and the other squadrons at a satellite airfield, Rattlesden. Bury St Edmunds aerodrome was to the east of that town, sited in the parish of Rougham, about seven miles south of the Wing station at Elveden Hall. The flight echelon of the 322nd was still training at MacDill, Florida, and receiving new B-26B2 and B3 aircraft for combat use. Deficiencies in men and equipment caused long delays and the first squadron did not move overseas until January. In the meantime 3rd Wing had undergone two changes of commanders and learned that initially only B-26 units would be received. From his study of RAF tactics and information obtained by skipping the Wing's sole B-26, *Hornet's Nest* over the English

countryside, Nye prepared a training directive. Basically, this advised strikes on small targets with not more than 12 bombers at a time, using very low-level flight with the advantages of avoiding radar detection and making the aircraft difficult targets for both flak and fighters. Surprise, however, rated the major factor in surviving in a hostile environment. A high degree of bombing accuracy should be obtained if a target had been correctly identified.

After a month in transit 14 B-26B-2s of the 322nd Group arrived at Bury. To avoid tail heavy loadings, tools, armour and equipment had been left behind to be transported later but the 450th Bomb Squadron had the distinction of being the first Marauder unit to make the crossing – via the southern route – without loss. Brigadier General Fred Andersen came down to Bury to see the first crews to reach his Wing and learned from the 450th's CO, Captain Othel D. Turner, that the 322nd Group had no authorised commander. Andersen thereupon made Glenn Nye acting Group CO and gave him the job of preparing the 450th for combat. Nye was disturbed to find that the pilots had not undertaken training flights below 1,000 feet and had little experience of formation flying.

Top: Chickersaw Chief in which General Brady flew as observer with Cpt Rezabeck on 14 May; and Lt Wurst piloted on the 17th. Only aircraft undamaged on the first raid and the only one lost on second from which the complete crew survived. Bump under nose of this B-26B-4 is wheelwell extension accommodating long leg, common to this and future B-26 models./*H. Posson*

Above: Colonel Stillman briefing for the first mission, using a sand table model. Major von Kolnitz, Intelligence Officer, in front of window./*USAAF/Gen Stillman*

Many gunners had never fired their weapons in the air. It was apparent that an intensive programme of low-level flying had to be undertaken with emphasis on pin-point navigation.

The B-26 suddenly became a familiar shape hedge-hopping over the farms and fields of East Anglia at 50 to 200 feet. Most pilots found it exhilarating, but due to its high wing loading the Marauder was slow to respond to changes in altitude and there were a few frightening encounters with tree tops.

Early in April the flight echelon of a second squadron arrived, less a Marauder that ditched through engine failure near the Portuguese coast. Major Gove C. Celio's

452nd Bomb Squadron had B-26B-4 models, the first to arrive featuring externally mounted gun 'blisters' on the fuselage for ground strafing. These newly arrived crews also lacked low-level flight experience and were quickly drawn into the training programme. On 28 April Colonel Robert M. Stillman arrived from the USA to take command of the Group and after a few days, when his successor was fully conversant of the situation, Nye returned to Elveden Hall. 'Moose' Stillman had previously been the Group Executive of another new B-26 group training in the States (the 387th), where he was noted for his 'bright outlook and enormous capacity for work.' Higher command must also have been aware of his qualities, for the selection of a commander destined to initiate a new dimension in the US air operations over Europe was a significant appointment. The responsibility was heavy and three days after assuming command a misfortune added to Stillman's problems. Lt Clyde H. Larey and crew were killed in a crash near Cambridge and the old image of the 'Widow Maker' was revived. Rumour had it that part of the tail had come off while the aircraft was engaged in simulated evasive action close to the ground. The 322nd Group had already suffered earlier casualties, six B-26s having been lost training in America with only two men surviving. Nevertheless, morale was generally good, aircrew finding the zero altitude flight exhilarating if exacting.

The staff officers at Elveden Hall were aware that VIII Bomber Command was too preoccupied with the problems of conducting high altitude bombing missions with its heavies to give much time to the medium bombardment role. While the Marauders practised for low attack, the method of their commitment to battle was still uncertain.

There had been some preparations to use them for anti-shipping strikes. Lt Col Jack E. Caldwell, who headed 3rd Wing Operations, was sent down to North Africa at the end of February to study B-26 usage. On his return early in April he reported that low-level operations had been successful against enemy shipping, but that most missions to land targets were now flown at medium level because of enemy defences. Indecision by 3rd Wing was not helped by having four changes in commander in nearly as many months.

In April Brigadier General Francis Brady, who had been serving in the Philippines when the Japanese attacked, took over. By early May there was still some doubt as to the actual level at which the Marauders would be employed even though crews of the 450th and 452nd Squadrons had reached an acceptable standard in low-level flying. Matters were brought to a head when VIII Bomber Command informed 3rd Wing that the two B-26 units would be placed on operational status in a few days. Frenzied activity followed at Bury St Edmunds, for if the crews were ready the aircraft were not. Because forward firepower was essential in subduing ground defences, only B-26B-4 models with side guns were deemed suitable for combat and these required other modifications. The normal D-8 nose sight was found unsatisfactory for zero altitude bombing, so a modified N-6 gunsight was fixed in the cockpit for use by the co-pilot. A cord cable with release button was rigged up for the co-pilot to use in dropping the bomb load. A compass had to be installed in the nose compartment for the navigator who was to ride there and not at his usual table behind the pilots. Changes in radio equipment and the installation of IFF (Identification Friend or Foe, a radar warning device) were also being made. Flight crews

helped the ground crews with this work in an effort to fully modify as many aircraft as possible. Another problem was bombs. To avoid civilian casualties in occupied countries, delayed action (DA) fuses were essential. The available American bombs had chemical fuses that had been found unstable and highly dangerous to use. Instead, 3rd Wing arranged for delivery of 100 British 500lb Mk VIII bombs with 30 minute delay fuses, plus a small party of RAF armourers to instruct the US ordnance men in fusing them.

On Sunday 12 May, 322nd Group Hq knew the first mission was imminent and on Monday afternoon Colonel Stillman returned from Elveden Hall with news that it would

Above: Celio and Porter's 41-17996, at Honington after the first raid. A 20mm hit on the left main wheel doors caused a flat tyre that led to a buckled wing on landing. The long nose wheel leg of the B-26B-4 increased the angle of incidence (wing to ground) and helped shorten take-off runs./*USAAF & R. Ward*

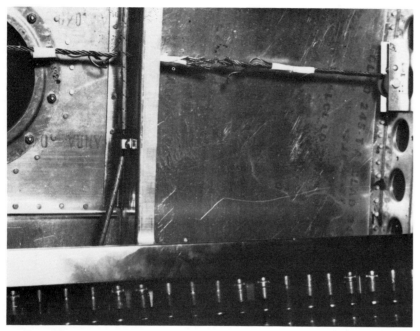

Above: A shell splinter almost severed the right-hand elevator control cable above the ammo' track to the tail guns in 41-18075, ER:J, flown by Lt George Watson. This aircraft took three 20mm hits on 14 May./*J. Statts*

be flown the following day. The target, the PEN generating station at Velsen adjoining IJmuiden, supplying the greater part of northern Holland with electrical power, was to be bombed at noon. Although only a few men shared this information, others sensed that the first mission was near.

The field order from Wing, giving precise details for the operation, came through at 0345hrs in the dark hours of 14 May. The maximum number of bombers available – 12 – were each to carry four 500lb DA bombs. Crews selected were called to briefing at 0715 and learned the target and route, which ran from Orfordness on the Suffolk coast to Noordwijk, a Dutch coastal resort 12 miles north of The Hague. After crossing the coast a wide left turn was to be made to pick up and follow canals and railways to the target but circumnavigating Haarlem known to have anti-aircraft defences. The target would be reached from the south-east at 1100hrs and after bombing the formation would veer north to avoid a flak area before turning out to sea and returning to England over Southwold. No fighter support was available but 8th Air Force heavies were operating elsewhere and might be expected to occupy the attentions of enemy interceptors.

The leading flight consisted of four 450th aircraft and two 452nd, one of the latter operated by a 450th crew as this squadron did not yet have sufficient B-4 models of its own. The trailing flight was all 452nd Bomb Squadron. The espective squadron commanders would lead each flight although Othel Turner had tossed a coin with his Operations Officer, Captain Roland Scott, as to who should fly left seat. Scott won and piloted the leadplane, Colonel Stillman flying the Marauder on his right wing. In the same

relative position in the 452nd formation was Captain Rezabeck's aircraft in which General Brady had elected to ride as an observer. Apart from the natural apprehension of men about to be initiated in battle, the crews displayed a general confidence in their ability to carry out the job.

At 0950hrs Captain Scott took-off and the whole force was airborne in six minutes. Climbing to 250 feet they assembled into two javelin formations and headed east for Orfordness along a route already familiar through training flights. Over the sea altitude was reduced to 50 feet and a course of 085 degrees taken for 121 miles to the Dutch coast. Only a little alto-stratus hung in the spring sky; the weather proved better than forecast. Nearing Holland a few fishing boats were observed through the sea haze shortly before Scott and Turner picked out the coastline some three miles ahead. At first they recognised no landmarks, then away to the north the large hotel and prominent features of Noordwijk were spotted. Scott gently banked to the left, the formation following, then turned right to make correct landfall over Noordwijk. The time was 1052 with six minutes and 25 miles to the target. Skimming over the flat landscape of fields and dykes the leaders turned left to locate the briefed 'pinpoints'. Some machine gun fire, visible by tracer, came up from ground emplacements and as the Marauders passed north-west of Lisse they were met with 20mm cannon fire. Lt Robert C. Fry's *Too Much Of Texas,* positioned left of the lead in the 452nd flight, took direct hits in the rudder and port engine. Fry was no stranger to piloting B-26s on a single engine, but nothing quite as precarious as with full bomb load at 50 feet. Realising he would not be able to maintain either speed or altitude, Fry skidded the aircraft out of formation and headed for the coast under full power on the good engine. Surviving bursts of machine gun fire from coastal defences, the bomb load was jettisoned in the sea. Fry then headed his ailing Marauder towards England.

The remaining bombers – reported by the German defences as Bostons – had meanwhile skirted Haarlem and veered slightly off course east of the briefed route. They did not make the turn for target approach until the leaders recognised the Noord Zee canal. This placed the formation on a 270 degree approach to the target, and not 300 degrees as planned. As soon as the tall smoke stacks of the generating station appeared ahead the Marauders climbed to 250 feet to clear. The first flight released their bombs and went squarely over the target. Immediately after the target heavier ground fire was encountered. A 20mm shell struck the top of the pilot's windshield on the lead aircraft blasting

the cockpit with fragments and badly wounding Scott in the face and chest. Turner received only slight injuries and quickly took over the controls. The second flight, some two miles behind and more dispersed, ran into more intense flak causing heavy damage to the leader and Lt John Howell's aircraft following to the left. The right two-plane element in this flight was also hit, pilot Lt Paul Shannon and his co-pilot receiving slight scalp wounds, while Lt Watson's aircraft took three 20mm hits. Dropping down low to reduce their vulnerability, the Marauders regained the sea within a minute. Light anti-aircraft fire from a few coastal vessels marked their passing.

The 135 mile return across the North Sea was uneventful; the formations climbing to 2,000 feet before regaining England about three miles north of Southwold. By this time both Celio's and Watson's damaged aircraft were trailing, while Howell, though not far behind the formation was having great difficulty as the aileron controls were damaged and severed hydraulics had caused the bomb doors to open. Seven minutes later Fry nursed *Too Much of Texas* over the coast near Lowestoft and flew towards base. When an airfield appeared ahead Fry lowered the undercarriage and went straight in for a landing: this turned out to be Great Ashfield, still under construction and with runways that had only just been cleared of obstacles.

The main formation reached home base just before noon. Howell circled the field while efforts were made to lower the undercarriage, but only the nose wheel would come down. After orbiting for half an hour the decision was taken to abandon the aircraft and five men successfully parachuted. Then the aircraft suddenly went into a spiral, crashed and burned. Howell did not escape and it was assumed the bomber went out of control when he attempted to leave the cockpit.

Celio had flown on to the Honington air depot where he orbited for nearly an hour while the crew filled the emergency hydraulic system. Shrapnel had severed piping but prompt action by the engineer in clipping open ends kept most of the system serviceable. The undercarriage was eventually locked down and the aircraft made a successful emergency landing.

Howell's death and seven wounded crew members – one seriously – had been an alarming introduction to combat for the 322nd. The only Marauder that had come through unscathed was *The Chickasaw Chief* in which General Brady had flown, although inspection found that damage to one aircraft was due to a bird strike and not enemy action. Understandably the crews were concerned about their exposure to anti-aircraft fire in this type of operation although the mission critique established that when the bombers were flying 'right on the deck' flak was not effective: damage was chiefly incurred during the five mile target run at 250 to 300 feet. On the other hand all crews were confident of having done a good job of bombing the generating station; some claimed to have seen strikes on buildings. The photographic reconnaissance pictures of the destruction wrought were eagerly awaited.

On 16 May Colonel Stillman was called to a conference at Elveden Hall. When he arrived Brady informed him aerial reconnaissance photographs taken the day after the raid showed the Ijmuiden generating station completely undamaged. Only 17 bomb craters had been found, mostly short of the target. Stillman, incredulous, maintained that his crews had seen bombs go into the buildings. Brady then informed him VIII BC wanted them to repeat the mission next day. Stillman viewed this as highly imprudent as the enemy, aware of the failure, would be expecting another attack and increase defences. Brady sympathised with this view and queried the matter over the telephone with General Longfellow at VIII BC. But Longfellow insisted that the mission could not be changed as it was part of the overall plan of operations for next day. Stillman continuing his objections was, on his own admission, threatened

with the loss of his command at one point. Obviously disturbed at having to order his crews on a mission he thought impractical, Stillman returned to Bury at 2220hrs with the outline plan which differed from the first in one major respect. As the previous raid had shown that the second flight, lacking the benefit of surprise, was more at risk from ground fire, this time it was to bomb a smaller electrical plant at Haarlem and keep clear of known flak areas while only the first flight hit Ijmuiden.

Group officers at Bury were also disturbed by the news that the power house was not hit and as alarmed as their CO to be returning so soon to the same target. The general opinion as to the reason for failure was the British DA bombs. With 30 minutes delay fuses, a fact well known to the Germans, it was suggested that prompt work by bomb disposal experts allowed bombs in the target site to be removed to a safe place before they exploded. Many were suspected of being duds, and so strongly was this felt that arrangements were hurriedly made to obtain use of the RAF range at Rushford, near Thetford, so that a test dropping of live bombs could be made before the mission was run.

The 322nd Group's second Field Order was received at 0036 on 17 May and required a maximum effort and an identical route to Ijmuiden. Lt Col Alfred Von Kolnitz, the Senior Intelligence Officer and a veteran of World War I, was particularly alarmed at the choice of the same route and objective which seemed to him to invite strong enemy reaction. In the early hours of the morning he wrote a memo for Stillman pointing out the dangers. As a postscript he added 'Colonel: you are sleeping and I did not want to wake you up – for God's sake get fighter cover!'

The men awakened to fly the mission were, with four exceptions, drawn from 450th and 452nd crews who did not participate in the first raid. Those who had were Stillman, determined to lead, and S/Sgt M. F. Freeman (engineer gunner on Shannon's crew) and T/Sgt C. P. Willis (radio man on Fry's crew) who were considered the best in the Group at their respective jobs. The other airman who had been on the first raid was T/Sgt J. D. Thompson, Celio's engineer, who was to fly with Captain Converse, Stillman's wingman. This time the 452nd Bomb Squadron made up the lead flight and the 450th the second. Only 11 B-4 models were serviceable, the 450th using five, two of which were borrowed from the 452nd.

Despite the confidence of the crews that they could succeed this time, all expected to meet stiff opposition and many were convinced they would not return. An air of hopelessness pervaded the briefing room according to one witness. The mood was not

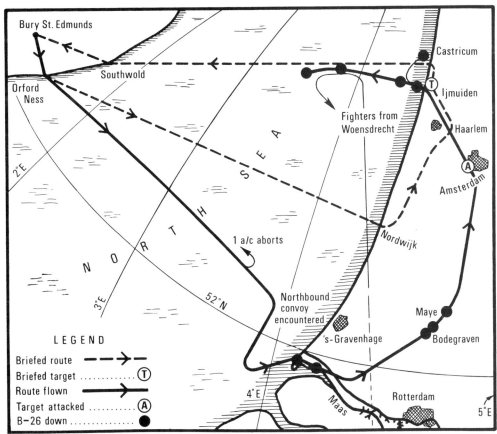

Bury St. Edmunds

Southwold

Orford
Ness

Castricum

IJmuiden

Fighters from
Woensdrecht

Haarlem

NORTH SEA

1 a/c aborts

Nordwijk

Amsterdam

2°E

3°E

52°N

Northbound
convoy
encountered

Maye

Bodegraven

LEGEND

Briefed route .... →
Briefed target .... Ⓣ
Route flown .... →
Target attacked .... Ⓐ
B-26 down .... ●

's-Gravenhage

4°E

Maas

Rotterdam

5°E

51

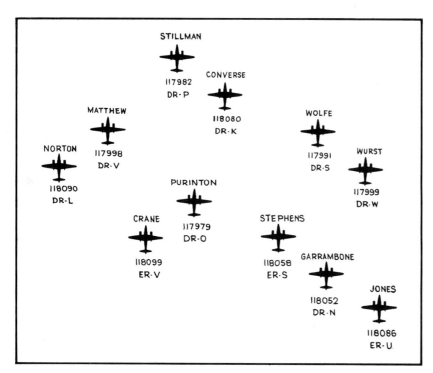

STILLMAN
117982
DR·P

CONVERSE
118080
DR·K

WOLFE
117991
DR·S

WURST
117999
DR·W

MATTHEW
117998
DR·V

NORTON
118090
DR·L

PURINTON
117979
DR·O

CRANE
118099
ER·V

STEPHENS
118058
ER·S

GARRAMBONE
118052
DR·N

JONES
118086
ER·U

Above: Formation as despatched from English coast, 17 May 1943.

Right: General Arnold, Chief of the USAAF, visiting the 2nd General Hospital, talks to Cpt Roland Scott who was recuperating from injuries received on the first B-26 mission in the ETO./*USAAF*

helped by hearsay that one officer, committed to the station sick quarters as an extreme anxiety case, had contemplated suicide because he was nominated for the mission.

While the crews were being briefed a Marauder took off with four 500lb DA bombs to drop at low level on the Rushford range. The results appeared to vindicate the delayed fuses as one bomb detonated 23 minutes after release and the others within 30 to 45 minutes. Efforts had been made to get VIII BC to authorise the inclusion of a few 100lb bombs with 45 second fuses in the mission loads with the idea of restraining the enemy from removing the DA bombs, but this was turned down for fear that Dutch civilians would be killed.

For Stillman, convinced the mission was sheer folly yet determined in his duty to

personally see the target hit this time, it was a dispirited departure from the intelligence section. Von Kolnitz said 'Cheerio' as Stillman was leaving. 'No, it's good-bye', the Commander responded. Ignoring the prophesy Von Kolnitz said, 'I'll see you at one o'clock.' 'It's good-bye' repeated Stillman and walked out.

At 1050hrs British Double Summer Time Stillman released the brakes on *Blueroad P-Peter,* advanced the throttles and sped the aircraft eastwards down the main runway. While the CO climbed away in a wide left-hand circuit of the airfield, following aircraft of his flight took-off at 30 second intervals. The Group Executive, Lt Col William Purinton headed the second flight and like the Group leader flew a wide circle of the airfield while each B-26 gained its correct position to effect the javelin formation. Assembly completed, at 1110 Stillman passed over Bury at 250 feet and set course for the coast. Soon the market town of Stowmarket came into view. There was no trace of cloud in the sky on this beautiful spring day as the dark shadows of the Marauders raced over the fresh spring greenery of the Suffolk countryside. Familiar landmarks of airfields under construction and the young conifer forests finally gave way to the coastline, the tower of Orford castle and the unmistakable shingle point that was Orfordness. A Royal Observer Corps post reported their passing at 1120. The bombers now turned east north-east on a heading of 085 degrees. Pilots fastened their safety belts and gunners charged their guns. Five minutes and approximately 15 miles later the IFF was turned off and the formations reduced altitude to 50 feet. Gunners fired test bursts into the waves. The enemy coast was a half hour away but already pilots and navigators tensely watched the oncoming horizon.

All was not well in Captain Stephens' *Snellgrove S-Sugar,* No 2 to Purinton in the lead element of the 450th flight. After take-off Stephens found the left engine was not giving the required power and he had to apply right rudder trim to maintain directional control. At approximately 1147, an estimated 33 miles from the Dutch coast, the top turret gunner reported his turret power had failed. Stephens decided to abort the mission, making a 180 degree turn out of formation. Major electrical failure was evinced by the radio, propeller feathering system and some instruments ceasing to function. Climbing slightly *S-Sugar* headed back to England.

An estimated five minutes from the Dutch coast as pilots prepared to increase engine speed to 2,400rpm, accelerating from 200 to 240mph, vessels appeared ahead in the line of flight. Stillman had to make an instant decision; he turned the formation south.

Some of the escort vessels of this north-bound enemy convoy fired at the bombers as they banked away. They radioed a warning to the shore from their position off Monster near the Hook of Holland – 18 miles south-west of the 322nd's intended landfall!

The ships lost from view, Stillman turned north-east, believing – as apparently did other pilots and navigators – that the formation would now make landfall some five to eight miles south of Noordwijk and near The Hague. In fact, when at 1150 the coast appeared ahead, the formation was 25 miles from Noordwijk, streaking towards the sand dunes of Rozenburg Island and the most heavily defended area in the Netherlands, the Maas estuary leading to Rotterdam. As the leading flight thundered over the sand dunes they were met with a hail of 20mm shells to which they responded by firing at gun emplacements with their package guns. The lead bomber took direct hits, one explosion severing all flight controls and apparently killing Lt Resweber, the co-pilot. The Marauder snap-rolled and Stillman saw the ground coming up to meet him. Miraculously, from the inverted wreck the Germans extracted three men, alive though badly injured – Stillman, Freeman and Willis, those on board who had flown on the first mission.

A mile or two to the south, the following flight also encountered intense fire on land-fall. Lt Garrambone in *N-Nan,* leading the second element, could not maintain control after being hit and the aircraft crashed into the Maas, he and three of his crew surviving. In the belief they were approaching the general target area pilots and navigators looked for briefed landmarks; but in vain as they were actually flying north-east between Delft and Rotterdam. The first flight was now led by Captain Converse whose bomber was rising and dropping in evasive action. Near Bodegraven, Converse collided with Lt Wolfe's aircraft which was heading the second element. Both B-26s went down in flames, two gunners surviving each crash, including Sgt Thompson the remaining first raid veteran. Parts severed by the impact of the collision struck a following aircraft, *Chickasaw Chief* in the nose and top turret. The pilot, Lt Wurst, finding the aircraft un-manageable belly-landed in a field at Meije, three miles north of Bodegraven. All the crew escaped, although Sgt Heski, extracted from the wreckage of the top turret, lost a foot.

Now only the third element of the leading flight remained. Lt F. H. Matthew leading Lt E. R. Norton. Norton's co-pilot was his twin brother, J. A. Norton. Lost and evidently believing they did not constitute sufficient force to attack Ijmuiden, Matthew and Norton turned to join Purinton's flight, but Purinton

too had no idea where the target lay. After some ten minutes overflying, and 45 miles into Holland he decided to turn for home and asked his navigator, Lt Jefferies, for a heading. Jefferies gave him 270 degrees then said, 'Hold it a minute, I think I see the target. Yes, there it is.' Bomb doors were opened and Lt Kinney, the co-pilot, sighted and made the drop on what they thought was the Haarlem works, but was actually a gas holder in the suburbs of Amsterdam. The four aircraft trailing Purinton also attempted to hit this installation, but all bombs fell short and caused no damage. A few pilots also strafed the target causing slight damage to buildings. Having climbed to bomb, some of the Marauders did not reduce altitude sufficiently as they raced for the coast. Unbeknown to the crews they were heading directly for IJmuiden. Some recognised it too late to avoid the murderous fire from two dozen naval and 15 other guns protecting the harbour. Purinton's bomber was hit but he managed to make a ditching two miles off shore near some boats. Jefferies was killed in the crash; the rest of the crew, including rear gunner Sgt Miller who had an arm shattered by flak, were picked up by a German patrol boat. The IJmuiden guns also claimed Lt Jones and Norton's aircraft. One with an engine on fire turned back and crashed into the sea off Castricum, the other went down a few miles west of IJmuiden. Tail gunner Sgt Longworth was the only survivor from Norton's aircraft and co-pilot Lt Alaimo from Jones'. Only Lt Matthew's *Blueroad V-Victor* and Cpt Crane's *Snellgrove V-Victor* survived the coastal flank and, at some distance apart, they sped towards England. But there had been other developments.

At 1155, four minutes after the Marauders had blundered over Rozenburg, 26 FW190As of II/JG1 took off from Woendsdretch, southern Holland, on a 'combat alarm'. They were vectored north at 3,500 feet to engage enemy bombers, and at 1218 two flights found the two Marauders flying low over the sea. An FW190 detached from each flight and went in to attack.

After crossing the coast Crane's crew had to jettison a bomb that failed to release. About three minutes after leaving the Dutch coast Crane called to Sgt Williams the engineer who was manning a gun: 'Pilot to turret gunner; George come up front, there is something wrong with the rudder.' Williams slid out of his turret but before going forward checked the rudder cables and saw that one was damaged. He decided to effect a repair, getting some safety wire from the rear of his turret. As he moved back he was horrified to see the sides and bottom of the fuselage perforated by bullets. Scrambling back into his turret he saw the port engine

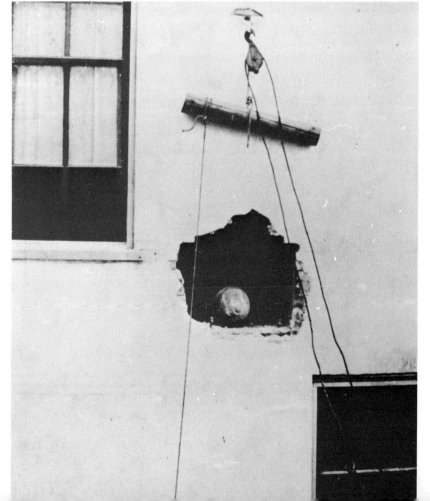

was in flames. He called the pilot but there was no reply. He then saw – as he thought – three Me109s pulling away and concluded a head-on attack had been made. The attack had actually been made from the rear and Sgt Lewis, the tail gunner, faced with a fighter approaching from nearly dead astern began firing when he estimated the enemy was 500 yards away. Although he appeared to be getting hits, the fighter came on and opened fire at 300 yards. Two 20mm shells hit the armour plate in front of Lewis, shell splinters wounding him slightly. The Marauder now lost altitude, dived, levelled out and dived again, hitting the sea and nosed in, leaving the tail sticking out of the water. The camera hatch had already been opened and Williams and Lewis climbed out and while struggling with their life-jackets were surprised to see the large liferaft was cut loose and inflated. They both succeeded in climbing aboard. The Marauder disappeared under the waves in about 45 seconds, as it did so the men saw seven fighters pass overhead. The time was 1224, the location some 40 miles west of Zandvoort, 80 miles from England.

Feldwebel Niedereichholtz of Stab. II/JG1 fired 700 rounds to bring down Crane's aircraft, coming in low and claiming to have hit both engines. Leading the second flight of FW190s, Oberfeldwebel Winkler caught up with Matthew's bomber and shot it into the sea at 1230 about 50 miles west of Zandvoort. There were no survivors.

Captain Stephens had landed his troubled aircraft back at Bury at 1212 having jettisoned the bomb load. Failure of the electrical power was quickly solved; the generators were switched off. Prior to this mission a new Standard Operating Procedure (SOP) was adopted whereby the ground crew chief would carry out pre-flight checks instead of the aerial engineer. The ground crew chief had in this instance, through force of habit, turned the switches off.

Estimated Time of Arrival (ETA) for the Group's return was 1250 and with no word at this time General Brady and other watchers on the Bury control tower were naturally apprehensive. Fifteen minutes later an RAF listening post reported interception of a German fighter radio transmission that two bombers had been shot into the sea. By 1330 it was obvious that the aircraft could no longer be airborne and the dreadful realisation of a disaster had to be accepted. All ten were lost.

During the next few days Bury St Edmunds air base was a place of gloom. Men looked for reasons; rumours were rife. It was said enemy agents had obtained details of the impending mission; Group security officers even compiled a dossier of suspicious characters. Suspects included were certain Royal Observer Corps members, two US ground officers, an American Red Cross official, a local newspaper employee and even a blonde who had been helping GI morale on the base at £2 a time. The favourite scapegoat was higher command that had callously, so it seemed, sent the Group back to the same target by the same route; then, of course, there was the B-26. What more proof was needed that it was suicide to fly one to war?

General Eaker, commanding the 8th Air Force, ordered his Inspector General (IG) to conduct an enquiry. Although the IG had the advantage of evidence from Sgts Williams and Lewis, picked up by a British destroyer after five days on a liferaft, no conclusions were drawn as to the primary cause of the fiasco. No one party was found negligent.

Relative to the scope of USAAF operations from Britain in succeeding months, IJmuiden became just one small mission that failed and there does not appear to have been a later survey to ascertain the reason why.

On the first mission the insistence of the crews that the target was bombed is partly confirmed by German and Dutch records. Of the 43 bombs dropped on 14 May (one failed to release), 32 were traced. A possible 18 fell on the Pen site, three producing major structural damage although only sufficient to cause the station to cease production for five days. Seven of these bombs failed to explode giving some credence to suspicions about British bomb fuses. At least four, perhaps five, bombers had dropped accurately on the target. Two bombers attacked the van Gelder south-east, but none of the seven bombs traced exploded. The rest of the known bomb strikes were in fields to the east and the harbour to the south-west of the target, all apparently released a second too early. Nearly half the bombs located failed to explode. It is assumed that those unlocated (11) were dropped outside the general target area. German bomb disposal teams did not defuse any of the bombs, in fact they showed a marked inclination to keep well away. Despite the efforts to avoid death and injury to civilians, one bomb, without exploding, killed three people and wounded seven others when it dropped in the doorway of a shelter.

Thus the facts are that the 322nd did find the target but less than half the bombs hit it and less than half those exploded. For in-experienced crews on their first mission the results were certainly quite reasonable.

As for the return mission to IJmuiden, there is nothing on record to show that the Germans were expecting a return raid so soon or that there was any strengthening of the defences for this reason. Instead of 30 miles and seven minutes planned over hostile territory the formation spent some 22 minutes and covered nearly 90 miles giving ample opportunity for defence systems to be alerted. The major factor precipitating the disaster of 17 May was the deviation from the planned route across the North Sea which would have meant a landfall of some 18 miles south-west of the briefed point even if a diversion to avoid the enemy convoy had not drawn the formation further to the south. On dead-reckoning Navigation alone, an error equivalent to about 10 per cent of the distance flown since the last reliable fix was not un-usual in those days, thus accounting for 12 of the 18 miles. The most probable explanation for the remaining deviation was a change in surface wind velocity which inexperienced crews were unlikely to spot – there was a 10 to 15mph north-easterly on this day whereas the wind had been south-westerly on the 14 May mission. While this is the most likely explanation, the truth may never be known.

Below: Taken from the same approach route as that flown by the B-26s on 14 May 1943, this pre-war view shows IJmuiden on the south bank and Velsen on the north bank of the waterway. The van Gelder paper factory can be seen to the east of the bridge adjacent to the river. The PEN plant is on the other side of the railway and to the right of the harbour basin – where some bombs fell./*Via A. de Jong*

A Change of Fortunes

Below: The last contingent of 323rd BG moved to England via the North Atlantic route. These B-26C-10 and C-25 models being serviced at Meeks Field, Iceland, on 27 May 1943 include 41-34970, *Raunchy Rascal*, which led the first B-26 medium altitude mission flown from the UK, and 41-34863, *Bingo Buster*, first 323rd aircraft to fly 100 missions./*USAF*

Rejected in the Pacific war, questioned in the Mediterranean theatre and now with the unenviable distinction of having composed the only USAAF task force to penetrate enemy airspace and incur total loss, the Marauder's image was never more tarnished than in the late spring of 1943. Serious misgivings were being voiced in high places back home; this and the distortion of facts brought by rumour did nothing to help morale of those men already committed to fly and fight in the B-26. Nowhere was this more apparent than with the 322nd Group which had flown the disastrous Ijmuiden raid. Although told there would be no more combat until the reasons for the failure had been thoroughly investigated, aircrews at Bury St Edmunds viewed the prospect of the next operation with a general air of hopelessness. A navigator likened the atmosphere to what he imagined a bunch of men awaiting the firing squad must feel. Some believed a reprieve was nigh – the withdrawal of the B-26 from combat, but it was not to be.

The situation brought a good measure of dispondency at Elveden Hall where the problem of tactical employment of the Marauder was discussed at a succession of staff meetings. Even in 3rd Wing there were a few men who saw the B-26 as the root cause of the current predicament. For the most part the senior staff recognised that the Marauder was simply the scapegoat and that

other factors were involved. Opinion centred on the return to the same target as a major error, with crew inexperience a contributory factor. Pursuing low-level attack with the B-26 was still considered viable though dependent on highly trained crews to assure good results and low losses. The RAF favoured lighter faster aircraft like the Boston and Mosquito for zero altitude attacks, preferring to send the slower more vulnerable mediums over targets at around 10,000 feet. This was also the policy for both RAF and USAAF medium units in North Africa.

Operations Officer at 3rd Wing, Major Jack Caldwell, had been sent to study 12th Air Force tactics during March 1943. He had learned how the B-25s and B-26s had been driven to operate at medium altitudes over North Africa with noticeable improvement in bombing results and a reduction in losses. Impressed by the evidence, Caldwell suggested on his return that British-based Marauders could be better employed at medium levels. He found some support but such a change was far from simple to effect. To start with the Wing had no supply of Model M series bombsights, the famous Norden, essential for attack from these heights. Bombardiers would have to be trained or refreshed on its use when available, while pilots had to be instructed in flying the PDI (Pilot Direction Indicator), an instrument that transmitted flight manoeuvres desired by the bombardier

while lining up his sight on the target. The two B-26 groups already in the theatre, and two more scheduled to arrive early in June, were trained and equipped for operations at altitudes under 2,000 feet: the Marauder had been developed for this role with all new models having fixed forward firing armament for ground strafing. Moreover, the second group to arrive, the 323rd, had aircraft tailored for single-pilot operation, as a co-pilot was considered unnecessary in low attack. A time consuming re-training and modification programme would have to be implemented. There was another aspect to be considered. With no surprise element in medium altitude operations, fighter escort was essential. US fighters were heavily committed to support the daylight raids by

heavies and if any fighters were to be provided for B-26 support they would have to be short-ranged RAF Spitfires.

While 3rd Wing struggled with the problems of tactical employment, higher command had come to a decision on control. The Marauders had originally been sent to the 8th Air Force to operate against short-range targets in the strategic campaign VIII BC was waging against the enemy. Their apparent inability to make an effective contribution to their campaign was a taxing problem VIII BC could well do without, at a time when its need was heavy bombers for the offensive then gathering momentum. In consequence, early in June, the 3rd Wing and its units were sent packing from Bomber Command to Air Support Command, hitherto a non-

Above: Initial movement of 323rd Group 'single-pilot' B-26Cs was by the long south Atlantic route. A refuelling stop was Rufisque, French West Africa, where replacement B-26s destined for the 12th Air Force also put down. In the foreground is a B-26B-10 which went to the 319th BG and saw extensive combat service. Note navigator compartment hatch removed to allow access to top of wings./USAF

Right: Undercarriage doors about to close on tucked-away wheels as *Ticklish Percy* crosses the threshold of Earls Colne. One of 60 'single-pilot' Marauders, this B-26C-6 was soon retired in favour of a conventional two-pilot model./*USAAF*

Below right: Buffalo Girl, a B-26C-6-MO 'single pilot' Marauder on her Earls Colne hardstand. Co-pilot's control column and armoured seat were not installed. A lightweight seat was fitted instead so that the navigator could operate flaps and undercarriage during take-off and landing. Navigational equipment was moved from the normal compartment behind the cockpit to the nose, leaving only the command radio, a small 'putt-putt' auxiliary starter engine and the life raft. An escape door (shown lowered in this picture) was built into the bottom of the radio room to afford crew egress – a feature most would like to have seen on conventional Marauders./*USAAF*

combat organisation engaged in developing air support for ground forces to be committed to a future cross-Channel invasion. At the same time 3rd Wing and its units were moved from bases in Suffolk and Norfolk, south to the county of Essex which would place them nearer the Channel area and prospective targets within a 300 mile radius of action. On 12 and 13 June 3rd Wing traded one English stately home for another, taking up residence at Marks Hall, while the combat groups moved to airfields in the same district. The 322nd took up station at Andrews Field (Great Saling), the 323rd at Earls Colne, and the 386th at Boxted – the last-named group being newly arrived in the UK. A fourth Group, the 387th, on its way from the States, went to Chipping Ongar.

A few days after settling in at the new Headquarters, 3rd Wing finally issued a directive on future B-26 operations. The main priority would be preparation for medium altitude bombing of land targets although low-level attacks on enemy shipping would also be carried out. Other forms of anti-shipping operations were to be explored and the possibilities of night bombing selected targets in occupied territory. The 323rd and 386th Groups were to be committed to medium altitude operations while the 322nd continued to pursue low-level tactics, training for shipping strikes in conjunction with British naval units operating from the ports of Felixstowe and Harwich.

Lt Col Glenn Nye, given command of the 322nd after Stillman's loss, had the difficult task of re-building confidence in the aircraft and the mission. In the weeks following the Ijmuiden debacle he led them in hedge-hopping flights, simulating combat missions, only to have progress marred by another fatal crash. Two weeks before leaving Bury St Edmunds a low flying B-26B-4 ploughed into the ground near a hangar on the airfield, killing all on board. This grisly accident, witnessed by many men on the field, was attributed to part of the tail breaking away while practising evasive action. The prophets of doom saw it as further proof of the Marauder's propensity to live up to the sobriquet Martin Murderer. Nye had to perform a tail testing flight in his endeavours to prove that this was an isolated accident: it transpired the crash was caused by bolts securing the fin to fuselage working loose, a fault peculiar to that particular machine. Factory changes were instituted to avoid similar failures, while in Britain a special strengthening plate was designed for installation on 'small tail' Marauders.

Before the move to Essex the other two squadrons of the 322nd had arrived and these were equipped with the new B-26B-10 and B-26C models featuring a 'big tail' and increased wing span. Both models were of similar specification and performance, being built at Baltimore and Omaha plants respectively. The general opinion was that the new models handled better, although the planned advantages in land and take-off runs were negated by an extra 2,000lb in basic weight. The 323rd Bomb Group had all Omaha Marauders as original combat equipment but these were the special single-pilot models, designated B-26C-6s with co-pilot's seat and controls removed to save weight. The Group was to test the single-pilot concept although there were misgivings in 8th Air Force at command levels as to the wisdom of this experiment, as the value of the co-pilot had been well proven in combat. In fact, any advantage in low-level operations was never tested, as the 323rd was to be the instigator of medium altitude bombing with Marauders in Europe. Training missions for this purpose, known as Doughnuts, were delayed until early July as 3rd Wing was unable to obtain Norden sights until late June. Much of the new technique was based on the experience of B-26 groups in North Africa, using the basic 3-plane vic, two of these forming a six-plane flight and three flights an 18-plane box. Flights were staggered within the box to give gunners the best possible fields of fire and enhance the defensive position of the whole formation. In general the grouping was based on the formations successfully evolved for the B-17 or B-24 heavy bombers when attacking targets as a group.

Apart from re-training navigator/bombardiers and practising formation flying, the 230 B-26s held by 3rd Wing by July 1943 provided a major engineering problem to embody modifications to meet the new operational proposals and counter weaknesses evinced by the first low-level raid. Special VHF radios had to be installed and anti-jamming noise suppressors fitted to other radio equipment; additional armour plate was fitted for protecting the pilots and a more suitable compass in the nose compartment were also major requirements. By the second week of July there was a list of 14 modifications for B-26s reaching the theatre plus another eight listed as desirable. These changes were made at air depots, but a few urgent modifications were carried out at bases. One was the provision of a wooden stop on the gun-mount of the Bell tail turret to prevent the guns breaking the plexiglass when swung to maximum depression.

During this training and modification period there were some changes in command. General Eaker had been successful in acquiring one of the most promising officers in AAF headquarters, the 38-year old Colonel Samuel E. Anderson who arrived at Marks

Hall to take over 3rd Wing. He had flown early B-26s at Langley Field and spent a brief spell in 1942 with the 22nd Bomb Group in Australia as a special observer. On taking up his appointment he learned that the USAAF had decided to postpone the movement of any further B-26 groups to England, giving priority to heavy bomber units. The movement of the 391st Group was cancelled and two other Marauder groups; the 394th and 397th, scheduled to arrive late in the summer, were relegated to further training. An additional three B-26 groups were earmarked for England, the 344th, re-forming after having originally been readied to move in April but whose crews and aircraft had been diverted to replace losses in North Africa, and the 21st and 477th Groups. This made a planned total of ten B-26 Marauder groups for 3rd Wing; the five B-25 Mitchell groups had

been diverted because of the demand for this type in other theatres. For the time being, Anderson's command would have to make do with the four groups already in the theatre.

On the eve of the first attempt to fly a medium altitude combat mission with the Marauder from Britain, yet more adverse criticism of the type was emanating from publication of the findings of the Committee set up by the US government under Harry S. Truman to review warplane procurement. What had been mooted on previous occasions, the termination of production, was now in hand with initial plans to convert the Omaha plant to manufacture B-29 Superfortresses early in 1944. The impression was given that the B-26 was being written off as a bomber that had failed.

In sunshine in the late afternoon of 16 July 1943, 16 B-26Cs took off from Earls Colne, Essex, to carry out an attack on marshalling yards at Abbeville in north-east France. Five Marauder co-pilot models flew mainly in lead positions of the three flights. Colonel Thatcher led his group to a rendezvous with a substantial Spitfire escort before proceeding to the target at 10,000 feet. While the bombing apparently did little damage, there was jubilation at Earls Colne when, two hours after take-off, 16 Marauders appeared over the field. The Spitfires had kept enemy fighters away but anti-aircraft fire had severely wounded a tail gunner. Anderson had himself flown in a bomber on this inaugural medium altitude mission.

Poor weather prevented further operations until the 25th when the 323rd visited the Ghent coke ovens. Again all aircraft returned. Next day another 18-plane box set off from Earls Colne for an enemy airfield at St Omer where over 100 Spitfires afforded protection. On the 27th it was Triqueville airfield and again all the Marauders came back. Next day Anderson made use of the long summer days by sending the 323rd out twice, morning and afternoon. This was attempted again on the 29th but the first mission was abortive as the bombers failed to assemble formation in time to rendezvous with the Spitfire escort.

The RAF stipulated a four-to-one ratio of fighters to bombers for effective protection which meant that escort might be limited to a single B-26 box on any one mission. Furthermore the Spitfire commanders insisted on the right to turn the bombers home if for weather, fuel shortage or for other reasons they considered it advisable. As radio silence was observed on penetration, the return signal was achieved by the Spitfire leader waggling his wings to the view of the Marauder leader. Some 3rd Wing officers tended to resent these restrictions but if the abortive missions were frustrating to the crews, none had any doubt as to the value of their escort, having seen

Spitfires tangle with FW190s on several occasions during these first few missions. Reduction in the fighter/bomber ratio was inevitable if 3rd Wing was to employ its whole force. On the 29th the 323rd had added another vic of three to boost its formation to 21 bombers, and for the operations of the 30th, when the 386th Group would be committed for the first time, 24-plane boxes were planned.

While the British-based US heavy bombers had been engaged in costly missions deep into Germany the 8th Air Force's ugly duckling had made eight penetrations of the most heavily defended coastline in the world and returned without loss. The bombing accuracy was poor, even so, it looked as if the right formula to attain success had at last been found.

Left: The crew of 452nd BS's *Jezabelle* had a small dog named *Salvo* which they took on parachute jumps over their home airfield. A special 'chute was made for *Salvo* who was said to enjoy the experience! Here crew and dog are preparing to enter the bomber to participate in another jump./*USAAF*

Above: The 323rd BG's Cpt Frank Kappler was an ex 17th BG 'Tokyo' flier./*USAAF*

61

Enter the Crusaders

Bottom right: Famous for his pioneering flight across the Pacific (in a Fokker C2-3 with Lt A. F. Hegenberger) which brought him the second American DFC ever awarded, Lester Maitland also had the distinction of being the oldest US bomber pilot flying combat from England. Extremely popular with his men, Maitland led or flew on most of the 386th's early missions. After leaving the USAAF he became a Presbyterian minister. */USAAF*

Far right: The remains of Lt Williamson's *Two Way Ticket* in a cultivated field at Severalls Hall Farm, Colchester. While the violent impact wrenched off both engines and crumpled the fuselage, none of the crew were severely injured. */Via L. McFarland*

Beyond the eastern boundary of Boxted airfield a lightening of the sky established a horizon and brought forth another dawn – that of 30 July 1943. The dark shapes of dispersed Marauders gradually emerged from the slowly lifting gloom. Here and there vehicles moved carefully along taxiways, the narrow beams from screened headlights stabbing through the ground mists. Beneath many aircraft figures were just discernible and occasionally a torch beam illuminated an engine cowling or undercarriage leg where inspection or work was performed. The faint, continuous drone of unseen RAF heavies coming back from a night's work over the Reich was, with most other sounds, periodically drowned by the roar of a Pratt & Whitney under test. The local population had learned to live with the sleep-shattering disturbance of aero engines being wound up during the dark hours, just as they had come to accept the other innumerable discomforts of wartime Britain. Little more than a year before their parish was woods and farmland; now 500 acres had been transformed into an airfield with meadows covered with camp buildings. This morning's early awakening was like so many others in recent days for the farmers and village people going about their normal lives; but on the other side of the airfield boundary's coiled barbed wire there was a difference. The atmosphere was tense and hurried; today the 386th Bomb Group – later known as the Crusaders – was going to war for the first time.

The combat initiation had been expected during the past few days. The Group had been alerted on the morning of the 29th, only to have the operation changed to a diversion flight. Twenty-five minutes before midnight the same day Headquarters was again alerted with a message to load eight 300lb bombs on each of 21 Marauders. Ordnance and armament men were awakened from their slumbers and set to hauling and loading the missiles in bombers selected from those in full commission. A long, slow and far from easy task in darkness.

The detailed Field Order chattered out of the teletype machine at 0035hrs and operations and intelligence sections began frenzied activity to produce the required material and information for briefing. Inexperience would mark most phases of this preparation; although guarded with the utmost secrecy the very nature of the activity soon led to even those personnel consigned to menial domestic chores being aware that 'the' mission was on. The engineering section had the line and crew chiefs out on the field by 0100hrs to pre-flight check the bombers. Each engine was run up in turn and the instruments checked. Meanwhile cooks were preparing breakfast for the aircrews, officially awakened at 0200hrs – but some had already been disturbed by the thunderous din of engines under test. Because of nervous anticipation and the early hour, few fliers did justice to their meal. Eager for briefing, most were assembling long before the roll was called shortly after 0300hrs. Briefing was delayed by a lighting failure and, as Major Thomas Haire, Group Intelligence Officer later commented, 'took something over two hours and probably all that can be said for it was that it was undoubtedly the most complete, if also the most disjointed, briefing the crews of the 386th ever had.' The target was Woensdretch airfield, a German fighter base 30 miles in from the island coastline of south Holland. Enemy fighter opposition was probable and eight squadrons of RAF Spitfires, some 96 fighters, would provide escort all the way.

The Field Order changed the number of bombers required to 24 and six aircraft from each of the Group's four squadrons was selected. The CO, Lt Col Lester Maitland, was to lead. He was a popular commander, a 'big bull of a man' and at 45 twice the age of most of his men. Already famous, having won his wings in 1916, he had established a world speed record in 1923 and four years later made the first flight from California to Hawaii of 2,000 miles.

As the eastern sky took on a pink hue, the weather forecaster's predictions appeared to be true; another fine warm day. 'Gas wagons' lumbered round the perimeter track, anti-static chains jingling against the concrete, topping fuel tanks. On some bombers there were snags; *Shadrack* had radio trouble which tradesmen were working hard to correct. Parachutes, Mae Wests and other personal equipment had been put in the Marauders by the time trucks brought the crews, shortly after 0500hrs. Pilots consulted with crew chiefs and carried out visual inspections of the aircraft as other crewmen put on Mae Wests and checked personal items. Engine start time was near and men climbed aboard, the majority using the ladder in the rear of the nose wheel well, but a few athletic gunners hauled themselves up through waist windows. Putt-putt motors strained and with a pro-testing whine of gearing, engines spurted life; first right then left. Co-pilots closed oil cooled shutters and checked cowl flaps. Pilots ran up right engines to 1,800rpm, watching the instruments for magneto fluctu-ation. Then propeller pitch was moved through its range. Standing in front of 'their' aircraft, where pilots could see them, the crew chiefs listened to the engine note and watched exhaust flames, then moving to the other side to repeat the procedure for the left engine. On releasing the parking brake, mixture control was changed and both engines opened up to 2,700rpm; pilot's feet jammed hard on the foot brake pedal as the whole aircraft vibrated and the nose pitched down on the front wheel strut. Power reduced and all checks satisfactorily com-pleted, the ground crew removed chocks and signalled each bomber out of its dispersal. Pilots watched for the call-letters on other aircraft so that they could be sure to taxi on to the perimeter track in the briefed order for take-off.

The 552nd Bomb Squadron flight moved out first; being at the south end of the air-field they had a long way to taxi round the eastern side to reach the head of runway 22. They were to be second squadron to take-off; the first was the 554th parked nearer the western taxiway. Behind the 554th, six air-craft of the 555th were marshalled, while from dispersals on the eastern side came the

553rd contingent bringing up the rear. By 0524hrs, the leading elements were in ranks on the perimeter track either side of the head of runway 22, with engines idling and sun-light flashing off the plexiglass, while long shadows began to take shape on the dew soaked grass. Seconds dragged by for the young men waiting tensely in the bombers, gunners now sitting with backs braced against the forward bulkhead in the rear fuselage until safely airborne. A pilot raised a hand to wave to a man setting off for work from a nearby cottage. The local nodded in acknowledgement, mounted his bicycle and rode off. A quarter of a century before he had been in a front line trench in France waiting to go over the top. Now outside his own back door 'bits of boys' were similarly setting out to face the enemy, but it was hard to reconcile the peaceful pastoral scene around with a battlefront.

At precisely 0525hrs the flare signal came from the tower. Captain Tom White, pilot of Maitland's personal aircraft *Texas Tarantu-la,* released the brakes and advanced throttles to maximum. The bomber gathered speed quickly: White held her down nearly to the end of the 1¼ mile runway and at 140mph *Texas Tarantula* lifted off. Maitland, riding the co-pilot's position moved the gear-up lever and the Marauder was clear, climbing steadily away south-west over Colchester, once capital of Roman Britain. The other five 554th Squadron aircraft followed at 30 second intervals. Men in the control van beside the runway could read the brightly painted nick-names as each began its run: *Question Mark* (2/Lt Petit), *Shadrack* (2/Lt Caldwell), *Cloud Hopper II* (1/Lt Curran), *Smokey* (Flt Off Casey) and *Litljo* (2/Lt Hillis).

Two minutes out from base Captain White began to turn *Texas Tarantula* left to start a wide climbing orbit of Boxted. Following aircraft of the lead element would turn 10 seconds sooner than the preceding B-26 to enable them to form a three-plane vic with the leader. *Cloud Hopper II* was to head the second element with the two following air-craft forming up similarly, while Lt Curran tightened his turn to catch up with the first element of the flight. The sky was cloudless but haze, precurser of a warm day, veiled the countryside below and misted the atmosphere for some 400 feet up, limiting visibility to about two miles. The haze was troublesome enough for 2/Lt Petit to lose sight of the lead plane and for the 554th flight to end up eventually with some aircraft in interchanged positions.

No sooner had the last aircraft of the first flight departed than the first of the 552nd Squadron pulled onto the runway from the eastern track and was on its way. Following *Crescendo*, commanded by Captain Thornton the Squadron Operations Officer, came *Dottie* (1/Lt Cox), *Danny Boy* (2/Lt Lambert), *Winnie* (Major Lockhart), *Margie* (Flt Off Albers) and *Hazard* (1/Lt Danforth). *Son of Satan* (Major Beaty), first B-26 of the 555th Bomb Squadron to roll, was followed, a half minute apart by *Hell's Fury* (2/Lt Sanford), *Perkatory* (2/Lt Perkins, *Man-o-War* (1/Lt Wilson), *Miss Muriel* (2/Lt Bartolain) and *Hell's Belle* (2/Lt Blackburn).

By the time 1/Lt Dewhurst, 553rd Bomb Squadron Operations Officer, led his unit's take-off in *Dinah Might*, White and Maitland were climbing for altitude at 200 feet per minute and 175mph with the rest of their flight in trail. After *Dinah Might* came *Grit* (1/Lt Saltsman) and *Elmer* (1/Lt Haber) to complete the 553rd's lead element. Then 1/Lt Williamson sped *Two Way Ticket* down the runway. Just after the undercarriage had been raised and some 75 feet of altitude gained, Williamson suddenly felt the right engine die. Immediately he tried to trim the aircraft for single-engine flight, but getting no response and seeing air speed fall below 140mph elected to belly-in straight ahead. The land dipped away to a small tree-lined stream then rose again to a country road. Williamson, managing to keep enough height to avoid farm buildings and a small house, swept over

the road. Trying to set *Two Way Ticket* down in a potato field beyond he struck an airfield marker post and a hedgerow tree which ripped off an elevator. When the bomber made contact with the ground both engines were wrenched off their mountings as the fuselage ploughed along scattering bombs and breaking in two at the navigator's compartment. No fire or explosion occurred and the worst injury was a broken finger for Williamson. With minor cuts and bruises the crew emerged from the wreck as *Rat Poison* (Lt Hochrein) passed over, closely followed at 0540hrs by *The Wolf* (1/Lt Glenn Zimmerman) making the 24th and final take-off of the mission. There was some confusion for these last two bombers, as they had no element leader to form on and *Rat Poison* did not catch up with the rest of the Group formation until 45 minutes later.

Watches and positions were constantly checked by those in *Texas Tarantula* for failure to make the appointed rendezvous with fighters would mean cancelling the mission. Because of this responsibility this aircraft carried both a bombardier and navigator, instead of one man combining both duties. While flying a box course in the vicinity of the base, Maitland and White gradually increased altitude. At Boxted an audience of

Left: The crew of *Man-O-War*, l. to r. Lts Ed Laube and Bob Owen, Sgt Charles Smith, Lt Jim Wilson and Sgt John Holmstrom, watch Sgt Jim Dugan demonstrate for the photographer how he 'bagged a Jerry' on the Group's first mission./*USAAF*

ground men, and aircrews not participating, only dispersed when the Group passed over the field for the last time heading north-east towards the rendezvous at Orfordness at 11,000 feet. The four flights were arranged in a diamond pattern in planform, but were slightly staggered in altitude.

To the relief of the leader, gunners reported Spitfires 5,000 feet above as the formation set course at 0627. Cloud had built up below as the 386th approached Orfordness, but during the 33 minutes it took to reach the enemy coast this gradually dispersed until the surf line far below was visible through the heavy haze of the summer day. Speed was increased to 200mph and evasive action started; changes of direction every 20 seconds, taking the formation to and from its course – and apparently somewhat too abruptly for the escort who had difficulty in keeping track of their zig-zagging charges, occasionally losing sight of them completely.

Black and white smoke puffs appeared behind and below; one tail gunner viewed them with curiosity until remembering the lethal nature of flak: 'Somebody's trying to kill us!' he exclaimed over the interphone, which brought chuckles although no one really thought it funny. Far below Flak unit 1/847 had fired ten well directed rounds of 37mm, close bursts making a few holes in aircraft in the 552nd and 553rd flights. The Initial Point (IP), a coastal landmark, was recognised, course adjusted and bomb-doors opened. A bombsight was carried in the lead plane of every element with the intention that formating aircraft should drop their bombs when the leader did, signalled by a red light on engine nacelles. While all bombardiers would sight for range, only Lt Dunn in *Texas Tarantula* would sight for both range and deflection. Through the haze the unmistakable shape of the coastal indentation near Bergen op Zoom presented a check point for the target. Looking over the bombsight the Command bombardier picked out the enemy airfield. Twenty-five seconds from release time the Group ceased evasive action and made a straight run. Unfortunately ground haze and refraction from the sun prevented Lt Dunn from locating the target through the Norden's telescopic viewer until it was too late to line up the instrument correctly. Neither the first nor second flights bombed because of sighting difficulties, but the third and fourth flights did release.

Immediately after crossing the target the formation turned right as briefed, but *The Wolf* dropped back apparently having been hit in the left engine. Tail gunners in the rear formations became aware of fighters rapidly approaching. The sun was to the advantage of the enemy and the B-26 gunners were hindered by glare as they opened fire. An FW190 flown by Fw Willius of 3/JG26 came up under Zimmerman's straggling bomber and blasted it with cannon shells. The right engine smoked and *The Wolf* fell off into a spin. Seconds later it was seen to strike the water far below with no sign of anyone parachuting to safety. (Willius was later killed in action near Kampen on 8 April 1944.) In the confused action with the German fighters many claims were made by gunners who expended over 9,000 rounds of ammunition against some 15 FW190s and Me109s estimated to have been involved in a three-minute battle. S/Sgt McQueeny, tail gunner on *Hell's Belle* put an accurate burst into the FW190 thought to have attacked *The Wolf* as did Sgt Dugan in the tail of *Miss Muriel*: it exploded in mid-air 'like an ash-can out of a twenty storey window.' Waist gunner on *Crescendo*, Sgt McKim, also claimed to have sent a fighter down in flames.

The Spitfire escort had temporarily lost the Marauders which were now several miles off their briefed course, apparently sufficiently divorced for the German fighter control, with the advantage of radar and ground observers, to vector fighters for an interception. The Spitfires were soon back on the scene and the Luftwaffe did not return. More flak; seven close bursts were from a captured British gun but 270 rounds of 20mm did not come within range. In a gradual reduction of altitude the Marauders crossed the coast out at 10,000 feet: they had been over enemy territory 13 minutes. Thirty miles out the lead-plane signalled to jettison bombs and the 11 others that had overshot the target followed suit.

The course back to England should have been via Orfordness, instead the Group crossed near Harwich and at 0753hrs the 22 Marauders arrived over home base, 14 minutes behind schedule. Taking a five mile circuit of the field, aircraft broke formation and made the long straight-in approach practised with the B-26. It seemed as if everyone at Boxted was there to witness the homecoming. As the crews emerged from the aircraft they were met by inquisitive groups of servicemen wanting to know how things went. 'Rough' was the general verdict. Ground crews searched for battle damage. *Rat Poison* sported a nick in a bomb-bay door and two more on the left propeller cuff. Flak had torn out a small piece of the trailing edge on *Crescendo*'s right elevator. *Dottie* had a splinter through the top of the right wing centre section and *Hazard* had one in the leading edge of the right wing near the root. *Elmer*'s liferaft cover also had a perforation. The only evidence of the engagement with the fighters was made by a single bullet through *Dinah Might*'s left elevator and rudder. Crew chiefs consulted pilots on any mechanical difficulties; the bomb racks in *Shadrack* failed to function properly while *Danny Boy* had low oil pressure on the right engine. *Hell's Belle* had a cylinder head temperature gauge go out. The pilots of *Hell's Fury* complained about dirty windshields.

Eventually trucks arrived at the hardstandings to transport crews to interrogation, coffee and doughnuts. Interrogation took as long as briefing as efforts were made to untangle the confused pattern of the air battle. Finally six destroyed credits and five probables were awarded air gunners. The problem of establishing the truth when several gunners were all firing at enemy fighters would always confound the most dedicated intelligence officers. The records of I/JG26 the German unit involved show that only eight FW190s attempted interception, two being lost in an action lasting only seconds; results not known to the 386th during hostilities.

While interrogation continued the room became a general debating chamber for those waiting. Many men were annoyed that they had risked their necks only to deposit bombs in the sea. There were complaints about the sun glare, poor visibility from the old type tail gun emplacements and suggestions that the glass panel should be removed to help matters. There were assertions that some gunners had fired at Spitfires and needed more recognition training. Most of the men on the mission voiced an opinion that the flak was heavy which, in the light of later experience, they would re-assess as light. The fatigue brought by excitement and fear finally found most newly fledged combatants seeking their beds. Even as they did, the Group received another alert for action later in the day.

The 386th had endured its baptism of fire, lost the first B-26 in medium altitude operations from the UK, and claimed the first enemy fighters. The operation had little success – bombs hitting Woensdretch did little lasting damage – yet much could be accounted for by inexperience. This mission would in its basic execution be similar to hundreds more that this and other B-26 groups in England would perform in the months ahead.

Just before noon a B-17 Fortress staggered out of the sky for an emergency landing at Boxted. On board were six wounded men. Large pieces of the aircraft had been blasted away by cannon shells and there were reputedly a thousand holes in its skin, the result of an air battle deep in Germany. After inspecting this wreck 386th personnel tended to revise their opinions of their own suffering this day. 'Say', said one B-26 gunner to another in the chow line, 'did you hear about those B-17 boys in that shot up Fort. The Old Man offered to fly them back to their own base in a B-26; know what they said? They didn't mind riskin' their necks fightin' the Jerries but they weren't goin' to be so screwy as to take a ride in a Widowmaker. Sure, they jus' darn gone wouldn't fly in it!'

Left: Cpt Charles V, Thornton who led the second flight on 30 July, poses for the camera a few days later. The enemy aircraft credited to *Crescendo's* waist gunner, Sgt M. D. McKim, is recorded on the score board – which also includes a duck symbol for a decoy mission. Thornton later commanded 555th BS but was killed crashlanding *Crescendo* in France after a flak hit caused another B-26 to collide with it./*USAAF*

A Place in the Sun

Having found a method of employing the Marauder without prohibitive losses, General Anderson next attempted to make maximum use of his force and improve bombing results. On 31 July 1943, his command was able to despatch 21-plane boxes to four different targets within 24 hours; the 323rd Group making two raids, the 386th one and the 322nd flying its first medium altitude operation.

The 322nd, only recently diverted from low-level training, had its mission to Tricqueville airfield contested by the Luftwaffe although eight squadrons of Spitfires beat off most attacks. In an exchange of fire between the B-26s and a few FW190s that did get through, waist gunner S/Sgt Clyde Maddox put a burst into one which an RAF pilot later confirmed as having gone down. On its second raid of the day the 323rd suffered the first Marauder loss to flak at medium altitude when the B-26C-6 piloted by Captain John Lipscombe was hit in the wing and went down on fire. Anti-aircraft fire was a regular feature of these Marauder missions. The 323rd received another rough passage on 2 August en route to Merville airfield when the formation was bracketed by a barrage of bursts and 11 aircraft were perforated. It was on this raid that the 323rd instigated what was to become the standard mission commitment for a B-26 group, 36 aircraft in two 18-plane boxes, the second trailing behind and below the lead.

Down at Chipping Ongar the fourth group assigned to 3rd Wing fretted to become operational. Doughnut training had been restricted by lack of fuel supplies pending the completion of the airfield's storage site in mid-July. The 387th Group had an excellent

Before *Mild and Bitter* departed for the US and a bomb raising tour 322nd BG personnel were allowed to apply 'autographs'. Also added at that time was the record of Air Medals and DFCs awarded aircrew members.
/V. Culhane

spirit after a fairly untroubled passage through Stateside training and being the first B-26 group to complete overseas movement without an accident. The early success of medium-level operations added to the airmen's confidence in the Marauder and their ability to make good in the bombing business. A 'wild bunch', according to one observer, 387th crews became increasingly frustrated as inclement weather in early August restricted flying and delayed their combat initiation. This frustration manifested itself in some over-exuberant low flying. The height at which Lt Jack Skipper skipped his *Booger Red II* over a camp living site is evinced by the fact that Lt Lou Sullivan, standing outside one of the huts, throwing his cap up at the oncoming Marauder, saw it slashed by a propeller. Unhappily the Marauder encountering an electricity supply line, suffered a shattered nose, holed wing leading edges and a mutilated fin. As Jack Skipper had been briefed for a low-flying sortie (although he admitted, not that low) the authorities had no grounds to 'throw the book' at him. Not so

other incautious members of his group. On the afternoon of 9 August, Captain Roger Ray led his flight down for an unofficial buzz job well away from the eyes of his superiors at Ongar. Lt Caples went a little too low and at Sheering tried, so rumour had it, to fly under an 11kv power line. He returned to base with a smashed nose glass and cables wrapped round the forward fuselage and wings. One length, wound around the right propeller hub, had smashed the governor. Later that day Lt Allen Sherman put on a spirited 'hedge height' display over the Essex countryside, including an attempt to turn the sails of an ancient windmill with the slipstream of his *General Sherman* – and achieved according to a witness! This led to Ray, Sherman and Caples, plus Major Charles Keller who was answerable for his men's conduct, all being fined by the Group CO, Colonel Storrie. The tree errant fliers were also grounded for the Group's first combat mission and even offered to pay twice the fine if they would be allowed to participate!

Storrie, a 'laconic Texan', was not above

showing his own desire to get the group operational. Having heard that an awards ceremony was to be held at 3rd Wing Headquarters he decided to impress the gathering as to the 387th's expertise. Enlisting the help of the Group Executive and a Squadron Commander, Storrie provided a fly past over the parade ground where onlookers were surprised to see three Marauders in formation, each with one propeller stationary. The 387th finally joined the fray on 15 August with the St Omer/Ft Rouge airfield their objective. Not to repeat a long straight bombing run was the principal lesson learned, for the German flak gunners had time to carefully direct their fire with the result that half the 36 bombers on the raid were hit by shrapnel.

Flak soon asserted itself as the chief antagonist of the Marauders. There were few places within their radius of action where flak was not encountered. The German anti-aircraft artillery defences were well established and proficient with many batteries linked to gun-laying radars. As Allied air strikes from England increased so did the number of enemy guns defending the Channel and North Sea coastal areas of France and the Low Countries. Marauder crews were having to operate in what was fast becoming the most inhospitable patch of sky on earth. Moreover they did not have the altitude advantage of the B-17s and B-24s which could put twice the distance between themselves and the ground guns.

For the B-26s, evasive action was essential to diminish losses. The time taken by a flak crew to re-compute and set-up changes in range was estimated at around 30 seconds, so to stand a better chance of surviving Marauder pilots had to change course or alter altitude every 20 seconds. To keep formation under these conditions required vigilance and untiring effort: no one complained once they saw a barrage burst in airspace they had occupied 30 seconds before. Evasive action could make difficulties for escorting fighters and often precipitated an inaccurate bomb release if care was not exercised on the target run-up. To minimise further the effects of flak, routes to and from targets were, wherever possible, planned to avoid unnecessary exposure to the heaviest concentration of guns. If navigation was poor it was very easy for a formation to wander from the prescribed route and into disaster. And navigation was not infrequently slightly off track, particularly when an undercast concealed landmarks.

The limited amount of armoured protection for the crew was designed chiefly to shield the bombardier and pilot when ground strafing. A curved steel plate on the outer side on the fuselage below the pilot's window

was a fixture on the 'big wing' Marauders, and a modification put in hand by the 8th Air Force involved fashioning a similar panel for the co-pilot's side. Earlier in the year special body armour had been developed in the UK for heavy bomber crews, but owing to demand it was not until the end of August that each of the four Marauder groups had sufficient sets to fit out every man on a 36-plane mission.

With all four groups operational and often launching three or four 36-plane missions a day, 3rd Wing should have produced a telling effect at targets visited. Results were, overall, disappointing during this initial period of operations at heights around 10,000 feet. The majority of targets were enemy airfields which, being in the order of a mile square, afforded a better opportunity of bombs causing worthwhile disruption even if a bombardier's aim was imprecise. The neutralisation of the Luftwaffe was a major priority, so in denying it the use of forward airfields the Marauder force was making an effective contribution to this campaign. The B-26 groups had made very good drops – such as the 322nd's second medium level mission when it caused major damage at Le Trait shipyards – and some very bad ones where bombs had fallen wide and caused deaths among civilians of the occupied countries. The principal trouble was that whereas the formation leader might achieve a reasonably accurate drop, bombs from other elements would be widely dispersed. Normally bomb sights were carried by the leader of each three-plane element and during August various formation arrangements were experimented with in an effort to improve both accuracy and pattern of drop.

After scattering bombs around Poix airfield on 27 August, the 386th Group decided to consult the B-17 group on tactics. Visits to the Fortress bases at Snetterton and Bury convinced the 386th of the policy of having their most skilled bombardier sight for a whole 18-plane box. *Texas Tarantula,* Colonel Maitland's aircraft, became a special leadship

Far left: Flak damage like this would become common but caused quite a stir at the 323rd BG base when *Miss Emily* returned from a raid on Merville airfield, 2 August 1943. A shell came up through the fuselage exploding against the right hand side of the cockpit and blasted out through the skin (blast and shrapnel from an exploding AA shell fanned up and out, not down.) Luckily this was a single-pilot B-26C and no one was hurt. When the crew picture was posed, *Miss Emily* was propped up on planks and being stripped for spares: l. to r. Tom Trainer, navigator, Jim Davis, pilot, and gunners Dick King, Joe White and looking out of cockpit window – George Lemberger. /USAAF

Left: The 36-plane formation introduced in August 1943 that became the standard group operational effort for the remainder of hostilities. Lower, trailing box is shown in white.

Above: The 'three-plane, feathered prop', fly-past staged by the 387th Group commander. /Via A. Crouchman

Above: As the first bombs hit during 387th BG's attack on Lille/Vendeville airfield, 31 August 1943, the strike camera of *Miss Ginger*, 11,000 feet above, also records the fate of *King Bee* falling in two pieces having taken a direct flak hit aft of the bomb-bay./*USAAF*

Right: Body armour, originally devised for heavy bomber crews in England, was soon available to B-26 crews. Made of overlapping steel plates it could stop most low velocity missiles. Demonstrators are 323rd BG's Lt Ralph N. Phillips (right), a navigator who later became the first Marauder man in the UK to complete a 50 mission tour, and Sgt William F. Vermillion, later a POW (see *Swamp Chicken*)./*USAAF*

with lights installed under the rear fuselage to signal a bomb release warning that would be in shadow and better seen than the nacelle light. Sights were carried by only two aircraft in each box, one by the lead and the other by his deputy in case the former failed. The first attempt was abortive due to difficulties in assembly but on 2 September the Mazingarbe generating station in Belgium was bombed by this technique. The drop was partly short of the target but the pattern achieved was far superior to the general run of previous results. At this time the box drop-on-leader was adopted for all groups in the Wing and as experience was gained so the Marauder strikes wrought telling destruction.

The most significant aspect of Marauder operations so far was their very low losses in comparison with the heavy bombers. A B-26 Combat Crew Replacement Center, set up at Toome in Northern Ireland in September 1943, groomed far more than the immediate need. By the end of August the survival rate for a B-26 crew was calculated as 37.75 missions as against only 17.74 for a B-17 crew. Heavy bomber losses during this period were chiefly due to fighters whereas the B-26s were troubled more by flak. Enemy fighters were active on several occasions, seldom reaching the Marauders due to the Spitfire escort. Captain Edgar J. Sauer, 323rd Group Intelligence Officer, echoed the feelings of the crews when, after witnessing the efforts of the escort, he proclaimed 'God bless the Spits.'

On 4 September crews from the four groups were assembled at Marks Hall to hear General 'Hap' Arnold, Chief of USAAF. He told them: 'The Marauder has found its place in the sun.' Indeed, there was some cautious reappraisal of the aircraft in high places, but steps taken to phase out production at Omaha and reduce the number of combat groups went ahead. Two groups earmarked for England, the 21st and 477th, were disbanded and four others in an advanced state of training were held pending a decision. The sun had begun to shine too late.

During the second week of September the Allies staged a feint-cum-exercise aimed at making the Germans believe a cross-Channel invasion was imminent. The Marauder groups played a major part in the air and on one day each put up three 18-plane boxes for a record number of sorties. The real invasion was planned for the following spring and as one of the initial moves a new Force was committed to a tactical role, and eventually the support of ground forces, was established in the UK during October 1943. This, the 9th Air Force, absorbed VIII Air Support Command whose only operational combat units were the four B-26 groups. The 3rd Bomb Wing became IX Bomber Command (IX BC) and a month later spawned two new wings, the 98th to administer the 322nd and 386th Groups and the 99th to look after the 323rd and 387th, accompanied by several changes in command at all levels. The commanders of the 323rd and 387th were given the new wings; the Group Executive, Lt Colonel Wilson Wood taking over the 323rd, and Colonel Jack Caldwell, originally 3rd Wing Operations, taking over the latter and obtaining the field command he had long sought. IX BC soon learned that it would receive the other four B-26 groups and the command would be brought to strength with three Douglas A-20 Havoc light bomber groups, pending the conversion of all groups to a new medium bomber. Up to these changes, the record of the 3rd Wing had been impressive. During the 13 weeks of medium level operations the Marauders had flown 4,000 sorties on 75 missions (averaging one a day) losing 13 aircraft. The loss per sortie ratio was 0.3 per cent whereas 455 B-17s had been lost, nearly 5 per cent of sorties. Significantly, the damage ratios were 18 and 23 per cent for the B-26s and B-17s respectively showing the B-26 as an aircraft that could absorb a good deal of punishment and come home.

While statistics presented an encouraging picture to the promoters of the medium level bombing campaign, an 0.3 per cent loss rate, reputedly the lowest for any Allied bomber in the ETO, was no comfort for those riding a B-26 through a flak barrage. Crews were soon aware of the heaviest flak concentrations – Boulogne, Calais, Dunkirk, and particularly Schipol on the outskirts of Amsterdam which was a priority airfield target. There the

Left: The 'Flak Suit' was worn over Mae West and parachute harness. Snap fasteners on shoulder and chest belts allowed quick release in an emergency as demonstrated by Cpt Norman L. Harvey, 322nd BG and later 1st PF Sqdn./*USAAF*

defences were formidable; 40 guns ringed the area and there was no approach that avoided their fire. Marauders made an attempt to hit the airfield on 3 October with limited success for the two groups involved, although no losses were sustained. Exactly a month later, four groups were sent. They met a murderous barrage – 'A huge cumulo-nimbus of black-assed flak' – which damaged 52 Marauders. To the participants it was a wonder that only one bomber went down, a 323rd Group aircraft which, said a witness, received a direct hit and blew up right before our eyes, a ghastly sight as it fell toward the ground – a huge red and yellow flame trailing what was a few seconds before a perfectly sound plane and crew.'

A third mission to Schipol was more successful, although from the enemy's stand-point their defences were more successful. It would be many missions before the Marauder men encountered anything to match the reception over Amsterdam on 13 December 1943. Four groups participated and put up 216 aircraft for a maximum effort to devastate the airfield. The 322nd had one shot down and 34 of its 54 aircraft battle damaged, plus two crash-landings; the 323rd lost *Raunchy Rascal* with Lt George F. Pipher's crew over the target, had six men wounded and 40 aircraft hit by flak of which three crash-landed. The 386th lost *Hell's Fury* and Captain Sanford's crew from a direct shell hit and had 35 B-26s damaged; *Man-O-War* so badly shot-up that the pilots had to belly it in at Stanstead depot. The 387th fared a little better with 38 damaged and no loss. The sheet metal men – the 'Flak Patchers' – were very busy after this episode.

Enemy opposition was not the only hazard. Winter brought mainly cloud-filled skies. Take-offs and landings frequently had to be made in poor visibility. Sometimes the cloud base, down to a few hundred feet, would extend to altitudes far above the Marauders' operational level. In such conditions collisions were a constant danger and while assembly procedures were planned to minimise the risk, survival depended on constant vigilance by aircrew and swift reaction by pilots. Most collisions resulted from aircraft in the same formation coming together in cloud. On the second Schipol mission there had been a very near miss in such circumstances. A 387th Group flight was circling base after take-off when the leader spotted a rift in the overcast and decided to climb through it. Due to other aircraft jockeying for position above, the leader had to check his climb at a conventional 180mph, 400 feet a minute. When he was able to resume his attempt to fly up through the rift it was necessary to increase the rate. Even so, making 1,200 feet per minute and airspeed

sacrificed to 150mph, the six Marauders missed the cleft and went into full cloud. The lead aircraft appeared blurred through the cockpit window for Lt Lou Sullivan and his co-pilot Lt Kelahan, following in *Lucky Lou*. Sgt Jeurgens, the engineer, was crouched behind their seats when suddenly he saw a Marauder loom close above the cockpit. He shouted a warning and both pilots simultaneously glanced up and pushed hard down on the 'wheel'. *Lucky Lou* shuddered, stalled and fell away in a spin; the crew believing that they were about to meet their Maker. A gunner, sitting in the rear fuselage, was pitched against the turret gear and badly injured. The pilots managed to regain control, checked the descent and gingerly climbed up through the cloud and out into a bright day. In the clear another B-26 radioed that *Lucky Lou* appeared to have a bomb hanging from the bays. On inspection Sullivan's crew found that two of their 1,000lb bombs had disappeared, evidently smashing open the bay doors. Sullivan, abandoning the mission, landed *Lucky Lou* very gently in case other bombs were insecure. The crew were also concerned that they had bombed England. Fortunately neither of the bombs exploded, having landed in the town of Braintree. Denied an explanation for 'security reasons' perplexed citizens may well have asked, 'On whose side are the bloody Yanks!?'

Cloud was the major cause of 'scrubbed' and 'abortive' missions. Cancelling a mission before it left the ground was one thing, but to find a target concealed by an overcast, having braved enemy defences to get there, was always a serious set-back. Like VIII BC, IX BC turned to the British for help with blind bombing aids. The heavies had priority for H2S, the most promising device which produced an image on a cathode ray screen of terrain below an aircraft. There was also Oboe, a highly accurate apparatus if used within good range of the two ground stations involved. This range limitation lessened its value to VIII BC who decided to turn Oboe over to the Marauder force. Oboe Mk I used in B-17s was British made, whereas the B-26s were to get Mk II made in the USA by MIT, the first sets arriving during December 1943. During the following month 8th Air Force turned over its Oboe technicians to the 9th.

Major Robert A. Porter, a 322nd Group Ijmuiden veteran, was selected to head a provisional unit specially formed to operate Oboe. On 25 January 1944 an installation was made in B-26B 41-31903 of the 322nd. The Marauder's spacious fuselage made it highly suitable to accommodate the bulky 400lb apparatus, with the antenna, modulator inverter and voltage regulator installed in the rear bomb-bay and the rest, receiver, filter and control junction box, were in the navigator's department. So secret was the project that when 41-31903, *The Trail Blazer,* returned to Great Saling with the equipment installed it was given a guard of three MPs. This airborne equipment was used to pick up signals from two widely separated ground stations in England. One transmitted an audio course signal; a steady tone so long as the aircraft was on course, becoming intermittent if it wandered. The second ground station sent out signals to alert the aircraft's Oboe operator of target distances and the exact point to release bombs. The position of the Oboe aircraft was shown on the control station screens to an accuracy of 200 yards in range. The great advantage of Oboe was that it was practically impossible to jam, unlike Gee, a navigational aid fitted in lead B-26s and operating with the aid of ground stations. Oboe was limited to no more than four such aircraft in an attack on one target, and aircraft concerned had to be spread 15 minutes apart for control purposes.

On 16 February 1944 the 1st Pathfinder Squadron (Provisional) was activated at Andrews Field, drawing its original 15 combat crews, three each, from the five groups then in the Command – the 391st Bomb Group having arrived at Matching in late January. Five days after formation of the pathfinder unit, Major Porter, undertook the first mission, leading 17 Marauders of the 322nd over a 'solid' overcast to bomb Coxyde airfield in Belgium. The technique was to place a pathfinder aircraft as lead or deputy in each 18-plane box, the formation releasing on the pathfinder's drop. Where everything worked as planned Oboe proved remarkably accurate. Unfortunately, the early days were marred by equipment failure.

Many of the early pathfinder missions were over V-weapon sites. Known simply as 'special targets' when the first – at Mimoyecques, near Cap Griz Nez – was attacked on 5 November, rumour quickly pronounced them 'rocket gun' sites. The frequency of these attacks soon led Colonel Wilson Wood's 323rd Group to dub itself 'Woods Rocket Raiders'. The significance of the small targets, mere pinpoints in the French countryside, was not revealed to crews as flying bomb launch pads until 20 November. IX BC was committed to destroying these sites to prevent or delay their use against England. As most sites were close to the Channel coast, they did not involve long periods in hostile air spaces. However, Noballs, the code name for these operations, proved far from 'milk runs' for the Germans increased the anti-aircraft defences to a point where these targets were as dangerous as any in Europe, evoking the quip among Marauder crews about the

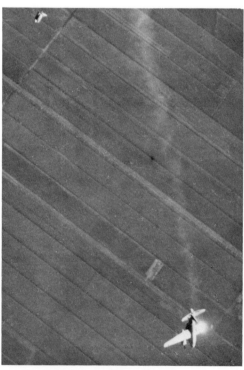

Above: Pounding the Luftwaffe. St Andre de l'Eure from **11,000** feet as *Lil' Pork Chop* banks away with a 322nd BG formation while trains of bombs explode along the aircraft dispersal area. A previous drop has ignited a fuel dump on the other side of the airfield: 3 November 1943. */USAAF*

Right: Despite a formidable flak barrage only one B-26 was lost on the second Schipol raid, 13 November 1943. A direct hit on 323rd BG's 41-34963, WT:Q, resulted in the left wing and engine breaking away and the stricken bomber spinning down, fuel tanks aflame, towards the drainage ditched Dutch pastures. */USAF*

apt choice of code name, in view of what could happen to their personages during such missions.

The Noball targets were chiefly in the Pas-de-Calais belt with another group in the Cherbourg peninsula, centred on Sottevast, and equally well defended by the deadly '88' guns. Fire from these guns brought about one of those incidents, albeit minor in the scheme of things, that helped dispel the myth about a Marauder's precariousness when flying on a single engine. On 15 February the 387th Group flew into the middle of a well directed barrage which brought down one bomber and damaged several others. Lt Allen Sherman (of windmill buzzing fame) suffered hits on the left engine of *Mitch's Bitch* causing him to quickly feather the propeller. Dropping behind the formation his plight was seen by four Spitfires that gave escort. The right engine of the Marauder then faltered under the strain. With rising gauges indicating a failure inevitable, Sherman risked unfeathering the left Pratt & Whitney in the hope it could be re-started and generate enough

Left: Bombs explode around camouflaged aircraft dispersal points during the third Schipol raid, 13 December 1943. Five light aircraft can be seen parked near covered revetments below left wing tip of last B-26. /USAAF

power to reduce boost on the other engine. To the pilot's great relief the left engine caught and ran giving adequate power despite the flak damage. At that moment the right engine cut out completely! Sherman was in no position to ponder this unique situation and nursed *Mitch's Bitch* home. Visibility had deteriorated by the time he arrived over the Chipping Ongar runway and his landing approach was too high for safety. Without faltering, in spite of power by a single engine, Sherman amazed the spectators, gathered at the news of his predicament, and witnessed the wheels and flaps tuck up again and *Mitch's Bitch* climb gently away on a single engine. The next attempt produced a perfect landing.

Mitch's Bitch, a combat original of the 387th, had 40 missions to its credit at this date; there were several IX BC Marauders that even topped that figure, especially in 322nd Group which, overall, had experienced less flak damage to its bombers. One, *Mild and Bitter,* a replacement for a Marauder lost at Ijmuiden, reached the 50 mission mark in January 1944. Crew members were also piling up the missions with Lt Ralph N. 'Red' Phillips of the 323rd being first to the fifty mark, early in the New Year, marking what was established as a 'tour of operations'. Six months previously few airmen in England would have rated the chances of surviving five missions in Marauders.

The four veteran B-26 groups were joined by the four delayed groups during the first quarter of 1944. The 391st Group became operational in February, the 344th coming into Stanstead the same month. The 394th arrived at Boreham in March and finally the 397th established base at Rivenhall in April. The Marauder force in Essex was then over 700 aircraft, the largest concentration of any type of medium bomber in any single Allied air force. In fact the total of B-26s in the UK by April, including spares and training machines, was in excess of 850.

To raise the experience level of the new units quickly, several crews from the old were temporarily transferred. Even so, the 'green' groups were not without beginners'

mishaps. On its third mission (25 February) the 391st failed to find Cambrai/Epinoy airfield due to poor navigation and had, as the official chronicler put it, the dubious distinction of touring France for 40 minutes without escort. The freshman group was lucky that enemy fighters were not vectored in by the German raid controllers who watched for such lapses.

Despite the inroads into its strength made by Allied fighters, the Luftwaffe could still hit back skilfully. On the same day that the 391st was · 'touring' France the 323rd and 387th Groups bombed Venlo airfield, Holland, and experienced a surprise interception by 20 Me109s as they turned for home. Four Marauders were quickly shot out of the 'Tiger Stripe Group', the 387th's sobriquet, bestowed because of its yellow and black tail markings. One squadron from the same group had inadvertently strayed $2\frac{1}{2}$ miles south of Venlo, discovering on return to base that its Marauders' had become the first to bomb Germany, if quite wastefully. At this time such brushes with the Luftwaffe were comparatively rare. In contrast, on the previous day the same two groups had gone to Leeuwarden, another German fighter field in the Netherlands, in the longest B-26 mission yet (250 miles from base) encountering neither flak nor fighters. The accuracy of the bombing caused the 323rd to enter in their records that it was 'the best raid we've yet made' and is supported by German documents which show that the station was devastated.

For every success there were a half-dozen indifferent results and some complete failures. Bad weather was the principal culprit for even with the growing use of pathfinders there was still the problem of assembling

Above: Jack Caldwell and his personal Marauder while commanding the 387th BG. This aircraft was lost with another pilot a few weeks before Caldwell was killed. Instrumental in developing medium level bombing tactics in the ETO, Caldwell was, in the words of one senior IX BC officer, 'a fine man'./*USAF*

Right: Cpt Robert Porter, veteran of the first B-26 ETO mission and chosen to form and lead the 1st Pathfinder Sqdn at Andrews Field. Here seen talking to the crew chief of *Flak Happy* on 1 February 1944./*H. Posson*

formations among the clouds. Such was the case on 8 March when none of the B-26s airborne bombed their targets. A dense overcast brought collisions. Two 387th aircraft came together soon after take-off, one crashing and the other being wrecked in a belly landing. The 344th Group, assembling for its third mission, had two collide and go down over Essex. Little could be done about avoiding these accidents in conditions of bad visibility, but collisions also occurred through error in close formation flying. After two further collisions involving 323rd Marauders during April, the Group was stood down for a few days to brush up formation flying.

With revenge in mind, the 322nd had long awaited the mission ordered on 26 March – Ijmuiden. The actual objective was the harbour and naval installations from which fast E-boats harassed Allied shipping in the North Sea. A maximum effort raid, 380 B-26s were despatched, including two boxes of 394th Group which had only become operational three days previous. Understandably 322nd Group, 'Nye's Annihilators' as they were known, led the mission with a crew in the van that included three veterans of the 14 May strike: Lt Colonel Gove Celio, pilot; Captain George Watson, co-pilot and Captain Sheldon Past, navigator. Another 18 'first

Left: Few 322nd pilots had quite such an eventful tour as Frank Remmele whose aircraft always seemed to be beset by flak or fighters. Flying Ben Willis's (449th BS CO) *Truman Committee* through Noball flak on 28 February 1944, shell splinters (hits arrowed) wounded him and killed the bombardier. Remmele and this aircraft featured in another episode described in the text./*USAAF*

Below: A crew member in the radio room top hatch combines keeping an eye open for obstructions beside the perimeter track with a breath of fresh air as *McCarty's Party* taxies in 8 March 1944. This B-26B-50-MA became the 391st BG champion with a grand total of 159 missions when the Group ceased Marauder operations./*USAF*

Left: Back from leading the 322nd BG's second box to IJmuiden, 26 March 1944, Othel Turner (cigarette in mouth) and Louis Sibille (cigarette in hand) talk with other crew members of the leadship (41-31975, ER:R). Both pilots flew on the first IJmuiden raid the previous year, as had Lt Ben Tillman, bombardier (second from left), and Sgt Harold Baker (far right). Sibille was killed flying a Mustang during the Korean War, the action bringing a posthumous Medal of Honor, highest US award./*USAAF*

Below: Part of the 380-plane force heading over the North Sea towards IJmuiden, 26 March 1944. The lead and low boxes (18 aircraft each) of 386th BG are photographed from an aircraft in the high box./*USAAF*

Right: Hasselt, 40 miles east of Brussels, was a main line rail junction and depot between Antwerp and Germany. This is what happened when 200 Marauders paid a visit on 10 April 1944. The white smoke shooting skyward is an ammunition train which left a crater 150 ft x 40ft. All through traffic lines were cut – one in 17 places – by 1,000lb bombs. /*USAAF*

raid' veterans were in other 322nd aircraft. Ijmuiden had lost none of its sting for although only one aircraft was lost – a 323rd machine suffering a direct shell hit – many aircraft were ripped by flak fragments and a few had to crash-land on return. One was the lead ship, *Johnny Zero,* and Celio was forced to belly in at the B-17 base at Framlingham.

As part of the pre-invasion programme for interdicting enemy communications, French railways and marshalling yards were made first priority for the Marauders early in March. Some excellent results and telling destruction was achieved at many of these. Even so, Sam Anderson knew that using the current drop on-leader procedure against small targets – such as bridges – which his command could be likely to have to destroy would be wasteful. In April he took a party of his officers down to the Mediterranean to study the highly successful methods of hitting bridges and viaducts developed by the 12th

81

Air Force B-26 units. Impressed, Anderson borrowed the 12th's star bombardier, Joe Perrin, who spent a month with the British-based Marauder groups dispensing his expertise on attacking small targets.

The man who, after his visit to the Mediterranean a year previously, had played a major part in getting the British-based Marauders to operate at medium altitudes, was killed in April. While leading his Group, the 387th, over Dunkirk on the 12th Jack Caldwell's bomber took a direct hit. German anti-aircraft defences in this area continued to grow in strength and efficiency. As an anti-flak measure *Window* – bundles of metallic strip – was introduced for Marauder protection six days after Caldwell's loss in an effort to defeat the gun laying radars in the Pas-de-Calais. Thereafter a flight of screening aircraft discharging *Window* in front of a following formation became a regular feature of many missions. The benefit was not always apparent until some formations crossed a V-site area without a screening force. Witness 21 April when the 322nd Group found cloud covering Siracourt and turned to find a target of opportunity. Of the 36 B-26s in the force one was shot down and 30 damaged by radar directed flak. Of these, six came back on a single engine, one crash-landing. Flt Off Gus E. Fuson outdid Allen Sherman's feat on return from the same target a few weeks earlier. Making his final approach at home base, Fuson found another B-26 cutting in front of his path to the runway. His options were a crash landing or to try and pull up for another circuit of the field. He chose the latter course and climbed away with his wheels jammed down owing to hydraulic system damage, having been pumped down by hand. To pull out on one engine with the drag of a lowered undercarriage would once have been thought impossible.

Another hoary myth about the Marauder was also being dispelled around this time – that its tricky handling characteristics made it unsuitable for night combat operations. Cross-country night flying had been undertaken in the USA but handling the B-26 with a full war load was a different matter. Yet the 322nd and 323rd found they had no more difficulty in handling the Marauders at night than in daylight. Indeed, the tricycle undercarriage made landings easier than with many 'tail sitting' aircraft regularly operating in darkness.

Having played the major part in denying the enemy forward air bases; been praised for a similar contribution in bombing V-weapon sites and currently turning in a better bombing record against communications targets than the US heavy bombers, the Marauder, by the spring of 1944, had quietly become respectable. Gone was talk of Martin Murderer, Widowmaker, Baltimore Whore and the other derogatory epithets, for they were hardly applicable to the aircraft with the lowest loss per sortie rate of any Allied bomber in the theatre, and one showing similar non-combat accident rate tendencies. Witness to this remarkable change were more than a hundred Marauders with over 50 mission symbols painted on their noses. With the coming of May interest was aroused in an

Left: Returning to base on a fine spring day, two 323rd BG B-26Cs pass over the Blackwater estuary, Essex. To the left of the far aircraft, *Wolf Pack II*, Bradwell Bay airfield can be seen. From March 1944 most replacement Marauders were received uncamouflaged but IX BC still considered some necessary in case of enemy air attack on bases. Many 'silver' aircraft – like that in the photo – were given a coat of medium green to the upper surfaces at UK bases or depots. /*D. Pepmiller*

Below: During the summer of 1943 the 322nd's 'Silver Streak' B-26B-4, 41-18014, DR:Z, was stripped of camouflage paint: an experiment engendered by news of benefits derived from this action in the SWPA./*J. Statts*

Andrews Field Marauder that had passed the 90 mark.

On 8 May a *Time* reporter witnessed a milestone in the story of the bomber, 'Just before dark, the sleek, fast B-26 Marauder circled her English air base and T/Sgt William L. Stuart, a taciturn, red-haired Texan, heaved an eloquent sigh, rubbed his grease-stained hands together, got out his tools and prepared to go to work. The ship rolling up to his dispersal station, the *Mild and Bitter* had just made history; she was back from her 100th mission. Sgt Stuart her crew chief had sweated out every one of the 100 for her; now he would check her over and get her ready for mission 101. . . . But *Mild*

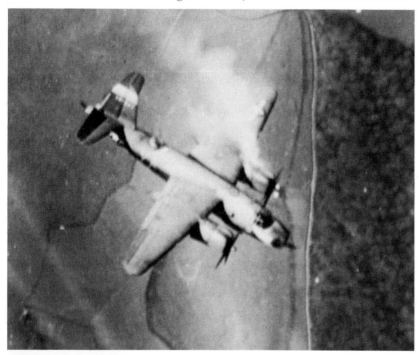

and Bitter had no record of hair-raising escapes. Her saga was one of good luck and almost monotonous efficiency. She had lugged 166 different airmen to battle; 26 were decorated, but not one got a Purple Heart. During her robust career she acquired some 50 flak holes, but never any damage that Bill Stuart and his ground crew could not repair overnight.

'On her first combat flight, last 28 July, she led a sweep over Abbeville; the 100th was to bomb an aerodrome near Paris. In between she had taken the targets as they came; power plants, E-boat pens, air bases, all around France up to Holland and back. She still had her original Pratt & Whitney engines. No one had picked any soft spots for the ship, even when she neared her record. Her last two missions were done between dawn and sunset, her last four in 36 hours.

'Stuart tried to think of something spectacular that had happened to his ship. On one raid a burst of flak fountained up right through the open bomb bay. Hot steel fragments rattled against cold steel bombs with a hellish din. But nothing happened! Captain Paul Shannon had the honour to fly *Mild and Bitter* on the 100th trip. He was the ship's original pilot and had flown it on 27 other missions'.

They sent *Mild and Bitter* home to the States to tour the Martin plants and other war factories. Its 100 missions made good news against the past reputation of the B-26. In some quarters it was acclaimed the first Marauder to fly 100 missions. These newspaper stories found their way to Sardinia where they angered Marauder men who knew it was not the first.

Swamp Chicken

Robert Mims

In Mississippi we have a game bird, a quail, that during the war was partly protected. You could shoot them to eat yourself but it was illegal to sell them. Hunters did sell them illicitly as 'swamp chicken'. The B-26 reminded me of a quail; it had a large body, small wings and had to flap real hard to stay in the air. So when I picked up my regular B-26 at Barksdale Field, Louisiana, for the flight overseas I named it *Swamp Chicken*.

A B-26C-22, she was an excellent aircraft and handled beautifully. Marauders varied considerably in their flight characteristics, some having to be constantly trimmed out. *Swamp Chicken* was so smooth she was often flown as a lead ship – Colonel Thatcher, the Group CO, used her quite a bit. Although it was my regular ship it was often flown by other crews and became the first B-26 in the Group to reach 50 missions – and without ever once having to turn back through mechanical failure.

I took *Swamp Chicken* on her 52nd mission which was my 26th. The target was a Noball, one of those V-weapon ski-sites hidden in French woods. With only a shallow penetration of enemy occupied territory it looked like a milk run, but the Germans were moving hundreds of guns into these areas so obviously they didn't like the way we were knocking the Noballs out.

My crew was co-pilot Leon Jackson, bombardier John Brush, engineer Michael Miyo and radioman Bill Vermillion. My regular tail gunner, Ollie Myers, had a cold and didn't fly that day. Instead we had Sgt McCandlish, a former ground man who applied for flight status and had just come in from gunnery school. This was his first mission.

We took off in the early afternoon, the Group putting up three boxes with more than 50 airplanes. There was broken cloud at around 3,500 feet which thinned as the formation flew south to our first checkpoint at Gillingham. Nearing the English south coast we turned at Shoreham and headed out over the point known as Beachy Head. It took 15 minutes to reach the French coast where landfall over Berck-sur-Mer was greeted with heavy but inaccurate flak. The cloud below us had built up again as we crossed the Channel although there were clear patches ahead. I could see the familiar French countryside below as the formation weaved in evasive action; it was a fine winter's day and visibility was good.

We were briefed for an eight minute run to Frévent where the formation would turn north-east eventually to locate our IP at Bruay and hit our targets on the run out to the Channel. *Swamp Chicken* was flying the No

Below: Engine gone and main wheel hanging, *Swamp Chicken* pulls to the right as another Marauder gets out of the way. /USAAF

5 position, lead squadron, second box. We reached Frévent and had just completed our turn when there was a tremendous crack and the airplane pulled violently to the right. The ring wing went up and I lost control. There was a seventh B-26 flying the slot in our element and we must have narrowly missed colliding with it as we went out of the formation. I don't recall seeing anything and assumed from the behaviour of the airplane that we'd taken a hit in the right engine. To counteract the pull we cut the throttle on the left engine and I told the co-pilot to feather the prop' on the right – normal procedure in this sort of emergency. Leon replied: 'We don't have any right engine.' I looked across and was horrified to see a tangled mess of metal and fuel lines protruding from a torn nacelle; the whole engine had disappeared!

With all the power on one side, the unbalance created by losing 2,500lb from the right wing and broken fuel lines spraying gas around to create a fire hazard, we really were in trouble! I applied left rudder and aileron and managed to bring the left wing down, while we both tried desperately to trim the plane for level flight. It needed all our strength on the controls. I knew I had to salvo the load of eight 500lb bombs fast as we were heading down all the time. I pulled the salvo knob above my head but nothing happened. By this time John Brush had come up from the nose – no place to be in an emergency. As the cockpit release wouldn't work John went back into the nose and managed to jettison the bombs with the controls there. It took a lot of courage in the circumstances as the plane might have gone into a spin at any moment. Free of that weight we hoped we could maintain altitude but when we applied full power to the left engine *Swamp Chicken* kept skidding to the right. We had a choice of holding altitude and flying in a circle, or holding a course and losing altitude. We decided to try for a course for if we couldn't make England we might get to the Channel and ditch.

After a few minutes we could see we were not going to get very far as altitude was being lost too quickly. To add to our troubles we were now all alone and being continually fired on by light flak. Our position was very vulnerable to say the least and sooner or later a shell was going to knock the plane out of control. There was now no hope of making the coast so at 4,000 feet I ordered the crew to bale out. I knew that if both pilots left the controls the plane would turn on its back and go in before either of us could jump. Somebody had to remain. So I said to Leon: 'I'll hold it if you would like to get out, or are you going to stay with me and crash land; it's your decision.' He said he would bale out. When he let go the controls to leave it became very difficult to hold the plane, taking all my strength on the rudder pedals to keep her straight.

With the strain I had to get down quickly and picked out a suitable spot ahead, slightly rolling farmland with woods dotted around. When the engine had been knocked off the main wheel came down. With no hydraulic power I could not lower the other wheel or raise the down wheel. It was a pretty precarious situation; if there had been time to reflect on the chance of coming out alive I guess I would have realised it was very slim.

I was down to about 500 feet, trying to line up on the open area ahead, when the aircraft twice jerked violently and I saw that a stream of 20mm fire was coming up at me. Then I realised that the field I'd chosen to belly into had a flak battery at one end! The only thing I could think of was to fire the five fixed guns in the hope that they would quieten the flak gunners or spoil their aim as I tried to get

Below: Still flying but losing height when last seen by the 323rd BG formation, *Swamp Chicken's* fate was discovered in a reconnaissance photograph taken a few days later. There is a well-worn track from the 4-gun flak battery site near a French country road./*USAAF*

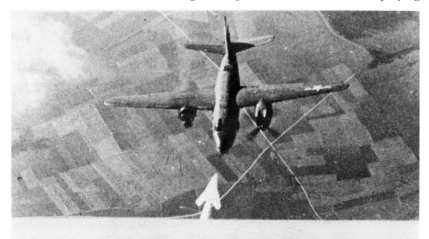

on the ground. I went directly across the site just a few feet from the ground, cut back on the power and dumped the aircraft onto the field which had a slight uphill gradient. I was doing about 160mph when she hit and really didn't think there was much hope of getting out because with one wheel down she would be bound to spin round, cartwheel and explode. After the first impact I didn't remember anything; either my head hit the control wheel or it came back and hit my head; I don't know – but I was stunned.

I awoke in a gold cloud, an eerie feeling until I saw I was still in the cockpit and not some celestial place. The fire risk immediately had me scrambling out through the top hatch and on to the ground. Half concussed, with a bad cut on my forehead, I was in no state to run and in any case the troops from the flak battery were soon there. They were certainly surprised to see a complete engine missing from the airplane. It turned out the gold cloud was made by the aluminium oxide powder from sea dye markers that had broken open in the crash. Old *Swamp Chicken* was still pretty well in one piece and evidently the lowered wheel had been hanging free and doubled up as soon as the plane hit the ground.

I was taken to the flak battery and after a while they brought in a body wrapped in a parachute. Of all tragic ironies, it was Leon Jackson; apparently his 'chute hadn't opened. Brush, Vermillion and McCandlish were captured but they never did get Miyo who contacted the French Underground and worked in a bakery until they got him over the Pyrenees into Spain.

In prison camp I learnt that the 5 February mission was one of the most costly our Group ever flew. The flak barrage knocked down two other B-26s after mine was hit by the first bursts. Another 30 planes were damaged, one so badly the crew had to abandon it over their home base after heading it out over the North Sea.

Below: Crew of *Swamp Chicken* on the occasion of the bomber's 50th mission: l. to r. (front row) Myres, Mims, Jackson; (rear row) Brush, Vermillion and Miyo. /*R. Mims*

We Proved the Ship

Having driven the Axis from North Africa the Allies, gathering strength, prepared to cross the Mediterranean into Europe; first Sicily and then Italy. The air forces on hand were, in most respects, sufficient to meet the requirements of the new campaigns when units had been brought up to strength and some re-equipment effected. Destruction of enemy installations to aid the progress of the land forces would rest chiefly with the medium bombers, predominantly the USAAF's three groups of B-26 Marauders and four of B-25 Mitchells. As in the Pacific war, the Mitchell had proved more suited to the rough airfields and limited base facilities available during the North African fighting and was considered better than the B-26 for the job in hand. As so often is the case in the face of censure, the B-26 veterans of the 12th Air Force had developed an almost unassailable allegiance to their charge and considered they had more than proved the bomber's worth: even if statistically the B-25 had a better record. For future operations B-25s and B-26s were concentrated in separate Wings which sharpened competition between them.

Much of the work on developing the best methods for employment of the Marauder stemmed from the 319th Group acting as an unofficial operational training unit at Oujda, French Morocco, after being withdrawn from battle in February 1943. In May the Group received several replacement crews and was re-equipped with B-26B-10 and B-26C-5 models featuring increased wing span and larger empennage. Many new crews came from the 344th Group in the States, being readied for England in April, only to have most of its flight crews taken to fill the gaps in the ranks of the Mediterranean B-26 groups. The 319th's old B models were transferred to the other groups or relegated to training. Deemed ready to return to combat at the end of the month the Group moved east to Sedrata, a dusty barren plateau in the Algerian mountains.

On 5 June the 319th's first medium altitude operation was flown, followed by daily participation in the bombardment of the Italian-held island of Pantelleria. Sedrata was shared with the 17th Group which, like the 320th based a few miles away, still had mostly the short tail, short wing Marauders. Thus in the early days of the 319th's return to combat its formations could be easily distinguished by the larger rear surfaces of its bombers, cryptically described by Sedrata tenants as 'big ass birds'. The 319th became enamoured with this label, later adopting it as a very unofficial group name which endured long after the other groups had shed their last small-tail models. Feeling the sobriquet too vulgar for general publication,

pressmen changed it to 'Big Tail Birds' in stories featuring the 319th.

For Marauder men, with experience of combat during the North African campaign, the missions being flown across the Mediterranean, though often of longer duration, were usually less fraught with danger. As one seasoned flier commented, 'We began to feel we could survive, which we didn't think possible earlier in the year.' Nevertheless opposition from the Luftwaffe was still encountered now and again during the summer of 1943. On 15 June the 319th and 320th were after Sicilian airfields when Me109s attacked, bringing down one and so damaging another that it crashed on return to base. The B-26 gunners claimed nine fighters destroyed. Three days later the 319th was jumped over Sardinia and in a running battle lost three of its aircraft for counter claims of ten. The Big Ass Birds also had a rough time at the hands of the Luftwaffe on Independence Day when an estimated fifty Me109s caught the B-26s on a bomb run over the satellite airfield at Gerbini, Sicily. Air gunners claimed no less than 19 of the enemy but one of the two Marauders that fell had the Group CO, Lt Col Wilbur Aring, flying as an observer in a tail gun position. Aring survived, as did the 319th's infamous reputation for losing its commanders. This did not daunt Lt Col Gordon Austin who, having completed a term leading a P-40 fighter group on the same field (the 17th and 319th Groups had moved to Djedeida, Tunisia, towards the end of June) accepted the post from General Webster commanding the 42nd Bomb Wing.

Compared with the long established antiaircraft artillery defences in north-west Europe, the flak encountered at most tactical targets visited by the Marauders was meagre, but effective at times. There were a few vital installations where the enemy bolstered his flak defences; one such was Messina, Sicilian supply port, where the 319th lost three of its aircraft on 14 July and had many more damaged, one so badly that a crash-landing followed.

Three days later the Marauders found the other end of the German supply route to Sicily could mount an even more lethal reception. Five B-26s were destroyed by flak, three of the 17th and one each from the other two groups. The 17th's CO, Lt Col Ross Greening, a Tokyo raid veteran, was among those taken prisoner. On medium altitude missions, approximately half the crew members of aircraft lost were able to parachute to safety.

On the completion of the Sicilian campaign, the Allies concentrated their bombing on Italian objectives and in August the 12th Air Force had its stiffest encounters ever with the Luftwaffe as the Germans endeavoured to

Left: Trains of fragmentation bombs fountain soil into the air at Alghero, Sardinia, a Luftwaffe transport base. Major Ross Greening led 24 17th BG Marauders in this successful attack on 24 May 1943. Ju52, Go242 and He111 are among aircraft types visible on the field 10,000ft below the formation. The three B-26Bs are 'small wing/tail' models./USAAF

check Allied preparations to invade. On the 21st the 320th Group lost four bombers near Naples while claiming 22 of their opponents. Next day the 319th making for Salerno marshalling yards were met by some 50 Me109s of which they claimed 24 destroyed and 14 probables for the loss of five Marauders; this was probably the most intense of all air fights in which Mediterranean-based B-26s were involved.

There were other occasions during the next week when Marauders again tangled with Me109s, and air gunners claims far exceeded enemy losses. While interrogators were anxious to obtain a realistic figure, estimates that emerged from the interviewing of some 100 combatants were much inflated. Several gunners firing on the same aircraft from their various points of view could appear as different aircraft to interrogators. German records of losses show that this must often have been the case. Factors not appreciated at the time were the fallible nature of combatants' reports, attributable to excitement, fear, restricted vision and, above all, the speed of the action. Even so, the situation afforded B-26 crews confidence in the ability of their aircraft to give better than it took in battle.

In August 1943, Colonel Austin moved to Wing Headquarters, relinquishing command of the 319th to Major Holzapple. If the superstititious considered Austin had broken the jinx on 319th commanders they were to be proved right, for Holzapple endured with his group until the end of hostilities. He and other survivors of the first Marauders sent to Europe had been actively engaged in improving the type's effectiveness by experimenting with formations and bombing techniques. This had a marked effect by the autumn of 1943, when the average accuracy and pattern concentration of B-26 bombing surpassed that of the B-25s. The Marauder was also showing its survivability. Early in July a 17th Group B-26B-2 *Hell Cat* passed the 50th mission mark. Later that month *Hell Cat*, plus the 320th's *Lady Halitosis*, an older B model, and the 319th's B-26C *Jabbo's Sky King the 2nd* were flown back to the USA by specially selected crews. The main purpose was to build confidence in the Marauder among trainees – many of whom showed a marked reluctance to fly the type – by letting them meet battle-seasoned men and see aircraft with extensive combat records.

Runner up to the 50-mission mark was another 17th Group B-26B-2, *Coughin' Coffin*, which had received a good deal of US press publicity for bringing crews safely back from many violent brushes with the enemy; a brief prayer for its safety had been scribbled on the bomber's nose by a mechanic before it left the States. The bomber flew its 50th mission on 11 July piloted by Lt Fred Mehner and with the original regular pilot, Captain Bill Pritchard, flying as an observer – although recuperating from injuries. One engine was hit by flak and the hydraulic system damaged. Difficulty was experienced in lowering the undercarriage and the right main wheel would not budge. Mehner had to land with only the nose and the left wheel extended. When flying speed was lost and the aircraft toppled over, the right wing was nearly ripped off. Nevertheless such was the publicity value of *Coughin' Coffin* that it was rebuilt and flown back to America in October by a veteran crew.

In November another 17th Bomb Group original, *Renaissance,* reached the 75 mission mark and also went home for publicity and Bond raising visits to USAAF bases. The crew were again men who had reached the prescribed 40-mission combat tour, and there

Left: Coughin' Coffin undergoing repairs after the precarious landing at Djedeida. /M. D. Preacher

Below: The Renaissance had more missions to its credit than any other Marauder by the late summer of 1943. At the date this photo was taken a Group identification band, red, had been painted round the rear fuselage (under the tailplane so as not to compromise camouflage). The 319th used white and the 320th yellow./USAAF

Group and its squadrons followed. Donald Gilbert, Operations Officer of the 319th, became the 17th's new commander. Taking charge in such circumstances was not an enviable task, but Gilbert's sense of humour quickly led to his acceptance. Much to the amusement of those in the know, at the same time as Gilbert was being advanced due to his undoubted contribution in developing B-26 tactics, the same office at Wing was also issuing a censure that (unbeknown to them) involved the same officer. In September Gilbert and Captain Harold Crow had initiated the use of B-26s for single-plane weather scouting sorties off the Italian coast, reporting observations by radio to base. On the first occasion the code message received stated 'Very poor visibility ahead, terrible thunderstorms, snowing at Brenner Pass and fog over England'. Unfortunately this piece of flippancy was also picked up by higher command where the details caused some alarm. A letter of rebuke eventually arrived for the unknown pilot to which the 319th adjutant wished to add the endorsement – but was restrained – 'Pilot has been severely reprimanded and is no longer with this Group.'

The 17th soon re-asserted itself and in January 1944 a particularly outstanding attack on an airfield near Rome brought a coveted Distinguished Unit Citation for the Group. One of the men transferred to revitalise the 17th was Joe Perrin. As Group Bombardier he developed a successful method for fast runs over heavily defended targets to minimise losses to flak. The technique involved climbing a formation 1,000 to 1,500 feet higher at the IP than the proposed bombing altitude, then losing 600 to 800 feet per minute on the bomb run, flying straight and level for 30 seconds to drop, then continuing to lose altitude. Without sacrificing bombing accuracy – as was so often the case when standard evasive action was practised – the diving run made it difficult for flak gunners to get an accurate range.

The bombing accuracy of the 42nd Wing was becoming steadily better during the winter of 1943-1944. The principal criteria of success was numbers of bombs falling within 600 feet of the aiming point. After hovering around the 10 per cent mark during the summer of 1943, in October it jumped to over 20 per cent, by December nearly 40 and to 55 per cent in March 1944. This was the average for all missions including failures and some 100 per cent strikes. Against bridges the Marauders were obtaining a one down for every two attacks by bombing with flights converging on the target. The improvement in accuracy was principally the result of lead bombardier skill gained through experience.

Luck played a part for a squadron of the

was no better way to dispel the stigma on the B-26 than to produce men who were living proof that the Martin was as durable as any other warplane. Indeed, there were many incidents to show that men had a better than usual chance of survival because of its sound construction. One 319th gunner had survived six crash landings in B-26s during his service.

The B-26 groups began bombing bridges and viaducts in Italy during August 1943 as part of a campaign to prevent supplies and reinforcements reaching the German armies. Overall, bombing achievement was erratic although several of the strikes were spectacular. In the 320th Group Captain Joe Perrin had emerged as a bombardier with persistently good results and encouraging ideas on tactics. During the autumn, battle weariness was beginning to show in the performance of the 17th Group which had been in combat since the previous December. It was failing on several missions and 6 October General Doolittle took the Group off operations and put it to an intensive training programme of bombing and formation flying for the rest of the month.

Changes within the administration of the

17th Group over Viterbo rail yards on 7 February. Low temperatures froze moisture on the lens in 2/Lt Ed Fitzgerald's bombsight. Nothing daunted, he proceeded to use, what he later termed, 'off the toe' aim. 'I had to do something in a hurry, so I just lined the target up to the best of my ability and let go.' The formation's drop resulted in 93 per cent of the bombs bursting within a 600 feet radius of the briefed aiming point!

With the battle line in Italy moving away northwards, the Marauder Wing moved to Sardinia in late October, taking over the very airfields it had once bombed. The 320th shared a base with the 319th at Decimomannu – usually Decimo to the occupants. The 17th was to operate from Villacidro, but this was so wet that for some weeks it operated from another group's field. Decimo's 2,000 yard runway was 500 feet wide and Holzapple utilised this to stage three-at-a-time take-offs on the first mission from the base. Cutting down assembly time by 13 minutes, this theoretically allowed another 50 miles of range. Winter rains put a stop to the procedure but in the following April Holzapple had the runway widened to allow six-at-a-time take-offs. Despite misgivings from some observers that this could be dangerous if an aircraft had a mishap, it proved workable. The chief practical advantage of a mass launch was that it allowed more time for dust to settle between take-offs, and could save 25 minutes assembly time. Later in 1944 six-plane take-offs were successfully performed in darkness. The compacted soil runways tended to become spongy with the winter rains and Sardinia proved very damp. These conditions caused additional stress on undercarriages increasing failures. Repair of crash-landed Marauders took many hours work to re-skin undersides of fuselages, re-build stoved-in nose sections and replace bent propellers or damaged engines. There were always a few aircraft undergoing 'bellied-in' repairs. To save man-hours Don Gilbert devised a scheme to lessen the damage when the nose wheel could not be lowered – a not infrequent happening. Ammunition was moved rearward to make the aircraft tail heavy, the main wheels were lowered and on touch-down the pilot kept the nose high, eventually letting the tail turret scrape the ground. This proved highly successful and resulted in a considerable saving in repair time as only the underside of the rear fuselage needed work.

The complex nature of B-26 systems was the principal reason for overall serviceability rates being lower than units equipped with B-25s; but the Marauder's status gradually reached parity by dint of far more rigorous maintenance activities. Oil changes were carried out every 100 hours on Marauder engines, whereas most B-25 mechanics only changed

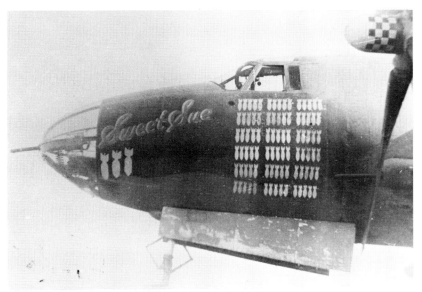

oil when an engine was changed. There were many in-the-field innovations to aid the servicing and operation of the B-26s. One was to correct the old bugbear of an inoperative turret when the main electrical system received battle damage. Sgt Charles V. Karlmann of the 319th devised a secondary source of power by running auxiliary wires from turret direct to batteries and generators.

By early 1944 few of the short wing B-26Bs remained in service with the 17th and 320th Groups, most survivors by then having been transferred to the training bases in North Africa. One of the 17th's first 'big wing' replacements had been a B-26B-10 which seemed set fair to reach the coveted goal of 100 missions. The aircraft, *Sweet Sue*, passed the 90 mark in February. On Leap Year Day, taking off on its 95th mission, *Sweet Sue* did not develop sufficient power and crashed off the end of the Villacidro runway, killing all six crewmen in the ensuing explosion.

If the many mission bomber was venerated through luck in survival, even more so was a many mission airman. While the combat tour of 40 missions had been extended to a tentative 45 in January 1944, later in the

Top: On a practice mission, 9 February 1944, the wing of one 319th BG aircraft struck the tail of another. The former crashed but 19-year-old 2/Lt Roscoe Nemer managed to keep control of *Modern Design*, although unaware of the extent of the damage as he had only a skeleton crew and no one in the rear of the aircraft. Every time he tried to level out for landing *Modern Design* nosed down. Only by increasing power and coming in at 175mph was he able to maintain control. On getting out and seeing there was no left elevator and very little stabiliser, Nemer said he nearly fainted. /G. S. Hunter

Above: Scoreboard of *Sweet Sue* on the eve of her 95th mission (94th symbol had not been painted on). Large bomb symbols anticipated this Marauder as being first to complete 100 missions. Red and white checkerboard on prop' bosses enabled crew chief, Sgt George E. Beaman, to identify his charge when in flight. /G. Beaman

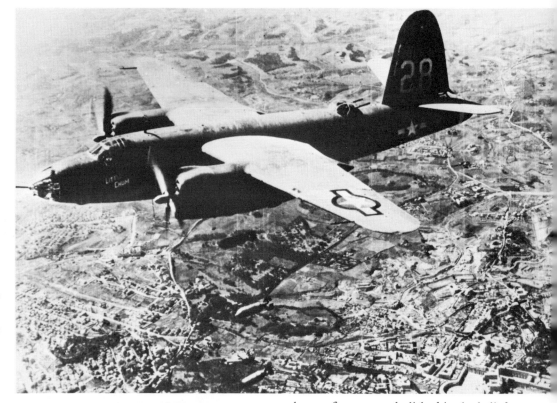

Right: The 320th's *Little Chum*, first B-26B-15-MA, passes over the Vatican to unload bombs on a Rome rail target./*USAF*

Below: Naomi Elaine turns with the 319th BG while smoke covers the Campo Di Marte freight yard, Florence, 2 May 1944. Cathedral and bell tower can be seen forward of left wing./*USAF*

month a set figure was abolished in the belief this affected tactical effort. Also with so many men reaching the 45 mission mark around the same time insufficient replacement crews would be available. Most crewmen went on to fly between 50 and 60 missions before being sent home (a similar policy was adopted for the English-based B-26 units). A few of the original men in the 17th and 319th Groups were still flying and on 28 March, Major Ashley Woolridge, 319th Operations Officer, completed his 71st trip, then a record for any B-26 man in any theatre. The 'killer' B-26, as in England, was now giving the fliers a better chance of survival than any other bomber type, 0.6 per cent of sorties.

The bombing accuracy of the Marauder Wing resulted in its selection to carry out attacks on targets in the Rome area, where cultural and religious considerations necessitated particular care in avoiding bombing errors. In March they excelled themselves with high accuracy on a Rome rail yard and then another such installation at Florence. This smaller city, dotted with buildings and monuments of great historic and religious significance, involved a particularly delicate operation. The Marauders lived up to their reputation putting a concentration right in the rail yards with little spillage, the 319th and 320th Groups obtaining 100 per cent accuracy. A few days later at the Abbey di Monte Casino, then believed to be a German stronghold checking the Allied advance to Rome, their bombing brought a commendation from General Eaker – who had taken command of the Mediterranean Allied Air

Forces at the beginning of the year – stating that the B-26s had achieved the best overall accuracy in bombing of any aircraft in his command.

The North African campaign had brought many former French Air Force fliers over to the Allied cause and their commanders desired that they participate in combat. Apparently it was their choice to fly Marauders. The first squadron, Groupe de Bombardement 1/22, conducted its operational training under the auspices of the 17th Group at Villacidro and after being equipped with bright metal finish B-26Cs, undertook an initial combat mission on 29 March, when 12 bombers attacked a harbour on Elba. Other French airmen were being trained on B-26s in North Africa with a plan to raise a formation equivalent in strength to a USAAF group.

The first natural metal finish B-26s had reached the 42nd Wing in January and by May all three groups had several on strength. The policy of discontinuing camouflage on aircraft, in the interests of economy and improved performance, caused some misgivings, particularly after a Luftwaffe night raid had destroyed several B-25s on a Corsican base. Following an experiment when flares dropped over Decimomannu were found to illuminate the 'silver' finished bombers to a high degree, green paint was applied to the upper surfaces.

On May Day 1944 *Hell's Belle II*, 41-18322, of the 319th Group returned from a raid on Florence railway centre having completed its 100th mission, first Marauder ever to reach this mark. The aircraft's first sortie had been 6 June 1943 and during the early months of her career she had often been damaged by enemy fire, so severe on her 23rd that she was nearly scrapped. There was resentment towards the USAAF's public relations offices when, a few weeks later, magazines reported the British-based *Mild and Bitter* as being first B-26 to the century. Several others of the 319th's original 'big ass birds' were also nearing 100 missions. The prospective runner up, *Duration Plus*, crashed on take-off 13 May on its 99th raid when a propeller feathering mechanism went erratic. Happily the crew escaped. A month after *Hell's Belle II*, *Big Ass Bird* reached the century and on 6 June unnamed '04' became the third aircraft in the Group to do so. 2 July found *Jersey Bouncer* the first in the 17th to reach 100, Colonel Gilbert going along on what was his 82nd operation. Gilbert then had flown more Marauder operations than any other man. On 20 July he led his Group to attack a rail bridge at Ostiglia in the Po valley. A burst of flak crippled one engine; to return home there were mountains rising to 4,000 feet to be crossed before the western coast of Italy

could be reached. In endeavouring to get the ailing Marauder over these the aircraft apparently stalled and went into an uncontrollable spin, crashing into a mountainside after only one man had parachuted. Don Gilbert, one of the most able and experienced men in the Marauder force, who had survived the early misfortunes of the 319th, was on his 94th mission. Two other members of the crew, Captain Elliott and Lt Lynd were on their 62nd and the last of their combat tours. Such were the misfortunes of war.

On 15 August 1944 the Allies invaded Southern France. The softening up, prelanding bombardment called for a maximum effort from 12th Air Force mediums and over 200 Marauders took part. The 319th Group

Top: Teton Special skirts the Alps. 319th BG squadrons were identified by coloured cowl rings and those on this 438th BS aircraft are red./*W. Corey*

Above: A 17th BG B-26C passes Monte Cassino, devastated by bombing and artillery during February 1944. Later in the year, when this photograph was taken, 17th BG was painting the battle numbers on its Marauders red as a further identification marking. /*M. Prusmack*

despatched its largest effort ever, putting a total of 74 aircraft into the air. The pre-dawn take-off cost the 320th Group three bombers which crashed, exploded and burned. The 320th were, in fact, the pioneers of B-26 night operations having flown the first such missions in the previous January.

With a successful invasion and rapid advance, the Marauders moved base again to be nearer prospective targets in France and northern Italy. This time the move was to Corsica where newly constructed airfields had steel plank runways. These were so short that on the opening raid many aircraft could not gain sufficient height to avoid brushing tree tops at the end of the runway. A reduction of bomb loads from 4,000 to 3,000lb was considered but finally Wing Hq ordered that the liaison radio, waist and nose guns be removed and ammunition reduced. The waist gunner was dispensed with and only five man crews flown. The weight saved shortened take-off runs, but after an engagement with enemy aircraft the following month, the guns were re-mounted.

Corsica was a stepping stone to France, for in mid-October Command decreed that the Marauder force would move to support that campaign while the B-25s looked after Italian front requirements. The French had now raised the equivalent of two three-squadron B-26 groups, 31 and 34 Escadre

Right: Planning the Rome mission of 3 March 1944 where the 319th BG achieved 98.7 per cent accuracy on the Ostiense marshalling yards. Back to camera is Major Ashley Woolridge, Ops Officer; on his left, Col Randy Holzapple, CO; and beyond Holzapple Major Charles Robinson, who became mentor to the French Marauder units. Robinson was lost on a transit flight between France and Corsica later in the year. */A. G. Woolridge*

Below right: Brig General Samuel E. Anderson with Lt Col Joseph Randolph Holzapple during a visit by IX Bomber Command staff to Sardinia, 12 April 1944. */Via E. Oyster*

which were to become part of the new 1st Tactical Air Force, making up its medium bomber element with the USAAF Marauders. However, only two of the American groups were to be assigned, the third, the 319th and the oldest group, was to remain in Corsica and convert to the new Douglas A-26, as B-26 Marauder production was tapering off and replacements were expected to shortly become scarce. In the event, A-26 production was insufficient to meet demand and the 319th had to exchange its beloved Marauders for, of all things, its rival B-25s. When Holzapple announced this to his men on 5 October he was met with a clamour of protest. Conversion began right away and on the last day of

October the 319th sadly flew its last Marauder mission, the 417th, only to miss its targets. The aircraft were either retired to training units or passed to a depot for re-assignment to the other groups as replacements. Among the veterans were 15 'big ass' originals with over 100 missions, *Zero Four* having 148.

The 319th did not remain in the Mediterranean area for long. At the end of 1944 it was taken off operations, returned to the USA to train on the A-26 and in July 1945 went into action from Okinawa against Japan. One of its distinguished members remaining in Europe was Ashley Woolridge, who was given command of the 320th Group. In November the 17th and 320th

Left: Rodger Dodger and five other 440th BS Marauders ready to begin their run down the Decimomannu oiled strips. Other flights are lined up behind./*USAF*

Below: Six-plane lift-off by 437th BS after a 5,000ft run. For safety it was essential all six aircraft kept near line-abreast so that in the event of a tyre or engine failure they would not collide with another B-26 when swerving. /*USAF*

moved their Marauders to Dijon in central France and – in military terminology – went from MTO to ETO. Both B-26 forces were now in the same country, over a thousand of them.

It was in the Mediterranean theatre that much of the successful technique for operating the B-26 had been developed. The groups had pushed their average bombing accuracy figure to nearly 87 per cent strikes within a 600ft radius of the aiming point before the weather deteriorated in the autumn of 1944. If in scale the 12th Air Force Marauders never matched their kin in the 9th, the crews had some justification to their claim 'we proved the ship.'

Top: First 320th bomber to the century was this B-26B-10-MA resplendent in the red and white 'shark nose' markings carried by all 444th BS aircraft. Note where side gun packs have been removed. Crew Chief was Sgt. W. D. Rossen. /USAF

Above: With flak bursting above and another Marauder flying alongside, the 17th BG leadship (silver aircraft) with Col Don Gilbert on board rapidly loses height over the patchwork of the Po valley. Only one man parachuted to safety before the bomber (42-96021) crashed into high ground./USAAF

Right: First Marauder to reach the coveted 100 mission mark, *Hell's Belle II,* unloads 260lb fragmentation bombs on enemy troop concentrations./W. Corey

In The Grip Of The Elements

Above left: The 320th BG's *Eight Ball* (a popular nickname carried by Marauders in at least four different groups) shows its 'dirty ass', the result of take-offs from Decimo's rain-soaked 'dirt' runways. This was the first 441st BS aircraft to complete 100 missions./*M. Deavor*

Left: Stress pattern showing on the wings of this 319th BG B-26B-50-MA results from turbulence encountered over Italian mountains./*A. Woolridge*

Below: Fine trails of vapour streak back from the wingtips as *Martin's Miscarriage* speeds over the Mediterranean./*W. Corey*

Right: Probably the most famous picture of a Marauder's demise. 17th BG's 42-107735, '50', was on the bomb run over Toulon, 20 August 1944, when an 88mm shell severed the engine with a direct hit. In the lead aircraft of 95th BS, Sgt Peter J. Holmes had a K-20 camera ready at the flank hatch to take obliques of the target. The result of his quick reaction when '50' was crippled also happened to be his first ever aerial photograph. Two men managed to parachute from the blazing Marauder./*USAAF*

Below: A 320th B-26C rides over a flak barrage. Crew member's head can be seen in the astrodome. /*USAF*

The Technique of Bridge Busting

Edgar Pewitt

When our B-26s began bridge busting, before the first landing on Italy proper, the only opposition came when bridges were close to other targets, such as marshalling yards, or were near the front lines. In the next four months anti-bridge raids increased in intensity. The Germans were forced to do something about it, even diverting heavy flak batteries from other targets, as we found in December 1943 when our formations began to run into flak at the start of their runs against bridges.

Bombing bridges became an elaborate art; a pinpoint target requiring unusual accuracy. The difference between a bridge and other pinpoint targets is the rectangular shape of the former, a factor affecting the axis of attack. Using the length of the bridge to compensate for lateral deflection of our bombs, we might hit a small bridge (under 200 feet long) broadside. Larger bridges we often hit at about 45 degrees, depending on the range or string spread of the bombs to achieve a number of direct hits. But factors other than shape determine the axis of attack such as wind and flak. An upwind approach improved accuracy by decreasing the formation's ground speed so that a standard length bomb run could start at a point close to the target. This gave bombardiers a better view of the bridge during the run. An upwind, or downwind, approach also avoided drift so that the bombsights needed to be set for dropping angle (affecting range) only, whereas on a crosswind axis drift had to be pre-set as well.

A route to avoid flak positions around other targets near a bridge could usually be worked out, but there was no way of avoiding guns protecting the bridge itself. However, over a well-defended bridge, we could send in different flights on slightly different axis. While the gunners below fired on one or more of the flights, the other flights might have an unmolested bomb run.

A number of items could wreck accuracy. There was always the chance of a bad 'met' forecast or it could be wrong on wind direction and strength, resulting in a pre-set error which the bombardier may, or may not, correct in time. Or it could fumble barometric pressure over the target, preventing bombardiers from computing correctly their true altitude.

Another pre-planning item was bomb interval setting. On a 30ft wide bridge, bombs of the lead ship of each element, carrying a bombsight, could be set to fall at, say, 60ft intervals. Wing ship bomb intervals might be set at 30ft. This was because the

Below left: Cpt Pewitt in his 'workshop', bombsight removed. /E. Pewitt

Below: Big Ass Bird and *Twenty Niner* returning from their 71st and 58th mission respectively, an attack on the Pontassiere rail bridge, 7 April 1944. Two of fifteen 319th original 'big tail' Marauders that survived operations, they had completed 145 and 105 missions respectively by October./USAF

wing bombardiers dropped as soon as they saw the lead ship's bombs dropping. The lead ship's string was set to start short of the target, to compensate for the dropping lag between lead and wing ships. The 60ft interval would bring the last few bombs of the lead ship across the bridge. Wing ship strings had to be directly across the bridge, the 30ft setting preventing any 'jumps'.

Appropriate fuses and bomb sizes had to be decided. Generally 1,000-pounders were carried for solidly built bridges and lesser sizes for frailer spans. On concrete bridges the fusing was usually less than 5-100ths of a second, just enough to permit penetration so that the explosion pushed the concrete outward, crumbling the bridge. This small delay was sufficient for a 5-10ft penetration. Steel was harder to knock out; instantaneous fuses were used to prevent bombs crashing

through girders and exploding in the open air beneath.

The actual job of bomb aiming and dropping began when the formation reached its Initial Point (IP). This was a pre-arranged point where bombardiers planned to pick up the target, bomb-bay doors were opened and flights changed from route to attack formation. The route formation was a standard defensive pattern to mass firepower against enemy fighters, but the attack formation had to be planned for each target. It was normally a compromise, since bombing accuracy and flak evasion called for different tactics; nor could the possibility of fighters in the target area be overlooked. For accuracy the ideal formation was a long line of bombers attacking in single file, all equipped with bomb sights. But that would have left them open to flak and fighters. A compromise was

Left: Josephine II makes her diving turn off target to evade flak as a road bridge in the Po valley crumbles. This was another of the 319th's fifteen distinguished veterans./*USAF*

Above: Hell's Belle II pulls away from a successful strike on the Sarzana rail bridge, 13 March 1944. Road bridge nearby stands intact but four spans of the rail bridge were knocked down. /*USAF*

Above: Bombardier's view of Norden M-7 bombsight. Nose gun is swung out of way and retained by a banjo cord while sight was in position. (387th BG). /W. Niezhalski

Right: Nose gun was fed from magazine box fixed to plexiglass. Flexible pipe carries warm air for gun heating. (322nd BG). /USAAF

to have flights attack not far behind one another, using slightly different axis, with sections such as three-ship elements making their own rungs.

This plan got a number of ships over the target almost at the same time, and achieved dispersal sufficient to confuse the anti-aircraft gunners. At the same time it permitted us to join up again quickly after the run to combat fighters. Over the target itself, flak usually kept the fighters away.

By the time the IP was reached and the turn in to the target made, the enemy knew what we were making for, but he didn't know how we planned to hit it. So we went into evasive action, changing altitude and zig-zagging to keep him guessing. Feints at the target were also made. This deception continued until we only had 35-50 seconds left for the bomb run. Then the flight leaders gave a wing waggle and those bombardiers with sights were on their own. Those in wing ships watched leaders closely, to release their bombs the instant the first missile fell from the lead ship.

The most delicate factor to control on the bomb run was lateral drift. With the pilot maintaining the planned speed and altitude, the bombardier could get the range with his sight by dropping at precisely the right moment. But both the bombardier and pilot had to work on drift, allowing an opportunity for either, or both, to over-correct. The bombardier 'corrected' for drift with his sight, but this correction alone had no effect on the bombs until the pilot turned in the given

direction. The bombardier's correction actually was an indication of a called-for correction and appeared in the deflections of the Pilot Direction Indicator (PDI) needle on the instrument panel. Bombardiers were trained to talk their pilots onto the correct heading: 'Left, left, steady, now you've got it, right a bit, steady steady, hold her . . .' If pre-mission computations were right and the bombardier

killed his rate of drift before dropping, he would hit the target. When these corrections were made, the bombardier was synchronised. That didn't only mean that his sight cross-hairs were on the target when he dropped, but that his cross-hairs were on the target and were set there as the plane moved steadily on course.

In combat it was not our standard procedures that went wrong, but the problems presented by each new target. Some bridges were so small, or so well hidden in folds, that picking them up at all became the main problem. Even on the most obvious targets, clouds frequently interfered with sighting. Sometimes an open space over the target enabled bombardiers to pick it up just in time for a short run. Sometimes cloud layers forced us to make a run at other than briefed altitudes. We hedged against that in two ways. One was to set up data for altitudes varying from the briefed altitude by multiples of 500 feet. If pilots dropped 500 feet at a time bombardiers would still have pre-arranged data for the bomb run. But if the pilot actually started on the run at an off altitude, he was instructed to stay there; then the bombardier made a quick correction, noting the altitude and figured how many feet on the ground to compensate for – his bombsight being pre-set for another altitude. Knowing the dimensions of the bridge he could judge the necessary correction by the size of the bridge in his sight. For instance, he might estimate the correction in feet on the ground to be 150 feet. Then, if he was bombing a 300ft bridge,

he would release his bombs with the sight's cross-hairs off the target by half the length of the bridge.

Flak could be more than a lethal or psychological hazard. Even without causing damage the plane could be bounced around, so thwarting a steady run. Once a direct hit not only sent a ship down in flames, but blast from the explosion affected the sight mechanism of an adjacent bomber which dropped anyway on the chance that the bombardier was already synchronised when the upset occurred – but his bombs hit beyond.

On a normal mission we expected to secure a bomb concentration within 200yds of the target, plus a few scattered bombs inevitably straying because of mishaps to individual planes; such concentration rarely left a bridge undamaged. Our campaign forced the Germans to muster expert engineers to speed repairs. In some cases they completed reconstruction of badly damaged bridges within 24 hours – but even that delay to enemy supplies could be critical to the land battle. We carried a few delayed-action bombs to hinder repairs that might explode as long as 24 hours after dropping. Embedded in the ground around the bridge they served as a psychological hazard to workers and might cause casualties and further damage on detonation. These bombs also gave our own crews a boost. It felt good to be playing a comfortable game of poker the day after a raid and be able to say, 'That big sleeper's probably going off right now.'

Above: Bombardier's 'pop gun' with bag to catch spent cases. Hinged door in plexiglass enabled bombardier to reach out and wipe flat 'bomb sight' panel. Armourers utilised the door for getting .50-cal trace into the nose. */Via E. Oyster*

D-Day and into France

Around mid-May 1944 a topic of conversation among flying men at Marauder bases was of a new model, the B-26F. They looked much the same as the familiar B and C models, until the wing and fuselage relationship was studied, for the angle of incidence had been increased by $3\frac{1}{2}\%$ giving the engines a slight upwards tilt. This change may have appeared insignificant, but pilots soon testified to its value in shortening both take-off and landing runs. With comparable loadings, the F would come 'unstuck' a hundred yards sooner than a B or C, while its roll from touch-down cut the usual 1,000 yard run by a quarter. Engineering the change enabled fuel cell capacity to be increased. The extra 40 gallons made little practical difference to combat range because the new wing setting gave the B-26F a slight tail-up attitude increasing drag. The F was also a little slower than its forebears, enough for some seasoned pilots to proclaim their preference for the older types.

Minor changes incorporated in the F model included the re-arrangement of some cockpit instruments and an all-electric bomb release. More important, a mechanical emergency system for lowering the main landing gear reduced the need for a belly landing when the vulnerable hydraulics failed.

The 'twisted' wing was the last major structural change to Marauders, in view of the phasing out when the Douglas A-26 became available in quantity later in the year. Martin at Omaha, having rolled out its 1,585th and last B-26C in March 1944, went over to B-29 production, a move planned many months before when the Marauder's whole future was in question. The extraordinary change in the bomber's fortunes had brought an additional contract for Martin at Baltimore in February 1944, but the 120 being turned out there each month was unlikely to meet the needs of USAAF and Allied operators for long. The Marauders' longevity was surprising; over 60 per cent of those with the groups when medium altitude operations were begun in the summer of 1943 were still in combat units compared to under 2 per cent of B-17s and B-24s.

In May 9th Air Force Marauders were directed against river bridges in northern France, principally those on the Seine, a prerequisite for the forthcoming invasion. These small targets required a different bombing technique from that of airfields and marshalling yards. With advice from Joe Perrin, the bombardier General Anderson had borrowed from MTO, the British based B-26 units emulated the tactics of their kin in Sardinia. To increase the probability of hits, a bombardier sighted for a reduced formation of six or four-plane boxes, flying converging runs onto the target. By the end of the month IX BC had destroyed 12 of the 13 bridges allocated, and damaged the other. Some of the best work was done by the youngest B-26 group, Colonel Richard T. Coiner's 397th, which completely destroyed five. For this show of expertise the Rivenhall-based group dubbed itself the 'Bridge Busters'. In later weeks when Colonel Thomas B. Hall's 394th Group, a few miles down the road, knocked down several bridges, they too called themselves the 'Bridge Busters'.

The Germans, in no mind to have vital lines of communication broken, increased anti-aircraft defences covering the bridges. By mid-May there was hardly any part of the area between the Pas-de-Calais and Paris free from radar directed flak and the incidence of loss and damage rose. The 323rd Group caught a devastating barrage near Dieppe on 20 May bringing down three B-26s and puncturing 20, four of which made single-engine landings in England. The extent of the smoke from the bursting shells led one pilot to jibe: 'If the flak had been any thicker we'd have had to go on instruments to get through it.' Over a bridge near Paris on 28 May ground fire was so intense and accurate that an 18-plane box of 344th Group was broken up, five being destroyed and the rest damaged. Some aircraft were literally blown off target course by the concussions.

Flak damage brought about what was probably the most frightening landing ever experienced by a Marauder crew. The 322nd Group was returning from a Seine bridge attack on 27 May when two shell bursts struck *Truman Committee*. One exploded under the right wing blasting the main fuel cell, the aileron, hydraulic lines and putting a great many small fragments through the bomber's skin. A splinter ripping into the cockpit tore away the main fuel gauge. Lt Frank Remmele was no stranger to such a situation having had more than his share of 'wing and a prayer' situations during 61 missions. Nursing *Truman Committee* back over the English coast he spotted the small fighter field at

Above: Adorned with freshly painted 'D-Day stripes', a 397th Group formation heads for France. Leading bomber is *Seawolf II* flown by 598th Bomb Sqdn CO Franklin Allen. This aircraft was the first 'silver' finish Marauder off the Martin production line after camouflage was discontinued./*Via B. Stait*

Left: A sight to remember. The 323rd BG over part of the invasion fleet on 6 June 1944. /*D. Pepmiller*

Centurians

Left: Back with *Bingo Buster*, the second UK based Marauder to complete 100 operations, pilot 1/Lt Robert Lind 'mits' crew chief Wendell Polonski while the rest of the crew look on. *Bingo Buster* then had a total of 466 hours 40 minutes flying time, one of her original engines, and a record of never having a crew member wounded. Ordnance are M38 practice bombs./*IWM*

Below: Mission Belle wings over southern England, the second 323rd BG aircraft to the century. Dark area around radio room top hatch was made by grease-stained hands of mechanics. This point provided the easiest means of access to the top of the aircraft for repair and maintenance. /*J. Perlinski*

Left: Wake over *Geraldine*. Albert Smith looks on as one of his crew points out the symbol for a truck destroyed by the bomber. Parents of the real Geraldine returned the naming gesture by having their baby son christened Martin!/*USAAF*

Below: Cpt E. E. Curran's *Privy Donna*, one of several 386th BG aircraft to reach 100 missions in July 1944. This Marauder had earlier been 'adopted' (unbeknown to its crews) by a 15-year-old English boy (the author)./*USAF*

Friston, just beyond the cliffs. There was some difficulty in getting the right main wheel to release and when this was finally achieved the flaps were found inoperative. Remmele had no option but to bring the crippled B-26 in for a touch-down at 175mph on the runway. With no hydraulic action, only the emergency air bottle brakes could be applied. They failed to hold the aircraft which coasted across the field at great speed. Remmele saw the sea and the edge of the cliffs coming up fast. Spotting a concrete pill-box to the left, he made an instant decision in an attempt to forestall a plunge into the Channel. Quickly restarting the right engine he swung the aircraft left. The impact was violent; the undercarriage was sheared off as *Truman Committee* sailed over the top of the pill-box, digging its left wingtip into the ground and skidding round to a stop. From the shattered wreck Remmele and crew emerged shaken but safe.

The imminence of the cross-Channel invasion was realised when orders were received to paint black and white stripes around wings and fuselages of all aircraft, a colossal undertaking in the few hours allowed. The job was completed on time and during the early hours of D-Day the Marauders were given the task of bombing coastal defences ahead of the first troops to land on the beaches. It was a maximum effort with take-off in darkness. Led by pathfinders, the 344th Group 'Silver Streaks' went in first and the 386th, the Crusaders, last (this latter Group having the best overall bombing record at this date), dropping from an altitude of 4,000 feet to get under clouds 6½ minutes before the first troops landed. One 322nd aircraft, *Pickled*

Dilly, flew with only a three-man officer crew due to some confusion after briefing.

Thereafter Marauders devoted the majority of their sorties to targets beyond the beach-heads, mainly bridges, ammunition dumps and troop concentrations. Despite the intensive flak an overall low loss to sortie ratio was maintained and as added proof of B-26 survivability more long service aircraft reached the 100 mission mark until, by the autumn of 1944, it was almost commonplace!

The second B-26 to reach the coveted figure had been the 323rd's *Bingo Buster* on 16 May. This B-26C had taken part in the initial medium altitude operation flown by Marauders in the ETO; like *Mild and Bitter* it was sent back to the USA early in June. Third British based Marauder to reach 100 was *Flak Bait* when 1/Lt Horace C. Rodgers' crew brought her safely back to Andrews Field on 1 June. *Flak Bait* and following century-makers were to soldier on, for in mid-1944 so many Marauders achieved this status that it was no longer a novelty. On 4 June *Impatient Virgin,* another 322nd aircraft, became the fourth; on 75 of its trips it had been peppered with flak splinters. During the next few days five other B-26s in the same unit (451st Bomb Sqdn) reached 100 – *Lil' Po'k Chop, Bluebeard II, Pickled Dilly, Satan's Sister* and *Clark's Little Pill* – and other squadrons of the group produced another five before July was out. Early in July six 386th Group Marauders had 100 missions to their credit: *Littlejo, Rat Poison, Bar Fly, Ye Olde Crocke, Blazing Heat* and *Slightly Dangerous.* Within two more weeks *Mert, Seductive Susie, Hell's Angels, Privy Donna, La Golondrina, Smokey, Bomerang* and *Bad Penny* had got there too. Not to be

Twisted Wings

Below and below right: One of the 100 B-26Fs made, on dispersal at Great Dunmow and B-26G, 43-34194, K5:S at Holmesley South. Bombs were stacked around hardstands in the spring of 1944 to speed up loading of aircraft./USAAF

outdone, during the same period the 387th Group produced *Stinky, El Capitan, Roughernacob, My Gal Friday* and *Mississippi Mudcat* as equally distinguished. The significance of many of these names was often apparent only to the initiated, but they endowed their inanimate aircraft with more of a personality than the official serial number. A crew chief and his men had to work hard to keep a B-26 in trim and, understandably, a loss was particularly hard felt when the aircraft had long and distinguished service. When the 322nd's battle damaged *Piecemaker* ran out of runway and came to rest in a sprout field on 6 August, returning from its 99th mission, it is said her crew chief wept.

On 7 July the 322nd Group undertook its third night operation, the target being the headquarters of the flying bomb command at Chateau de Ribeaucourt, northern France. Three Oboe-equipped pathfinders dropped marker flares to illuminate the target, in answer to which the Germans lit decoy flares although, allegedly, these did not confuse the crews. In the clear moonlit sky cones of searchlights caught and held many of the 35 Marauders flying singly. This time the Luftwaffe were on hand and night fighters made 14 attacks shooting down nine bombers, surprising them by coming in from below – a rude introduction to the fact that by 1944 night operations were more dangerous than daylight. Among those shot down that night was Captain Robert 'Fearless' Fry (he survived), something of a legend in the 322nd having made six single-engined landings in Marauders, the first after the Ijmuiden raid in May. In addition to the nine aircraft missing, one extensively shot-up B-26 put

down at Tangmere and never flew again, while the damaged undercarriage of another collapsed upon touch-down. This latter was 80 mission *Geraldine,* named after a six-year old English girl who lived near Andrews Field. Pilot 2/Lt Albert W. Smith and crew escaped unhurt. Smith was another 322nd pilot who was often in a tight spot. On the Group's fourth night mission flak put an engine out of action. Two of the crew parachuted over France but Smith made a safe single-engine landing in darkness at Warmwell. Eight days later he and the whole crew had to parachute over Witham when their shot-up Marauder went out of control.

During July the first B-26Gs appeared at the Essex Marauder bases. This last production model differed from the F primarily by the re-plumbing of the hydraulic system, using the standard Army-Navy fittings to facilitate maintenance and supply for both services – the US Navy having acquired Marauders for target towing. Among a few equipment changes was provision of an auto-pilot, a mechanical means for lowering the nose wheel in an emergency and an improved liferaft. A year previous, when the B-26 force was being established in England, it was discovered that liferafts would frequently fail to release, inflate inside the stowage hatch and explode. Urgent representations were made to have this situation rectified quickly as ditched crews faced the prospect of having only Mae Wests for water support. Lt William Bertsche, a ground officer at Chipping Ongar, took it upon himself to investigate the problem. Experimenting on the base, he found the reason for the blow-outs, re-arranged the release mechanism and devised a concertina

fold for the inflatable raft. With these modifications the trouble was overcome and Bertsche's ideas were adopted by the command.

It was generally considered that the twisted wing F and G models were prone to more mechanical troubles than the B and C, and most pilots preferred to fly the older, faster models. But, in any case, the much heralded replacement was at hand. On 6 July the first of the square-cut Douglas A-26 Invaders arrived at Earls Colne from Wright Field. Others followed during the next few weeks and B-26 pilots who flew them grudgingly agreed they handled well and had a good turn of speed. Also powered by Pratt & Whitney R-2800 engines, the A-26 had the advantage of being 4,000lb lighter unloaded. The chief complaint was the limitations of the bomb-bay in accommodating only two 1,000lb bombs, against the B-26's four, even though the Invader had the capacity to lift the same weight. The A-26s and their crews were assigned to the 386th Group at Great Dunmow for experimental trials where the aircraft soon exhibited a tendency to catch fire and for undercarriage failures. Such teething troubles were to be expected of any new warplane hurried into service – shades of the Marauder itself – but it was apparent at IX BC that there would be no early replacement of the A-20 and B-26 as planned.

The principal advantage of the A-26 was range, a practical radius of action of 350 miles as against 250 of the B-26. From July 1944, with the need to reach deeper into France, the four B-26 groups of the 98th Wing (323, 387, 394 and 397) moved 50 miles from Essex to bases in Hampshire near the south coast. The 387th, the first to move, suffered a tragedy on the evening of its departure from Ongar. Lt Col Thomas Seymour, who had taken command after Caldwell was shot down, was killed in a crash near the base while on a local flight. Colonel Grover C. Brown, who had flown the first B-26 to England nearly two years before, and was currently Chief of Staff with 98th Wing, persuaded General Anderson to let him have the 387th. Most group commanders were drawn from experienced men in a group headquarters and understandably their outlook was usually parochial. Brown had the advantage of having studied operational matters from higher command level and was more attuned to the problems involved in achieving the destruction of a target. He soon made his presence felt – not without incurring some unpopularity amongst those under him. Aware that some pilot-bombardier teams worked more smoothly than others and obtained better strikes, he picked these crews to lead formations, often over the heads of flight and squadron commanders. If this upset the normal pattern of advancement it was justified by the superior bombing results achieved; hitherto the Tiger Stripe Group's overall record was not impressive; now this was to change.

Expertise was the basis of this improved bombing but good fortune still played its part. Perhaps the most extraordinary instance of the latter occurred on 15 August when 36 Marauders of the 387th flew to attack a rail bridge at Auvres-sur-Oise. Old *Booger Red II* (of cable-clipping fame) with 100 missions behind it, had trouble from the outset. The engines were not giving full power but the pilot, 1/Lt John Sivert, decided hopefully to continue the mission. Over enemy territory he could only stay with the formation by reducing the evasive twists and turns. To add to his troubles shrapnel hit an engine and by the time the other five aircraft in his flight had reached the target and dropped, *Booger Red II* was trailing behind too far away to drop on the flight leader's release. T/Sgt Miller Peterson, the togglier in the nose, noticed that bombs were missing the bridge, so he estimated on release point and flipped the toggle switch. To the amazement of all, *Booger Red II*'s two 2,000lb bombs scored a direct hit on the centre of the bridge and broke it apart. Some of the other flights in the formation failed to identify the bridge and others that dropped failed to score hits.

Sivert feathered the propeller on the flak damaged engine and flew home. Thereafter Peterson had to take a lot of ribbing about his 'precision guesswork'.

An attack on a French rail bridge on 9 August resulted in the only Medal of Honor awarded to a Marauder crewman. Captain Darrell R. Lindsey, box leader in the 394th Group, was on the bomb run when a shell-burst ignited fuel in the right engine. Although realising that the flames could quickly spread to the fuel tanks, Lindsey continued to lead his formation over the bridge at Compeigne. After his bombardier had done his work Lindsey ordered the crew to jump. The bombardier offered to lower the nose wheel to give Lindsey a better chance to bail out but the pilot declined for fear the extra drag might throw the aircraft into a spin

trapping them both. The bombardier para-chuted successfully, but Lindsey did not leave the aircraft before it crashed. The bridge was destroyed.

During the last week in August, the four groups of 98th Wing moved from Hampshire to landing strips in the Cherbourg Peninsula and the following month, when Allied ground forces had liberated most of France, to former Luftwaffe airfields north-east of Paris. In late September the four groups of 99th Wing moved from Essex to airfields in the same region, the last Marauders leaving Great Dunmow in the first few days of October. During the summer and autumn of 1944 a great many airmen were returned to the USA having flown far more than the relief mark of 55 missions. In practice most veterans had flown considerably more due to

Above: Dellwin Bentley was a superb pilot and is said to have been the only man to have deliberately rolled a B-26 and lived. Commander of 497th BS 344th BG, he preferred to wear a pair of cowboy boots instead of regulation flying boots./*USAAF*

Below: The Allied beachhead in France saved many Marauder crews whose aircraft were too badly damaged to cross the Channel. The leader of a 397th formation received a 'hot reception' over a French bridge on 19 July 1944. *By Golly* had an engine disabled, hydraulic reservoir hit, and rudder control severed. Cpt Quinn West (right with prop') managed to bring the aircraft down for a crash-landing on a Normandy airstrip where all the crew escaped a fire. There were nine men on board including two special radio operators./*USAAF*

replacement shortages. When the situation was becoming desperate, an influx of pilots straight from advanced flying school arrived – the 323rd Group were astounded to receive 51 pilots who had never been in a B-26! The groups had to fly the newcomers as co-pilots to gain experience while there were some harsh things said about air force planning.

The Pathfinder Squadron fliers had to be in top form, and it was policy to relieve them after 55 missions. For two such crews their departure from the Squadron was a particularly memorable event. Both Richard Ulvested and John Hipp and their crews were original members of the unit. Having completed

tours they were to fly home on 15 October in Marauder 42-96206. The two pilots flipped a coin as to who should take the left seat in the cockpit and Ulvested won. Thirteen men climbed aboard the aircraft, engines were started and warmed up and with instruments checked Ulvested taxied out to the runway. The small crowd of well wishers that had gathered watched and waited for the anticipated buzzing that usually accompanied such farewells. After the aircraft had made its run down the Beauvais-Tille runway onlookers noticed delay in the undercarriage retracting; this was felt to be due to lack of normal co-ordination with two first pilots in the cockpit.

However, the Marauder seemed slow in gaining altitude. When it executed a shallow 90 degree turn to the left, ground watchers knew something was wrong; the engine sound suggested a runaway propeller. Another 90 degree turn and two red distress flares were fired as the aircraft flew downwind past the airfield at less than 200 feet. Watchers climbed on vehicles and anything that would give them a better vantage point of the drama. In the distance the ailing B-26 was observed to make a third sharp turn as if to bring the aircraft round towards a landing approach, but it was then lost to view behind trees along the airfield boundary. Men waited apprehensively; with no further sight of the bomber after 10 minutes everyone hoped a safe force-landing had been made. Then someone scanning the horizon from the roof of the intelligence hut shouted that there was a B-26 on approach. Two more distress flares confirmed hopes that U-Uncle was still airborne. A safe wheels-down landing followed and there was a general rush by the crowd towards the hardstand as Ulvested taxied in.

It transpired that there had been two runaway props – a fault in the energising switch that automatically adjusted pitch to compensate for speeds and altitude. The propeller blades had remained in an over fine

Below: Booger Red II at Ongar earlier in 1944. Men on the wing are her original pilot, Jack Skipper (right) and co-pilot Lt C. L. Syverson./*J. Skipper*

Bottom: A visitor to the 397th BG in July 1944 was Peyton Magruder, Project Engineer of the Marauder design. He was a friend of Lt Col Franklin S. Allen who had flown B-26s in the SWPA and now commanded 598th BS: l. to r. Lt Col R. M. McLeod (CO 596th BS), Magruder, Allen, and Lt Col E. H. Berkenkamp (CO 599th BS)./*Via B. Stait*

On 13 August 1944 an accident claimed two 391st BG B-26s on their bomb run at Cherisy, France. The strike camera of a higher aircraft recorded the tragedy. The low flight was under the high flight at the moment of bomb release and bombs (arrowed) smashed off the right engine of the No 4 plane. In the third photo the severed engine can be seen on the right side of the fuselage, falling away as the torque of the remaining engine pulls the crippled bomber violently to the right. In the next frame this aircraft had collided with No 5 aircraft, shearing off its tail assembly. In the final frame No 5 is going down minus the rear half (No 4 has spun out of camera scan) while other bombs nearly down the lead B-26. In fact, one nicked a propeller necessitating an emergency landing at an Allied strip in France./*USAAF*

pitch angle for take-off, causing engine revolutions to rise to 3,200 yet the reduction in thrust was such that the aircraft could not climb. More power might have produced an engine failure. When Ulvested had tried to make his final 90 degree heading for the runway he found that such a turn at his low height was too risky. So, out of view of the airfield, he had elected to make a very wide circle for the approach. Ulvested's skill and coolness had overcome a very critical situation which might have proved fatal for a less experienced pilot. Strangely, a year before his B-26 had been badly shot up while bombing this very airfield and he had made a spectacular crash-landing in England.

Electric feathering mechanisms did not respond well in damp conditions and were a continued source of trouble. Another engineering problem during the summer and autumn of 1944 involved carburettors. After aromatic fuel had been found to cause carburettor diaphragms to fail on the early Marauders, diaphragms made from new materials were thoroughly tested for the adverse effects of fuels. It transpired that one make fractured under pressure, leading to faulty mixture and sometimes complete engine failure. The trouble was first experienced in June 1944 and had become so common by November that orders were issued to change every carburettor with more than 200 hours use. Another production change on carburettors also caused troubles on occasions – a change from metal to rubber caps on the needle valve brought about a tendency for floats to stick.

Shortly after the last B-26 group moved to the Continent, western Europe was beset with an unusually wet and cold period, the worst in France for 40 years it was said. But for the pathfinder aircraft which accompanied formations most operations would have failed in the cloudy conditions. Oboe was producing consistently good results with bombers averaging drops within 400 feet of the planned centre of a target. Of failures, only 20 per cent could be attributed to Oboe equipment breakdown – most common failures were through operator lapses and atmospheric conditions affecting the strength of signals. By October the RAF had set up new ground stations on the Continent to give the 1st PFF Squadron an extended offensive range. Its activities were confined to supporting 9th Air Division (a designation change for IXBC in August) medium bomber groups, the B-26s of 1st TAF not having this advantage when they arrived in France in November. With all USAAF first-line B-26 units now in the one theatre, the only other Marauders in combat were the few RAF and SAAF squadrons down in Italy. They fought a rather different war.

Close Call

Jack Havener

Uncle Sam always wanted value for his dollar, and this certainly applied to the payloads of his World War II bombers. A combat overload was more the rule than the exception and we regularly flew our B-26s off at 40,000lb gross, when the manufacturer's maximum recommendation was 37,000lb. Every bomber pilot's dread was the loss of an engine on, or soon after, take-off. We B-26 men were almost conditioned into believing that if this happened a crash was inevitable. Confidence was maintained because you hoped it only happened to the other guy. It didn't.

On 12 September 1944 we were briefed to bomb strongpoints at Foret de Haye near Nancy. I was flying *Terre Haute Tornado* with 1/Lt William Hunter as my co-pilot. We had just taken off to the north and were about halfway through the first turn to join up with the balance of the flight on our left, when the right engine started sputtering and losing power. As we frantically clawed the pedestal controls, trying to get some life back into the engine we realised we had a serious problem. Naturally we couldn't gain altitude so abandoned the attempt to join up with the flight and completed the turn to the downwind leg of the traffic pattern, trying to maintain flying speed. When it was obvious that the engine would not respond I gave Hunter the order to feather the prop. By the time I had trimmed for single-engine operation we were still losing altitude, so I gave Sgt John Skowski, our engineer/gunner, the order to pull the emergency bomb salvo lever. He always stood between the two pilots seat on take-off to keep an eye on the instruments. He immediately reached up and pulled the lever and greatly relieved the tension in the cockpit when he yelled out: 'We got a haystack, Lieutenant!'

Hunter kept calling out airspeed as we continued on the downwind leg and called the tower, informing them of our situation and requesting permission to land immediately. In a very cool tone the tower operator came back, telling us he had a formation taking off and could we please hold for a bit until all the ships were off? Hunter replied 'Hell No! We're on one engine just above stalling speed and we're coming in, if we have to land on the taxi strip!' We were so low that we couldn't see the field to our left, but knew we were on a correct downwind heading and would begin our approach turn when we sighted a church steeple just off the end of the

runway. Then pre-stall vibrations set in and I told Hunter: 'We can't make it. Let's land on the RAF fighter field just ahead of us.' Before he could answer the RAF field loomed ahead where tractors were pulling mowing machines across the centre of the grass. How do you decide what to do in a situation such as this? Sacrifice two lives on the ground in hopes of saving six in the aircraft – possibly wiping out the aircraft in the process – or save the two on the ground and try for the good old Stanstead runway.

As if reading my thoughts, Hunter said: 'We've got to make it! Just keep her from stalling and do a pylon turn around the steeple!' I agreed and began a gentle turn to the left with the steeple as my bearing point. Not wanting to lose any more altitude than necessary I kept the turn very shallow; as a result we rounded out the turn just south of the steeple and homed in on it to the north looking for the end of the runway.

It's hard to believe but the rest of the crew swear I lifted the right wing to clear the steeple, dropped the gear and flaps, all in one motion and chopped the throttle over the end of the runway, still managing to unwind the trim to keep her straight.

Luckily, we had consumed enough time with the slow flying and wide turn to allow the rest of the formation to take off and the runway was clear for the landing with the exception of crash trucks, ambulances and the inevitable Group Commander's jeep racing down the side of the runway as we touched down and braked to a half about halfway down the strip.

With my preoccupation in winding out lateral trim I didn't have time to adjust elevator trim on the round-out and can thank Hunter for helping me pull back on the control pedestal to keep us from going in too steeply. The usual ground-kissing ritual was performed by the entire crew as we exited the aircraft and my right arm was already quivering from the crew shaking my hand when Colonel Vance drove up, shook my hand and thanked me for saving the crew and the aircraft. In the next breath he asked: 'What happened, Lieutenant?' I recounted the loss of power and the bomb salvoing and told him we still hadn't been able to figure out why the power loss. He told us to all go over to the flight surgeon for a shot of whisky. Just at that time our crew chief arrived and was looking at the engine and giving me a jaundiced look, so I asked the Colonel for permission to go with the aircraft while our crew chief checked it out to try and find the trouble; this was granted.

Back on the hardstand as the crew chief ran the engine up to full power time and again with no drop in manifold pressure or the faintest hint of sputter, I had the uneasy

feeling that he was thinking: 'Well, another pilot with feather-itis.' The next time he ran her up there was a definite spluttering and loss of manifold pressure. This repeated itself after more run-ups and he admitted that there seemed to be fuel starvation. Subsequent investigation revealed a perforated carburettor diaphragm which prompted a maintenance directive to go out and all engines in the group were checked for this fault. I never did find out how many more were faulty but know that they found some on other aircraft. It was one of those things that doesn't show up on a ground check but would only come under full power load in flight.

After a meal at the mess, Hunter and I and an intelligence officer took off in an Airspeed Oxford to plot the location of the jettisoned bombs. Re-tracing our previous calamitous flight pattern, as best we could, we found that Skowski was right. We had completely demolished a large hay stack in a farmer's field but had caused no other damage or injury. The armament crew went out and retrieved the bombs and our personnel officer made arrangements with the farmer to pay for the damage.

By the time we were ready to take off in the Oxford I had finally recovered from the shock of the experience and had developed a bad case of the jitters, so prevailed upon Hunter to fly the Oxford. Old steel-nerved Willy rose to the occasion and as we were starting our left turn after take-off I slyly reached over and pulled the right throttle back just enough to create a noticeable loss in rpm, yelling: 'Oh no! Not again!' Hunter's startled look changed to a grin as he saw what I was doing and we laughed like idiots, bleeding off plenty of pent up emotions.

Cockpit

Right: Co-pilot flies formation, left hand on throttles. View from radio room. (386th BG)./*USAAF*

Below: Co-pilot viewed through bombardier crawlway. (320th BG)./*L. R. Welch*

Below right: Easy with the right hand. A pilot (Lt Evans) eases the throttles. (320th BG)./*E. Evans*

A Gunner's Tale

Denny McFarland

I came in the service strictly as an adventurer but I'm prepared to admit that when I got into combat I was as scared as any man. The first time we were really under heavy attack from fighters I just froze up and didn't fire my guns. Just a spontaneous action of fear. Really ashamed of myself afterwards. Made up for it later. Fired many rounds at enemy fighters and saw hits though can't say I ever shot one down.

Trained as a tail gunner on B-24s before being switched to B-26s as a gunner instruct-or, I got my chance to go overseas with a combat group when the tail gunner on Lt Mullins' ship went for pilot training and I took his place. Most of my 72 missions were in the tail, although I did fly the top turret several times.

The original B-26s in our squadron, the 553rd, nearly all had the hand-held tail guns. Replacements used the powered Bell turret. I liked the hand-held tail guns best; didn't like the Bell turret at all and don't know of anyone who did. The Bell had a wider field of fire

Below: Original hand-held tail gun position on B-26B and C as preferred by many gunners. (319th BG)./*USAAF*

Above: S/Sgt Leroy 'Denny' McFarland (far right) after *Rat Poison's* 121st mission, when Col Joe W. Kelly (386th BG CO) piloted the bomber and its crew chief T/Sgt Herman Levy was allowed to fly as a gunner. Over the Thames, Levy, in the tail turret, tested the guns thinking he was over the Channel. On return to base Col Kelly, believing McFarland to be in his usual position in the tail, 'chewed him out' for testing the guns without permission. When Levy explained he was the culprit, and in error, Kelly said that that was all right and that McFarland now had 'a chewing on deposit for next time he screwed up.'/*L. McFarland*

and was supposed to give the gunner a better chance of a kill by way of its reflector sight. Like most gunners I preferred the ring and post of the hand-held guns. It gave you a direct line of sight on target and swinging the guns by hand was more natural. In the Bell the guns were placed low and power-operated through a remote linkage. I suppose firing them didn't give the same psychological assurance that you got from really being behind those twin fifties and letting fly.

The ammunition feed to both types of tail gun position was the same and was one of the best in any bomber. Instead of all the clutter of ammunition boxes around the gunner, Martin designed a patent track which ran along each side of the fuselage above the waist windows, all the way from the tail guns back to the ammunition boxes in rear bomb-bay. There were 800 rounds per gun, double that in a B-17 or B-24 tail, and a gunner had to be busy to use that lot. The track was out of the way and with no belts or boxes around the tail gunner there was a lot of room.

Each ammunition track was powered by a small electric booster motor and if this worked too fast or too slow the guns would probably jam. Biggest cause of jams were the link chutes down which links and spent cases were ejected after firing. The links and cases

would sometimes bridge, cause the guns to jam, and were hell to clear. I finally removed them completely from my regular plane, *Dinah Might*. In the original type tail gun position the links and cases fell into a small compartment under the guns and were cleared out back at base. On the Bell they were ejected from the underside of the turret and could be a hazard to lower aircraft in the formation. A point fifty case could smash through plexiglass. Later they put a metal tray under the Bell turret to catch the cases and links.

We were trained to fire in short bursts of no more than a second or two otherwise there was a danger of burning out the barrels. The armament section threatened to fine any gunner who burned out barrels $50 to try and get them to go easy, but when you were in combat you didn't have time to think and acted automatically. One day when our box had made a second run on a target and was without escort we were attacked from the rear by Me109s in line abreast. They made one pass and the fight lasted only a few seconds. When I got back on the ground the armourer asked if I fired many rounds and I said 'No, not many, 50 or 60.' So he took a box, went back under the tail and slid the panel back and around 300 cases fell out. No idea I'd used so many. The twin-hand held guns were fired electrically via a solenoid switch. The switch was on the right-hand gun grip and on the left-hand one was an identical switch that worked your interphone when you wanted to speak. I never could get it through my head that I didn't have to push both switches when I wanted to fire, as when there were fighters coming in I'd be screaming foul epithets at them – and our pilot would be having a hard time getting me to shut up!

There was no seat for the tail gunner in the original type position and a little swivelling stool in the Bell. I used a 50-calibre ammunition box to sit on and that suited fine. A split canvas with a zipper was fixed across the opening in the bulkhead just behind the tail gunner's back so you could cut yourself off from the airstream through the waist windows. I didn't find the breeze that bad and the canvas looked like trouble if ever I had to get out of the tail in a hurry. So I removed the canvas and got rid of it. This gave me an unimpeded entrance and exit and I could move in and out pretty fast keeping stooped over. I'm 5 feet 5 inches and slightly built so perhaps a larger man might have found it more difficult, especially dodging under the two ammo' cans for the waist guns that were suspended from the roof. I practised getting out quickly and if need be could do a back flip and be at the waist windows ready to bale out. There was a

tail gunner's escape hatch on the right hand side of the aircraft but I always considered it too small.

I wore a British harness for a chest pack parachute which I laid on the floor just behind me. Over a bridge on the Seine one day the flak became – as our pilot Dave Dewhurst always put it – 'heavy, heavy and unbearable' so I thought I'd better put the chest pack on. As I reached around to pick it up it was knocked about two feet into the air. When we got back to base I took it into the parachute shop, they popped it and found the piece of flak that had buried itself through several folds of silk. Kept the fragment in my pocket for good luck. Incidents like this made you superstitious. I had a little talisman tied on my gun grips. It was a little ceramic doll a girl in the village had given me. When I went to London on pass another guy was flying in the ship and a hunk of flak came through the side and smashed the doll.

They told us flak was mainly a deterrent, I don't know why, for an awful lot of Marauders were knocked down by this deterrent. With flak you just sit there, duck, hope, pray or whatever but when enemy fighters appeared it released the tension; you could call them every name you could think of and fight back. During my tour quite a few shell splinters hit near me; through the tail cone, in the rudder above my head and once against one of my guns. Dented the gun

Below: Bell M-6 tail turret with canopy raised, showing flexible feed track to guns and armour plate in front of gunner's position. /*AFM*

so much it wouldn't fire and when the lump of flak hit, my hand was really stung – just like when you hold a bat and a ball hits it hard. Funny, as scared as I was of flak I never wore a helmet or flak vest. Tried them both, only found them too heavy to move around in. Remember, we had no oxygen and at 12,000 feet any prolonged exertion can be really tiring. Like most gunners I had a fixation about the safety of my genitals so always spread the flak vest on the floor under my box seat. There was a quarter-inch armour plate in front of me and above that a four-inch thick sheet of armoured glass, only these were against fighter attack. They would stop a 20mm but happily that's an experience I never had.

The view for the tail gunner was excellent, better in the Bell but still good in the original type. I could see down pretty well and even either side of the rudder if I craned my head back. Only blind spot was directly under the turret at 6 o'clock low. I never felt separated from the rest of the crew and I only had to turn to see the waist gunner. Could also see the legs of the guy in the top turret.

The Martin top turret was fantastic and I liked flying that slot. It was pretty close-knit in there, you couldn't move around a lot and the gun were mighty near your head. It was a job to squeeze in and so you could exit fast in an emergency the folding seat

you sat on had a quick release which, when pulled, dumped you out on the floor. A bar was provided to put your feet on. The electrical mechanism was noisy; made a whirring sound when you spun the turret around – and it would traverse fast, much quicker than hydraulic models. You could have fun with that turret on days when we were on a non-combat local flight. I'd spin the turret so the guns were on one side and wait for the pilot to trim the aircraft. Then I'd spin round to the other side and watch till he'd trim again. After a while he'd catch on what was happening and chew me out over the interphone. The B-26 was very sensitive to any movement in the rear of the aircraft. The pilot always had to re-trim when the radioman went back to the waist guns or left them. Normally I'd take off and land sitting in the waist. If for some reason I took off or landed in the tail I had to inform the pilot so that he could compensate with trim.

She may have needed a lot of handling and wasn't the sort of plane to make a piloting error in but she was tough, really tough. Nothing less than a direct flak hit would bring her down. Once saw a shell burst right under a B-26, it went nose up, wing over, and passed inverted over another plane before the pilot levelled it out the other side – a complete barrel roll and it still stayed in one piece!

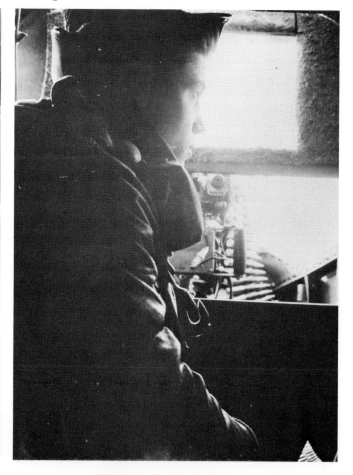

Below: Tail gunner's escape hatch on late model Marauder. Small ring allowed it to be opened from the outside in an emergency. /USAF

Below right: Tail gunner in position with bullet proof glass in front of face, and centre panel of armour plate removed for access to guns (322nd BG)./USAAF

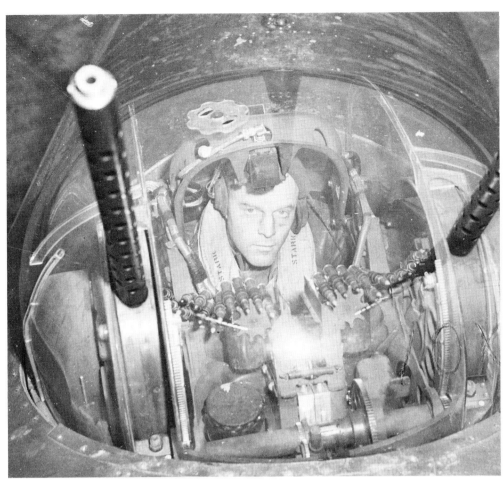

Left: Martin upper turret with reflector sight removed to show ammunition feed in front of gunner. (Sgt Stark, 322nd BG). /USAAF

Below: Only the gunner's head projected into the plexiglass dome. (Sgt Chester Klier, 386th BG)./C. Klier

British and Commonwealth Use

The British Air Ministry, making a careful appraisal of all US military aircraft that could be secured, held a surprisingly favourable view of the early Marauders. While concurring with the concern emanating from USAAF quarters about handling qualities, virtues of high speed and good payload were recognised. Happy to acquire more, 52 B-26As (designated Marauder Is in British service), was the limit of the first allocation and these were ferried to the Middle East where other Martin bomber types, Marylands and Baltimores, were in service. With little prospect of receiving further Marauders until USAAF requirements were met, the RAF decided to equip only one squadron initially and thus allow a sizeable replacement reserve to sustain the unit. The squadron selected, No 14, completed transition with only one mishap – an aircraft piloted by its USAAF mentor, Colonel Flint Garrison, crashed into a lorry that tried to cross a runway.

First British operational employment of Marauders was shipping reconnaissance where its turn of speed was expected to help in evading enemy opposition, and the extra tankage installed in the B-26A's rear bomb-bay allowed good range. The first sortie was

flown over the eastern Mediterranean on 28 October 1942 to gather meteorological data. Subsequently the Squadron extended its activities to the Bay of Tunis where it suffered a first loss, not to the enemy but to misidentification by Spitfire pilots. By the end of the year the Squadron's Marauders were making use of bombs, mines and torpedoes in anti-shipping operations, chiefly in the Aegean. This offensive role was of short duration for early in 1943 the Squadron transferred to the North West African Coastal Air Force, reverting to shipping and weather reconnaissance sorties. Later in the year and during early 1944 the Squadron operated detachments from Italy, Sardinia and Sicily, locating and shadowing enemy coastal vessels until an air strike force arrived. Losses were light and several of the original Marauders supplied were still flying two years later. By the autumn of 1944 the need for shipping reconnaissance in the western Mediterranean had diminished to a point where the Squadron was out of a job. It was ordered back to England to train on Wellingtons for Coastal Command, although only the flight commanders of the original squadron went to the re-formed No 14.

Below: Torpedo slung on a 14 Sqdn Marauder I at Shalufa prior to a shipping strike./*W. Tong*

Right: Single .50 hand-held gun for rear defence of Marauder I. The gunner (F/Sgt W. Hurstbourne) took a kneeling position. Perspex canopy was removed to allow a greater field of fire./*R. Gilbey*

In 1943 Britain had obtained 100 B-26C-30s which, under the designation Marauder II, were made available to re-equip two South African Air Force (SAAF) squadrons, Nos 12 and 24, in Italy. Before becoming operational No 24 and its complement of 16 aircraft was ordered to Gambut in Libya. No explanation was given, and the prospects of desert living sapped morale. In fact the Squadron, together with other British and Commonwealth units, was part of a deceptive force planted in the Middle East to divert enemy attentions from invasion preparations in England. Of the air units involved, only No 24 had bombers with sufficient range to reach objectives in the Aegean, the area where it was hoped the enemy would believe Allied intentions were focused. Even so this would entail a round flight of some 800 miles and with the Marauder's consumption of a US gallon per mile, reserves were dangerously low. These missions were only possible at all because the $1\frac{1}{4}$ hours required for a bomb-laden Marauder to reach the combat altitude of 10,000 feet could be part of the flight out. The defensive armament of the Marauder II was considered good by the RAF, sufficiently so that a formation of six Marauders could be reasonably secure in an area where only a few enemy fighters were still maintained.

Commencing on the last day of January 1944, No 24 Squadron started to fly bombing raids on German military installations in Crete and the Aegean islands off the coast of Turkey. The opposition was much stiffer than expected, with accurate anti-aircraft fire and persistent fighter interceptions. On an early raid the Squadron lost its CO when a direct flak hit blasted the fuselage of his aircraft in two. By mid-February fighter interception was encountered on nearly every occasion and in most the Marauders gave a good account of themselves in long running battles. After bombing shipping in Portolago Bay, Crete, on 25 February, four Marauders were intercepted by fighters; Captain A. F. Shuttleworth seeing an opportunity to reverse the situation, left formation and blasted an FW190 out of the sky with the full weight of the Marauder's forward firing package guns.

Considerable trouble with the Bell tail turret guns jamming was deemed a factor in the losses sustained. Matters came to a head on 6 March when a formation of six bombers was under attack by a dozen fighters for 90 minutes, to and from the target on Santorin Island. Although four of the enemy were claimed destroyed, four Marauders were lost and a fifth crash-landed at base. Only the leader, Captain Shuttleworth, returned unscathed. It was estimated that half the tail guns in the formation jammed, rendering defence

ineffective. After this serious reverse, operations ceased while efforts were made to sort out the gun problem. Advice sought from US authorities led to a check on the ammunition feed booster motor speed, and the fitting of a pan deflector under the turret to prevent the slipstream flow causing spent bullet links to foul the discharge chute exits. There were still stoppages and the problem was not overcome until larger link chutes had been constructed and modified. Because of this, operations did not recommence until early April.

No 24 Squadron stayed in the Middle East until June, operating from Cyprus on occasions. Latterly long range fighter escort was available and the raids were less hazardous. Even so, the personnel were delighted to learn that they were to return to Italy and rejoin No 12 Squadron in tactical bombing. No 12 had begun Marauder operations from Campo Marino on 2 March but early raids were sometimes unsuccessful due to difficulties with the Mark XIV bombsights. The enemy's communications network provided most targets over which the Squadron often had a rough passage through flak. The unit's most grievously felt loss occurred on 13 July when a direct hit exploded a Marauder and brought down another two aircraft, one the CO's.

By mid-summer the RAF was receiving the first of its 350 Marauder IIIs. These were 100 B-26F-2, 100 B-26F-6, 75 B-26G-11 and 75 B-26G-21 models, all incorporating refinements to suit British requirements. The model T-1 bombsight was installed in place of the Norden, shackles to take British bombs, some changes in radio equipment and more portable oxygen units, were the principal differences from those of USAAF B-26F and

G models. Marauder IIIs were used as replacements in Nos 12 and 24 Squadrons and to equip two more SAAF squadrons making their No 3 Wing at Pascara an all-Marauder formation: No 21 Squadron converted from Venturas in July and No 30 was a new unit formed in August. The Wing then had an active strength of 70 aircraft and as such became the major daylight bombing force in British and Commonwealth air commands supporting ground operations on the eastern side of Italy. During the final months of hostilities these Marauders were based at Jesi and in April began using Shoran (a radar device) for pathfinder lead bombing raids.

No 3 Wing occasionally operated against targets in Yugoslavia and Austria during this period, although Yugoslavia was usually the domain of the Balkan Air Force, specially set up to assist Tito's partisans. Late in 1944 a medium bomber element was added in the form of two Marauder III squadrons. A South African unit, No 25 Squadron, went into action in November followed by 39 Squadron RAF the following month. During their brief period of operations these squadrons claimed a 90 per cent serviceability rate for their aircraft and No 39 never lost a Marauder to enemy action. No 25 Squadron was unable to equal this latter record for over the Dugo-Selo to Popovaca rail line on 4 May 1945 – which proved to be its last raid of the war – Marauder HD667 'P' went down after a direct flak hit. It is believed that this aircraft was also the last Marauder with any force lost in action. With peace most RAF and SAAF Marauders eventually found their way to 107 Maintenance Unit at Kasfarect to be 'Struck Off Charge'. They never flew again.

Left: Marauder I, FK111, showing substantial fuselage and comparatively small wing for a propeller driven aircraft. Some wits said that what passed as wings were really cooling vanes for the large Pratt & Whitney radials./*British Official*

Below left: Marauder I, FK144,M, served with 14 Sqdn from April 1943 to November 1944. Seen on a local flight with a crew member's head in the astrodome. /*Via T. Allen*

Below: An Me323 transport shot down by Wing Commander Maydwell's Marauder on 23 July 1943. The enemy aircraft crashed on a Corsican beach and later a propeller blade was retrieved, polished and mounted to serve as a 14 Sqdn trophy./*W. Tong*

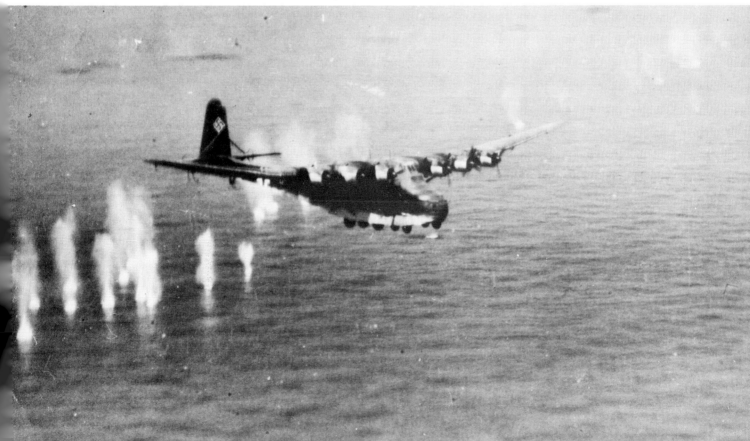

Left: Bridge at Chiaravalle over the Asino river gets clobbered by 12 Sqdn SAAF. The Marauder II is FB 442, D./*IWM*

Right: Blikstem; one of several SAAF Marauders that passed 100 missions, seen with air and ground crew and 21 Sqdn SAAF administrative officers. The aircraft is a Mk III, HD561. It flew 108 sorties between 15/8/44 and 24/4/45./*Via T. Allen*

Below: Disaster at Pescara, 9 September 1944 when a 21 Sqdn Marauder (HD409, F) blew up while a bomb was being fused. Seven men were killed. /*N. McGregor*

Right: Marauder II, FB422, L, of 24 Sqdn SAAF after returning to to base with 400 shrapnel holes. /N. McGregor

Below: The last aircraft lost by 24 Sqdn SAAF in WW2. A direct hit severed the left wing of HD481 during an attack on Ficardo, 21 April 1945. There were no survivors. /*Via N. McGregor*

Dominion Squadron

Dick Maydwell

When No 14 Squadron was re-equipped with Marauders, the morale of air and ground crew improved tremendously since the unit had been selected to receive their aircraft by the C-in-C Middle East Air Forces (Sir Arthur, later Lord Tedder) because our intruder operations with Blenheims over Crete had been so successful. On 10 August 1942 the first nine aircraft from the United States arrived at LG 224 near Cairo and from that day the Squadron never looked back. The Marauders proved to be easy to handle provided they were flown in the proper manner. A high standard of serviceability was maintained with remarkably few accidents, and during one three-month period in 1943 the squadron's Marauders had the best flight safety record of only one accident per 1,560 flying hours in Mediterranean Allied Coastal Air Forces.

In September 1942 the Squadron moved to Fayid and set up camp on the side of a hill overlooking the Bitter Lake. The intensive training of pilots and crews continued under favourable conditions. On 6 November the Squadron Commander carried out his first operational flight on a reconnaissance from Fayid to an area in the Aegean Sea which necessitated flying at 50 feet all the way, a round trip of 1,600 miles taking eight hours. A few small ships were seen, but nothing important.

The Squadron had about 120 aircrew, nearly two thirds being Australians and others including a few New Zealanders and three South African Air Force pilots – truly a Dominion Squadron. In December HQ Middle East decided that the Marauders should be used as torpedo bombers, rather unpleasant news but, nevertheless, all pilots carried out the torpedo dropping course at Shallufa with enthusiasm. As soon as it became known that our operational task would be in the role of torpedo bombers, I instituted a programme of naming each aircraft. To symbolise our integration and future operations aircraft were named after submarines operating in the Mediterranean; hence, *Dominion Thunderer, Dominion Upholder* etc. My aircraft, *Dominion Revenge,* was subsequently intercepted by enemy fighters near Crete and shot down. Lt Young of the SAAF was captain of the aircraft and the wireless operator managed to transmit two panic messages before the aircraft crashed. All the crew were killed except the pilot who was taken prisoner.

In early January 1943 Flt Off Elliot successfully torpedoed a 1,500 ton ship in the Aegean Sea and escaped from the enemy fighter escort. Other flights were made all over the Aegean, the furthest north was flown from Gambut near Tobruk to Lemnos island near the Dardanelles.

On 10 January 1943 the Squadron Commander led a formation of three Marauders in a daylight operation to drop mines in the Burgi Channel, north of Athens. The aircraft took off from Shallufa in the Canal Zone and

Below: Wg Cdr Dick Maydwell's *Dominion Revenge* in desert camouflage./*IWM*

completed the 8½ hour trip of 1,650 miles at 100 feet. None of the aircraft were intercepted. The raid was planned for mid-day because knowing the Italians were manning the AA guns we thought they would be having a siesta, which proved to be the case. As we had to fly the Marauders as slow as possible and at only 50ft before dropping our loads, we would have made 'sitting ducks' for alert AA Gunners. The purpose of the operation was to place magnetic mines in a narrow channel at Khalkis and force enemy ships out into the Aegean where Royal Navy submarines could attack them. I led a follow-up mine-laying operation to the Burgi Channel on 14 February and the results were most encouraging. Later information indicated that one ship was sunk and another damaged. The channel was blocked for some time and must have caused the enemy a great deal of trouble.

In the same week another successful daylight raid was carried out by nine aircraft, three armed with torpedoes and six with bombs. The low-level raid was led by Major Lewis of the SAAF against the harbour and defences on the island of Milos, north of Crete. Two ships were sunk but unfortunately two of our bombing aircraft were lost.

About this time a very unfortunate accident occurred on the bombing range at Shallufa. Half the fin and tailplane of a Marauder broke away in flight and the crew of six were killed. It was deplorable that the Marauders were not grounded immediately for investigation, as soon after two more crashed with the resulting loss of 15 lives, the second aircraft was on a transit flight with nine personnel aboard. Peter Good, a Flight Commander and Flg Off Stewart, the Intelligence Officer, were killed and the Squadron historical record was lost in this crash. It was the saddest day I ever remember on the Squadron. Eventually all aircraft were grounded and a reinforced strip was rivetted up the leading edge of the fin which overcame this disasterous structural failure.

In mid-February the Squadron was ordered to Berka near Benghazi but no sooner were the ground crew underway than the aircraft was ordered to fly to Telergma in Algeria! The 16 Marauders had set off from Fayid to Algeria via Castel Benito, and all arrived at Telergma on 2 March where they were met by Air Chief Marshal Tedder and General Spaatz. During our ten days at Telergma we had no mess and meals were served in the open and officers and aircrew used billy cans, however the American rations were a pleasant change. The aircraft were next flown to Blida, Algeria, and on 10 April the ground crew arrived in Dakotas from the Canal Zone.

Marauders were then used in a different role exploiting their range; torpedo dropping and daylight mining were forgotten. They were used exclusively to reconnoitre coasts south of Naples and around Sardinia and Sicily. Later, when the Squadron moved to Bone, the aircraft were sent on reconnaissance along the south of France, Genoa, Spezia and Corsica. Numerous enemy transport aircraft were seen and some were attacked; the Squadron Commander destroyed a six-engined Me323 and a three-engined SM82 and probably destroyed a four-engined Ju90. Sqn Ldr Donovan even knocked down an Me109 and other pilots got at least another SM82 and two Ju52s. Sqn Ldr Law-Wright also caused considerable damage to three Me323s. It was great sport but the primary object of the operation was reconnaissance, particularly information on the Italian fleet. One pilot flew past a double-Heinkel (two Heinkel HeIIIs built together with a fifth engine in the centre mainplane) pulling two gliders. It is a pity that he did not have a shot at knocking it down.

On 10 June 1943 the Squadron Commander and Flying Officer Johnston were detailed for a cross-over patrol at sea level between Sicily and Pantellaria. This flight was necessary to give warning of any Italian forces proceeding south to intercept Allied forces already on their way to capture the island of Pantellaria. No sea forces were sighted by No 14 Squadron but both aircraft were intercepted by Me109s from Sicily. Flg Off Johnston had six after him and I two! Quite enough. I thought it was going to be my last flight. I jinked up and down and sideways and my rear gunner Flg Off Graham said our aircraft on two occasions only just jinked away in time before the water was churned up with cannon fire! I turned the aircraft into the sun, but I could see one of the Me109s very close on the port side. The enemy aircraft had yellow spinners and I could see the cannon 'puffing' away but our aircraft was not hit. The battle at sea level lasted 12 minutes and but our aircraft escaped.

From Bone the Squadron moved to Protville near Tunis and on 19 July the Squadron Commander carried out an important reconnaissance at dawn over Rome. This was the prelude to a heavy American bombing attack on the marshalling yards later in the day, which caused great havoc. After flying over Rome at dawn, I continued north to Lake Bracciano where my gunners shot up some Italian seaplanes at anchor.

The squadron morale was excellent during the whole time that we had Marauders. Serviceability was consistently good and the double Pratt & Whitney engines averaged 480 hours each before overhaul. In August 1943 I handed over the Squadron to Wing Commander Law-Wright. It was a fine Squadron with a splendid record.

A Springbok View

Tom Jenkinson

Trained on Marauders in North Africa, I was one of the crews sent to Pascara when No 30 Squadron SAAF was formed in August 1944. We were given a Marauder III and flew this from North Africa, landing at an airfield near Naples to re-fuel. One runway although usable was closed for extension. Our skipper asked the Americans if they would open up the runway as we were heavily laden. At first they said this couldn't be done but when told we were flying Marauders there was a complete change of attitude. They thought we *really* had got a problem!

I must admit I wasn't very keen when I was put into Marauders. Most of us had heard of its reputation and didn't like the idea. When we started to fly them it was different, the more I flew in them the more I liked them – I really did. If hit upstairs they could take plenty of punishment and still stay up. Landing and take-off could be awkward on those PSP runways because a Marauder came and went fast and hard. There was a lot of trouble with runaway props, particularly in winter when the electrical contacts were affected by damp. If your Second Dicky wasn't really fast and pulled the prop back into manual you'd go right in. A runaway

prop could be overcome but the Second Dicky had to really be on the ball and watch them like a hawk at take-off.

I put in 46 raids as a signaller/waist gunner, mostly to targets near the bomb line in Italy of between 2-4 hours duration. We usually went in from the sea. The signaller's position was behind the pilot in what we called the well. This was the radio and navigator's compartment separated from the cockpit and bomb bay by bulkheads. Radio equipment was fixed to the forward bulkhead and the signaller sat facing forward behind a receiver. On the route out my job would be to listen for coded messages and pass these to the pilot or navigator. Mostly they passed us a lot of wind change findings which were important if our bombs were not to drift off the target when released. Being close to the engines it was very noisy in the well and you could only talk to the navigator through the intercom. There was bags of room, particularly compared to the Boston I'd previously flown.

The signaller's only outlook on the world was through a small window at head level, even then the view was restricted by the engine. I spent most of the trip here, up front.

Below: Flank or waist gunner ready for action. Ammunition fed from magazines attached to top of fuselage. Post and ring sight was preferred by most gunners./*H. Posson*

About five minutes before we crossed into enemy territory the skipper would tell me to transfer petrol and he would switch to receive radio messages. Four minutes of petrol would be transferred from the outer auxillary tanks into the mains. This complete, I walked along the bomb-bay catwalk, climbed through the rear bulkhead opening and went to the waist gun position. The hatches pulled in and slid up inside the fuselage so the two .50 guns could be unlocked and swung down into openings. Once ready I would repeat this to the skipper on the intercom.

I never saw a fighter and rarely did any come near our squadron. Some of the other squadrons encountered a few on raids and it was comforting to see that the tail armour plate really did stop 20mms. There was no armour at the waist guns and we didn't have armoured vests or helmets. You felt rather naked when flak started to come up. It was necessary to kneel to sight and fire the guns. A cushion was provided for your knees; still it was a tiring position on a long flight. The waist guns could only get fighters coming up from below and to the side of the aircraft. It did afford a wonderful view of the countryside below and I was also issued with an F24 camera to take photos of the target after attack.

It was not noisy at the waist hatches and

Below: Radio operator at Command set. Radio operator's window visible over the shoulder of this 322nd BG airman./*M. Fitz*

you could often hear the crump of flak bursts. You always knew when the bomb doors were opened because of the change in tone due to the effect on the slipstream. It wasn't draughty unless somebody opened the bomb-bay bulkhead cover when the bomb doors were open. Then you got a gale and it was damned near impossible to stand up. It could be cold and in winter we wore fleece-lined Irvin flying suits – there were no electrics. Now and again I would have my moustache frozen which wasn't very pleasant. There was a lot of equipment around the waist position and you could knock yourself out on the ammo boxes suspended from the roof if you weren't careful. The upper-turret was just forward – near enough to reach out and touch the gunner's leg.

When we were back over the sea, the skipper would tell me to come forward again and take over the radio. Before landing he had the other two gunners come up to the well as this was safer for them and didn't interfere with landing trim.

Probably the most scarey thing that ever happened to me was having to dislodge a fragmentation bomb that had caught up in the bomb-bay doors while they were open. Hanging from that narrow catwalk and trying to kick the thing free with a foot was no fun, particularly when you knew it was armed.

We got plenty of flak. On the way out to one target we had a message passed from base to avoid Ferarra at all costs because that morning the Germans had moved in a large number of guns. Coming back the formation went right over it. First thing I knew was our skipper shouting over his radio to the leader 'For Christ's sake weave! You're getting us blown out of the bloody sky!' They loosed an estimated 500 rounds of 88 at us and we collected plenty of hits. As I went forward I could smell petrol and reaching the bomb-bay saw that one of the fuel hoses that ran through from the tanks had a hole and was spraying fuel all over the place. The fragment had gone clean through leaving a neat hole so I plugged it with my fingers and called up the skipper. The Second Dicky came back, pulled the cord out of his Mae West and bound it up with that. We managed to make an emergency base and found 39 holes, mostly big – and this is counting only where they went in; most came out the other side. Three days later we were able to take off for our home station. There it was discovered that we had missed finding a shrapnel hit on the rudder control cable, which was only held by a single strand.

Nearly always flew with the same crew and in the same aircraft – ours was *Capetown Charlie*. You developed a great trust in your skipper: I'd have flown to hell with mine if I knew there was a chance he'd get me back!

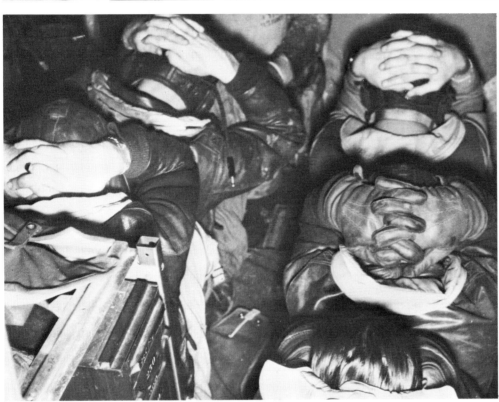

Black Day over the Bulge

The Battle of the Bulge became the popular name for the stemming of Hitler's last great land offensive of World War II. The German plan was audacious: by thrusting out from the forests of the Ardennes they planned to cut the Allied armies in two and reach the Channel coast. To negate Allied dominance in the air a period of bad weather was awaited, and that in mid-December 1944 was exceedingly so. Low cloud and fog cloaking the wooded valleys of the Ardennes also extended to most of western Europe and generally made flying too hazardous to attempt. For five days after von Runstedt's tanks came rumbling out of their forest cover most British and American bombers were fogbound at their bases.

On 23 December a high pressure area moved in from the east to bring brighter colder weather although conditions were still poor for flying. By then the ground situation was so serious no opportunity could be neglected to strike at von Rundstedt's supply lines from the sky. Priority targets were the bridges over the Moselle and western tributaries of the Rhine, to sever the enemy's supply lines. The job was handed to the medium bombers, renowned for their expertise in destroying bridges. Indeed, most of the targets selected had recently been knocked down or badly damaged by Marauders; their quick repair indicating how vital they were to German communications. Among the most important were four situated in an arc beyond the Eifel hills, 50 miles behind the front, at Euskirchen, Ahrweiler, Mayen and Eller. Two 9th Air Division B-26 groups were assigned to each bridge with a pathfinder aircraft in each of four 18-plane box formations, a much greater number than such targets would usually warrant had their destruction not been so urgent. American and French manned B-26s of 1st TAF were scheduled to attack other bridges further south, but having no pathfinder facilities their missions stood less chance of success.

The first mission to set out that morning was briefed for Mayen, 16 miles west of Coblenz. Two boxes of the 387th Group took off from Clastres at 0820hrs and were followed by two more from the 394th at Cambrai. The morning was bright but hazy. Near Bastogne the 387th was surprised to encounter accurate flak from guns the Germans had quickly moved into the area. The second 387th box became separated from the lead by three to five miles and after crossing into enemy held territory was suddenly intercepted by fighters. Four Me109s, sharply etched against the snowy landscape below, came from the rear in climbing attacks, concentrating on the trailing aircraft of the low flight. *Mississippi Mudcat,* on its 150th mission and one of the most venerated Marauders in the Group, took hits on the right engine and tail gun position from the leading Messerschmitt, another's fire ignited the left engine. The bomber's wounded pilot, Lt Staub, ordered the crew to bail out, only to perish himself in the crash of the stricken aircraft. In quick succession other Me109s appeared and shot down three more 387th Marauders, including the flight leader, and severely damaged two others in the 15 minute action. A fifth B-26 shot down was the pathfinder aircraft which, presumably for mechanical reasons, relinquished the lead of the second box just before the enemy fighters appeared and was out of formation when it was struck. This aircraft, flown by Lt W. F. Garbisch and crew, was the first lost by the 1st Pathfinder Squadron in 520 missions!

Despite the air battle the 387th's visual bombing hit the bridge, knocking one span into the river. Intense fire from guns, placed to defend the bridge, shot down one B-26 in the lead box and damaged several others as the formation withdrew. In addition to these losses, two Marauders were so badly shot up in the fighter attack that one was written off in a crash landing at base and the venerable *Booger Red II* was beyond economical repair. In contrast, the 394th Group, 15 minutes behind the 387th, did not see any enemy fighters or encounter accurate flak. It also made a visual run on the Mayen bridge and added further damage.

The P-47 escort for the Mayen raid had failed to appear even when called for by the beleaguered bombers. Neither were the scheduled fighters to be seen when the 397th Group arrived at the rendezvous point on its way to strike the Eller rail bridge, 15 miles south of Mayen. The Group flew on and soon after crossing the battle lines was caught in a vicious flak barrage that brought down three of its aircraft. Cloud and haze concealed the target so a pathfinder run was made. No sooner had the group turned off target at 1037 than the second box was subjected to

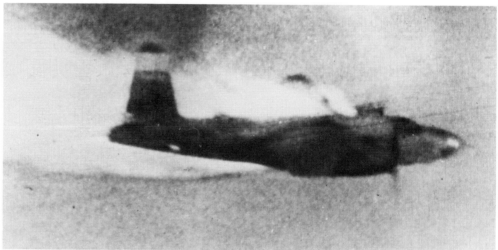

attacks by waves of enemy fighters. In a matter of a few minutes seven of the Marauders had been sent flaming down and although four of the enemy were claimed by return fire only the appearance of P-47s apparently caused the enemy to depart. Of the 26 397th bombers that landed at their Peronne base only five were undamaged.

The day had not started well for the 323rd Group when, during take-off, a B-26 had been wrecked when it hit a Cletrac tractor. Following a few minutes behind the 397th the 323rd escaped the fighter interception only to run into heavy anti-aircraft fire from the fully alerted defences near the Eller bridge. The barrage claimed one veteran Marauder during the pathfinder run while another was so badly smashed and uncontrollable that Lt Eastwood and his crew were forced to parachute near Laon Athies, their home station.

Meanwhile the 322nd Group at Beauvais/Tille and the 344th at Cormeilles-en-Vixen had despatched two boxes each to Euskirchen, 40 miles south-east of Aachen. Again the German fighter control was able to vector an interception when escort fighters were not immediately to hand. Me109s came in while the 322nd was on target approach and succeeded in shooting down one pathfinder and so crippling the other that its equipment was useless. Another B-26 went down before US fighters arrived on the scene. The Group was then subjected to heavy fire from guns ringing the area of the bridge, 28 of the 34 bombers being holed by shrapnel. Fortunately the visual bombing was good and the bridge claimed hit. The shot-up pathfinder was wrecked on landing and another 322nd Marauder so badly damaged by enemy action that its crew bailed out near Sedan in friendly territory.

As in the attacks on the other two bridges, the second group fared better. When 15 minutes after the 322nd had passed the 344th arrived at Euskirchen, enemy fighters were absent and the flak tended to be less accurate, for all aircraft returned safely.

At briefing the Marauder crews had been told that they might encounter enemy opposition, but its intensity and persistence came as a shock both to 9th Air Division and the bomber crews. Never before had the B-26s met such concentrated fighter opposition,

comparatively few interceptions having been experienced since D-Day. Although US fighters were assigned for escort and target support the haze made it difficult for them to locate their charges, beside which several had encounters with Focke-Wulfs and Messerschmitts diverting them from the bombers.

The worst was still to come. Destruction of the rail bridge at Ahrweiler was the res-

ponsibility of the 386th and 391st Groups, flying from Beaumont-sur-Oise and Roye/ Amy respectively. The 386th endured several heavy flak concentrations and at 1135 found conditions clear enough for one box to carry out a visual run, only to miss hitting the bridge. However, the 386th escaped the most lethal fighter onslaught of the day. In the three other missions the enemy fighter control had vectored their interceptors against the leading Marauder boxes in the hope of disrupting the bomb run. At Ahrweiler Staffelen of Me109s only arrived in time to catch the second group but with deadly effect. The 391st led by Captain J. M. Jansen comprised 31 aircraft, including an all-black painted pathfinder. Unable to locate its escort and several minutes late the group pressed on to the target where a visual run was made. Five minutes after bombing, several waves of Me 109s came in from 6 o'clock level, attacking the second box and continuing through to hit those in the first. For some 20 minutes a battle raged with one Marauder after another going down – and at least one or two of their assailants – to splatter across the white hillsides below. Attacks were concentrated on the low flights of each box which were completely annihilated. When the 391st formations finally regained friendly airspace and took stock more than half were missing, 16 of their own and a pathfinder. Eight were original aircraft including *Easy, Sky Hag, Lady Chance, Fifinella Dog* and an unnamed B-26 with over 100 missions each. Another 100 mission veteran crash-landed at base due to battle damage. Only one of the returning 391st aircraft was undamaged and there were 13 wounded men in the others.

Despite the ravages of their numbers, Marauders were sent out again in the afternoon of the 23rd, when even the battered 391st was able to put up 21 aircraft. The targets were troop concentrations and communications where less flak was encountered than in the morning raids. Only one Marauder was lost, and this a 394th machine while bombing a marshalling yard. Down at Dijon the 17th and 320th Groups with the two French Escadre had also flown against targets in their battle area earlier in the day. Weather had deflected most of the formations from their objectives but two Marauders, one each from the US groups, failed to return.

With many hundreds of fighter, bomber and reconnaissance sorties being flown, and the confused and changing situation at the battle front, it was Christmas Eve before the full extent of the punishment meted out to the Marauder groups the day before was fully appreciated. A total of 39 were missing in action, two had been abandoned over friendly territory, six had crash-landed or been written-off as beyond repair after landing and over 120 incurred battle damage. The enemy had put paid to 47, the establishment of nearly three squadrons; a veritable Marauder massacre. It was clear evidence of how vulnerable this and other day bombers had become to the advances in fighter armament and tactics. After this grim Saturday, group leaders rarely continued towards a target unless assured fighter escort was present.

Below: Cannon shell damage sustained by a 391st Group B-26B in the fight over Ahrweiler. */USAAF*

Bottom: Two 17th BG Marauders head for a target over winter cloud. B-26G, 43-34238 was the Group's sole loss on 23rd December.

A Matter of Confidence

George Howard

In the summer of 1942 I was sent to MacDill at Tampa, Florida to work on B-17 maintenance. On the other side of the field was a B-26 training outfit and I hadn't been there long before learning things weren't too happy with them. This was the time of the 'one a day in Tampa Bay' situation and it was common talk that crews were afraid of these airplanes. The Martin people sent test pilots down to demonstrate the B-26 was a safe and reliable airplane, flying and landing on one engine, but they didn't seem to improve confidence. The main problem was at take-off when a prop or engine would go out and the B-26 spun into the bay that lay off the end of the runway. No doubt, the Marauder was a killer.

Although I had been in aircraft maintenance since joining the Air Corps in 1940 I always wanted to fly. In September 1942 I finally got accepted and successfully went through basic training. On the day of graduating as a pilot they gave me a 'dream sheet' which listed thirteen types of airplane assignments you could take for advanced training. Like most graduates I favoured fighters. I waited all day for my turn to be called before the interview board and must have been one of the last to go in. There was no choice left; only number 13 – and that was the B-26! Having been conditioned by the troubles at MacDill I had a decidedly sinking feeling that my days were numbered.

B-26 transition was at Laughlin Field, Del Rio, Texas and here my fears were quickly dispelled. I had one of the best instructors anyone could wish; he knew just about all there was to know about the B-26 and how it should be flown. I guess a lot of this must have rubbed off on me for I was handling it on my own after 18 hours. The Laughlin people believed in the B-26 and had things pretty much under control. In the 2½ months I spent there I never had a problem with the Marauder and came to enjoy flying it. These were the short-wing models and they put in a lot of hours. One was the first B-26 off the assembly line; they called it *Gran' Pappy* and it was still going strong when I left. The later long-wing Marauder was more sluggish and didn't respond like the others. I preferred flying the short-wing Marauder as far as handling went but the long-wing was safer to fly in combat.

After Del Rio I was directed to Barksdale

to join an operational training unit, made first pilot and was assigned a crew to train. We got along and all went smoothly. Early in 1944 we received orders to collect a new B-26B from Savannah, Georgia, and then set off to fly via the south Atlantic ferry route to Europe. By this time I had complete faith in the B-26, but if I was becoming over confident an incident on this ferry flight soon checked that. We were flying the leg from Dakar to Marrakesh in Africa when we came up with a lumbering old B-24 heading the same way. I decided to fly a little formation with him but he was too slow for us. Perhaps I had momentarily forgotten that we were heavily loaded with fuel and equipment. Suddenly, the B-26 began to wallow a little bit so I put the power on and started to turn away, action similar to that taken many times before without incident. Just as I started to make that turn the airplane went into a high speed stall and before I could do anything about it we were spinning. We lost 5,000 feet in about a 2½ turn spin and the last time I looked at the clock it was past the red line and the plane still headed straight down. It took both the co-pilot and myself to pull her out of that dive and I still don't know how we did it or why that B-26 didn't come apart under the strain and stress.

We were all shaken up by the experience and decided to do some gentle turns to see if the airplane had any inclination to repeat this behaviour. We then discovered our fuel transfer pump would not work so we couldn't transfer fuel from our bomb-bay tank to the main tanks, depriving us of the necessary endurance to reach Marrakesh. We decided to land at an airfield near a little oasis town south of the Atlas Mountains. There was a sand storm blowing and it took three passes before we could see the runway. On the third we were off to the left but I wasn't going round again in an airplane that had taken such a beating so I hit hard right rudder and plonked her down. Guess I was a little upset for when I got out of that airplane I said I wasn't going to fly it any more and would walk the rest of the way! Then some of the mechanics on the field gave the B-26 an inspection. Couldn't even find a popped rivet! I didn't believe it but it was true. This was an early lesson on how tough the B-26 was. What the inspection did reveal was a lot of caked-up dirt in the cowlings and control surfaces that we didn't know about before take-off. The airplane had been parked near some dunes at Dakar and a storm wind had blown up grit and rain into the plane. This was a contributory cause of our stall and spin.

They gave us some fuel and we continued our journey. That B-26 was taken away from us at Stanstead when we reached England. As a replacement crew we then went to the training field at Maghaberry in Northern Ireland for theatre indoctrination; then to the 598th Bomb Squadron, 397th Bomb Group at Rivenhall in Essex county. I got this assignment as my cousin was a pilot in the same squadron.

We were one of the early replacement crews, the Group having been in combat about a month when we arrived. The original crews of the 397th mostly had their own airplanes but we Johnny-come latelys, so to speak, were outsiders and tended to fly any of the spare aircraft in our flight.

For experience my first missions were as co-pilot with the Squadron CO, Franklin Allen, who had been an original pilot with the 22nd Bomb Group in Australia before coming to England. I flew the full tour of 65 missions finishing up in March 1945. The average was 3 to 4 hour duration. Some were longer and you could squeeze five hours. Ten thousand feet was the optimum altitude of attack but I've known times when we would follow a Pathfinder leader who kept climbing and climbing and suddenly you find you're at 14,000 feet, no oxygen and straining the old beast to give everything she's got. On a few occasions where heavy flak wasn't expected we would bomb from seven or eight thousand feet – the operation against German communication centres in February 1945 was one and then, after bombing, we dived down· and strafed railyards – the only times I used the side package guns.

Coming and Going

Above: Props 2,400rpm, flaps down, 140mph over the threshold.

Left: Flaps quarter down, 3 degrees rudder trim. On the tower's signal, advance power settings, manifold pressure 52ins hg, 2,700rpm, and away.
/*Via T. Allen*

Our main task was interdiction – knocking out bridges, rail and road targets. Our Group had a good record over bridges but these were often the most well defended targets. Rare were the occasions that we didn't run into some flak, mostly it was heavy. Many times the aircraft I was flying was hit by shell splinters but no one in the crew was ever injured and we always got back to base. You never heard the explosion above the engine noise but you often felt the concussion and the rattle of shell fragments hitting the plane. Sometimes bits would come up, hit the armour plate at the back of your seat and rattle around – that was worrying. The worst we had was a flak burst below our open bomb-bay just before bomb release – you could always tell when they dropped as you felt the plane lift. As a result of the damage we couldn't get the bomb doors closed. The open doors caused so much drag that we couldn't keep up with the formation and it needed careful throttle handling if we were going to get home. There were certain areas of England which had to be avoided and one was London. With our depleted fuel I headed right over the city at about 2,000 feet. It brought us another worry when the guys in the back reported that they could see anti-aircraft crews tracking us with their guns as we flew over.

Pathfinder missions could be the most terrifying for if the cloud cleared and we were still committed to a pathfinder run, then we would fly straight and level for ten minutes giving the flak gunners ample time to get our range. We were never troubled much by fighters. Usually when they did appear, it was a pass by one or two. The exception was the 23 December mission to Eller. That day they hit us hard, knocking down several planes in our group, but I never saw a B-26 go down or an enemy fighter on that mission; there was so much going on your mind closed right up, the only thing you concentrated on was getting in and getting out.

For some reason the Marauder had an aptitude for getting the hydraulics knocked out by flak. There were several small hydraulic lines in the area beneath the cockpit and the shell fragments – which would blast upwards – frequently cut one of these. You could get the gear down but the problem was stopping the aircraft as you then had only the emergency brakes. These made use of an air bottle system but the moment you jacked it the wheels locked solid and peeled the tread off the tyres.

I soon learned that the Marauder could take plenty of punishment and keep going for you. I would say even a B-17 couldn't take the damage to its fuselage that a B-26 could. It looked after you in a crash too. I've seen them belly-in hard, end up a wreck and the crew come out not much hurt, if at all. The R-2800 engines could also take a terrific beating and still keep turning.

Take-off is critical with any airplane because of the possibility of engine failure. If that happened in a B-26 the pilot had to be quick to change the trim or the torque of the good engine would pull the plane into a snap roll and in you'd go. By the time I started flying the B-26 the R-2800 engines were well proven and I never had one fail. A fully loaded B-26 needed all the runway it could get to build up speed for take-off – the longest runway at Rivenhall was six thousand feet but the end still came up mighty fast once you turned her loose and applied full power. We'd fly her off at 150 indicated and get everything tucked up quickly and plane out to build up speed before climbing.

We took off at 30 second intervals catching a certain amount of turbulence from the previous aircraft which could affect control – quite a different situation than that if you were out there by yourself making a take-off. One time I didn't quite clear the boundary for as we were climbing away from the field the flight engineer called over the interphone that we were trailing lengths of barbed wire from the left engine nacelle. As there appeared to be no danger to the aircraft we elected to fly the mission. On return the gear came down and we landed without difficulty. We found that the left wheel had snagged the coiled barbed wire at the end of the runway and about 50 feet had been drawn up into the wheel well.

After we moved to France we were more appreciative of the runways in England. The first strip in the Cherbourg peninsula was terrible. It had PSP (pierced steel planking) and the field was so wet the weight of the planes made ruts in the planks. Miracle we didn't lose anybody in the four missions we made from there. Next move was Dreux, an old Luftwaffe base, where the runways were paved but conditions were still pretty grim.

The B-26 was a good flying airplane in spite of all the tales. True, it had to be flown all the time but so long as you kept the speed up there was no problem. It was all a matter of confidence and once you knew its flight characteristics you felt you could master any problem. In contrast to those early days at MacDill when many were scared to fly the plane, I'd say there wasn't a crew in my group who would have rather flown anything else. We were regularly flying through the most dangerous skies in any theatre of war yet our losses were probably the lowest for any type of plane involved in so much action. We had confidence that no other would look after us so well, and if one is honest that's what really counted for each man.

Crew Chief
Karl Berry

As long as a crew chief's airplane was flyable he was in good shape: when it wasn't and the flight crew kept bitching about something wrong with it, he had a miserable time. Most crew chiefs and their men took a pride in their plane and worked all hours to keep it in trim. The safety of the combat men was your first obligation: it would always bug you to think you'd overlooked anything that might cause their deaths.

All B-26s had peculiarities; but I wouldn't say more so than other types of airplane. I had five assigned to me during the two years my squadron was in Europe. The first was one of the original B models the Group took overseas, named *General Sherman*. Pilots usually named the plane assigned to them and in our squadron, the 557th, many of the original '26s had nicknames linked with that of their pilots: so it's easy to see how Captain Allen Sherman's got this one. I had *General Sherman* for around 30 missions until it took a flak hit in the wing on May Day 1944. The airplane needed a wing change and was in the hangar several weeks. Never did get it back and another ground crew took it over in September. They only put on one mission and it was out of action again. Flak finally finished the ship in February 1945 when it had been on about 48 raids. *General Sherman* always had some problem and gave us a lot of work. Sherman got a new silver ship, a B-26C which he christened *General Sherman II*. When his crew finished their tour other crews took over. On its 26th trip it collected a lot of flak and was washed out in a crash-landing at Tangmere in southern England.

Next I had a new B-26F and, as no flight crew was assigned when it arrived, I named it *Shirley D* after a girl in the States I thought was crazy about me. I could usually pick out *Shirley D* in a formation as she had been given an all-over olive drab paint job at the air depot. *Shirley D* was a good ship and I was sure sad when she took a direct flak hit on that bad day just before Christmas 1944. Several crews had flown the ship and I didn't know the one lost with her very well. You felt bad about the men who went down, but when you lost a plane you lost a friend.

The replacement was a G model, *Shirley D 2nd,* and the best B-26 of all, as she went 52 missions in 3½ months. At the end of the war she was taken away and I got *Mammy Yokum II*, an older ship that had flown around 85 missions with another group. This one became the Squadron Commander's plane. Had a lot of trouble with the radio; they never did get it right.

When we first came to England there were 16 airplanes to each squadron and four to a flight. My plane was in B flight. Each B-26 was assigned to a crew chief and he had complete responsibility while the plane was on the ground. We had good crew chiefs, mediocre, and some that were sorry – and I'm not classifying myself. No one man could take care of a B-26 as many jobs could only be done with two men. There were three of us in my crew, Joe Beaty and Johnny Brink being the others and they could do any job I could do. We worked as a team, sharing the duties and got along fine. Joe later made crew chief and was given *Ole Smokey,* an original plane that was in a rough state. He got it into trim and never once had it abort in 146 missions. Joe was replaced by Luc Langlais, a French boy who got his US citizenship papers in Paris. He caught on quickly – thanks to Johnny Brink's patience.

The crew chief and his mechanics were supposed to know a little about everything, but if we had any real technical trouble we got one of the specialists to give us a hand. There were electrical, instrument, radio and propeller specialists; they worked on all the planes in the squadron as required. A couple of guys did the sheet metal work and were kept pretty busy patching flak holes; armament and ordnance was a separate team.

The ground crew didn't normally repair,

Below: Sgt Karl Berry and *General Sherman.*/R. *Western*

only replace; we didn't have the time or facilities to repair things. Supply had orders only to issue a new part in exchange for the old. This meant lost time, as it was often a lengthy business fetching the new part from supply once the old had been removed – so we built up our own secret store of new parts. When a B-26 cracked-up on or near the base, we ground crew men would strip parts off it at the first opportunity, hide them and later exchange them for new at Supply. On occasions Joe Beaty beat the MPs to the wreck! We accumulated extra tyres, batteries, generators, access doors, plexiglass and in-struments. The instruments were the first things to go from a wreck; the compass and the clock in particular. As all this was against regulations we hid our store in a barn that belonged to a wonderful old English couple who lived in the woods near the base. In exchange we kept them supplied with coffee and sugar.

A ground crew had to pre-flight (check) their bomber every day regardless of whether or not there was to be a combat mission. First thing on approaching the plane we would check visually that the chocks were in place. Then that the main wheel locks were on – these prevented the gear from folding if anyone accidentally moved the gear-up lever. The batteries – there was one in each engine nacelle – were inspected, and if low we'd charge or replace. One good battery could carry the airplane; two poor batteries wouldn't and could cause a dangerous situation in flight as so many components depended on the electrical system. Next the locks on the empennage were taken away so the elevators and rudder could be worked.

The props would be pulled through, that is, we'd move the blades round by hand to get rid of the oil that had accumulated over-night in the bottom engine cylinders. If we

didn't it could blow a cylinder out when the engine fired. This done, two mechanics would get into the pilots' seats while the third stood down on the ground where he could see up to the cockpit and signal. When no one was near the props he'd give the okay to start the first engine. When both engines were running you went through a series of tests. The first thing was to wind the engines up and maintain a certain temperature on your oil. With the brakes set, as you started to give the engines gas and the power built up the plane would shudder and pitch down on the nose strut. The gauges – and there were a lot of them – were red lined and you watched to see that these weren't exceeded. Once the engines had been checked out all movable controls would be tried. While there was pressure in the hydraulic system you worked the flaps, engine cowl shutters and opened and shut the bomb bay doors. We also checked for leaks in the system. When the pre-flight was completed the Form 1 would be signed to signify all in order.

Regardless when a '26 was pre-flighted during the day, before night that airplane was topped up with gasoline to keep con-densation out of the tanks. When, for various reasons, we had to drain gasoline this was saved for washing down the plane, which we liked to do it now and again. The fuel tanks had drains under the wings and every so often they had to be checked. I knew one flier who filled his lighter from these vents!

The B-26 Tech Orders called for inspect-ions at 25 flying hour intervals. So you'd start over again, every 25 hours. When an engine did 50 hours the spark plugs had to be changed. Quite a job as all the cowlings had to come off and they were difficult to get back into place, especially after they got a bit bent. We got reconditioned plugs to fit and we'd often find some were faulty. After 300

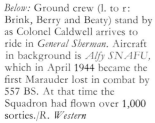

Below: Ground crew (l. to r: Brink, Berry and Beaty) stand by as Colonel Caldwell arrives to ride in *General Sherman.* Aircraft in background is *Alfy SNAFU,* which in April 1944 became the first Marauder lost in combat by 557 BS. At that time the Squadron had flown over 1,000 sorties./*R. Western*

hours there was a special inspection, pretty tough and more an overhaul.

The hydraulics gave us plenty of problems; there were a lot of lines and the connections were given to leaks. Biggest headache was replacing the actuating cylinders. Those that opened the bomb bay doors were placed in position before the fuselage skin was put on at the factory. If it hadn't been for Joe Beaty and his long arms I don't think we could ever have done the job. The cowl flap cylinders were easier to work on but always covered with oil and grease. Crew chiefs made a habit of going down to the end of the runway when a mission went out to watch their planes and see if the main wheels went up together. If one lagged we'd know the pressure system wasn't even. A lagged main wheel could affect the trim of a plane on take-off making it difficult for a pilot.

The B-26 landed fast and was hard on tyres. Changing one was a big job which nobody liked so we began to take an interest in how pilots made their landings. The better the landing the longer the tyre life. I took movies of almost every ship in our squadron landing and showed them to some of our pilots so they could see why they were ruining so many tyres. Some hit the runway several times, or with one main wheel first and then the other, burning rubber. The good pilots eased the main wheels on together and stayed down. Joe Beaty kept an accurate record of one of the tyres on *General Sherman* to see how many take-offs and landings it would go. When they took the plane to the hangar to repair someone ignored Joe's request not to change the tyre and put new ones on. When Joe found out he was somewhat mad and told off the engineering officer in the hangar. Rank didn't mean a lot to most of us. We knew what we were in the air force for and what our job was. When a flight crew came out to the plane we treated the officers as equals. Off base was different; we saluted and addressed them properly.

We were never told much about the outcome of missions and if we wanted to find out if they were successful we'd go to the nearby pub. There would often be a few fliers there and with a couple of drinks under their belts they let all be known. We got a little action on the line too sometimes. Once an armorer was cleaning the nose gun on Major Keller's ship when he accidentally fired a few rounds. The refuelling trailer pulled by a Cletrac was parked directly in front of the plane and a tracer bullet went straight into the Cletrac's fuel tank and set it on fire. Luckily several men were around to shove the plane back out of danger and disconnect the fuel trailer from the Cletrac, pulling and pushing to get that out of the way. The Cletrac burned out completely despite several people, including Major Keller, spraying it with fire extinguishers. When the Major was looking the other way two of the ground crew sprayed him good!

The unfortunate armourer was given the choice of a court martial or becoming the Squadron barber. Naturally he chose the option. Hair cuts were a problem as we had no barber and had to go off base to get one. We set this boy up in a shed in our area and he wasn't long getting plenty of trade. The whole group soon began to use him as he did such a good job. The charge was 35 cents and half this went to our squadron funds for parties and other things. I made him a barber's chair. Took the co-pilot's seat out of a wrecked B-26, rigged up a swivel and welded it onto a B-26 wheel rim for a base. When we moved to the Continent the barber seat went too. There's been more than a few 'hairy' incidents in B-26 co-pilot's seats but I guess this one topped them all!

Below Crew chiefs waiting near the end of the runway for take-off. /K. Berry

All Work

Then perhaps there was time for
some of that British . . . . coffee?
/USAAF

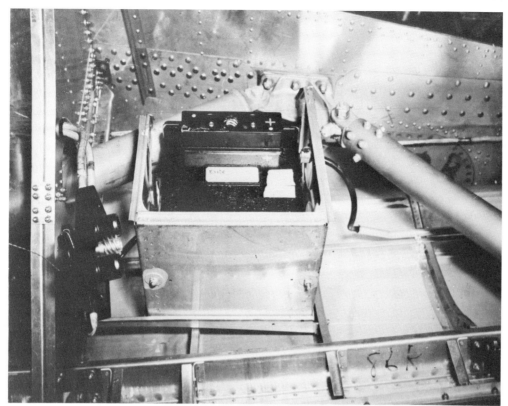

Left: Batteries had to be regularly checked. Each 24-volt Exide was housed in the engine nacelle forward of the undercarriage gear./*USAF*

Below: Engine cylinders had to be cleared of fuel. Sgt George Parks (right) and assistant pull the props through. Note aft bomb-bay doors are open./*G. Parks*

Right: Plexiglass needed regular cleaning. Top turret glazing could be removed and here Sgt Carl Palin and Pvt Karl Sutherland give one elbow grease. (323rd BG). /*USAAF*

Below right: Tyre pressures had to be checked. Cletrac compressor provides air./*USAAF*

Far left: Guns had to be rodded. A pair of home-made steps eased the problem in getting at this 322nd BG nose gun./*USAAF*

Below: The ubiquitous 45-gallon barrel served the purpose for the tail guns of 319th BG's *Rob's Reaper*./*E. Kantarski*

Left: Don Elbey chances his footing to work on the top turret of *Lady Liberty* (323rd BG). /*USAAF*

Below left: Changing spark plugs in winter was hell on the fingers (386th BG)./*R. Denison*

Above: Fixing a rudder could be tricky unless you were a mountaineer. (344th BG).
/*Via T. Allen*

Right: The excesses of North African rain or shine always made engine work difficult. (319th BG, Djedeida)./*Via E. Oyster*

Top: Riveting a fin-plate was easier – with the right tool (322nd BG)./*Via T. Allen*

Above: 'Flak patchers' had to work in difficult positions, especially on wings and tail. (344th BG)./*Via T. Allen*

Left: Changing a main wheel needed plenty of jacking. (387th BG)./*R. Allen*

Top right: For long trips a 260 US gallon self-sealing tank had to be fitted into the bomb-bay. (387th BG)./*R. Allen*

Right: When a prop' had to be shifted a crane was required. In the desert a jib on the front of a truck did the job. (17th BG). /*R. M. Schmid*

Top far right: An engine change also required a crane but the task could be achieved in remarkably short time with practice. (387th BG)./*R. Allen*

Left: Bombs were delivered on special trailers from which they could be easily placed onto jacking frames. (500lb M43s for 322nd BG's *Jolly Roger*)./USAAF

Below: If the weather was rough the Air Force provided a special tent for repair work. Few used it as it usually took far longer to erect and dismantle the tent than to do the job./R. Western

Right: Trolley jacks were used to lift bomb and frame and place under bomb-bay. These are 500lb M43s. (387th BG)./R. Allen

Below right: Tanks would be topped up before engine start. B-26B and C had total capacity of 962 US gallons, the F & G models 1,002 gallons. (387th BG)./R. Allen

Marauder Bases

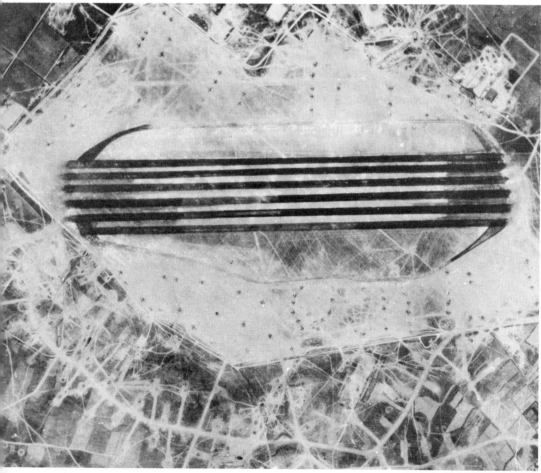

Above: A gunner's view of Earls Colne, typical of English airfields used by B-26 groups. Main runway was 6,000ft long and others 4,100ft, and built in reinforced concrete as were perimeter track and hardstands. The two hangers and technical sites can be seen on opposite sides of the airfield. Camp is in wooded park area where IX BC Hq, Marks Hall, is also situated (to right of B-26B, 41-31895, RJ:L's wing tip)./*J. Perlinski*

Left: A vertical of Decimomannu, Sardinia, taken from 10,000ft on 22 July 1944. The six 6,000ft long runway strips were regularly treated with waste oil to supress dust – hence the dark tone in photograph. An extensive system of aircraft dispersals had been constructed by the Germans but the Americans units preferred to be nearer the runways. 319th BG aircraft are on the east (right) of runways, 320th BG on the west./*USAAF*

Right: Cambrai/Niergnies, France, was a former Luftwaffe base with extensive and well dispersed aircraft hardstands. Most buildings untouched by Allied bombing were destroyed by the Luftwaffe upon departure. Many bomb craters can be seen around the parked 394th BG Marauders. /*J. Cahill*

Marauder Francais

The origin of the French Marauder force was l'Armée de l'Air light bomber units in French North African territories. Although personnel had expressed their willingness to join the Allied cause soon after the Torch landings, it was not until September 1943 that the first French Marauder unit was established for training at the USAAF bombing training centre at Telergma. The basic French unit was the Groupe de Bombardement, equivalent to a USAAF squadron with an aircraft establishment of 18. Each Groupe de Bombardement was sub-divided into a 1st and 2nd Escadrille corresponding to flights in Anglo-American units. Three Groupes de Bombardement composed an Escadre, corresponding to a USAAF group in purpose although having only three-quarters of the operational strength.

As each Groupe de Bombardement completed training at Telergma and satellite airfields, it was despatched to Sardinia and initially placed under the control of the US Marauder Wing. Major Charles G. Robinson, an experienced member of the 319th Group, became mentor and guide to these units, accompanying them on early operations. GB I/22 'Maroc' was the first to reach Sardinia, in March 1944 – as well as a number designation each Groupe de Bombardement was identified with the name of a French colony or province. GB II/20 'Bretagne' commenced operations in May and GB I/19 'Gascogne' the following month, forming the 31st Escardre. The fourth unit, GB II/52 'Franche-Comte' went into action in August, temporarily as a component of 31st Escardre p nding the arrival of GB II/63 'Sénégal' and the formation of a second Escardre, the 34th. This occurred early in September 1944 and towards the end of that month its complement was completed when GB I/32 'Bourgogne' joined the other units at Villacidro. The two Escadre were organised under the 11th Brigade de Bombardement which controlled its B-26 units in similar fashion to USAAF 42nd Bomb Wing once all had become part of 1st Tactical Air Force in southern France.

During hostilities the French Marauder force participated in 270 missions for a total

Entry to the Marauder was normally through the hatch in the rear of the nose wheel well. Leaving in a hurry while airborne left much to be desired. Escape from any of the top hatches was too dangerous with the risk of hitting the tailplane. Forward crew members had to lower the nose wheel to bail out but if the hydraulics failed it was not always possible to do this.

of 4,884 combat sorties during which 14 aircraft failed to return and 425 were battle damaged. There was little contact with enemy fighters, the most serious occasion was over Italy in July 1944 when a formation of Me109s made a single mass pass shooting down a B-26. Only three enemy fighters were credited to the French Marauder gunners in the 270 missions. Total casualties were 102 killed in action and over 50 wounded.

Right: Just equipped with brand new B-26Cs at a North African base, cross of Lorraine marking identifies GB II/20, the second French Marauder unit. Pattern on nose wheel door was due to manufacturing process.

Below: All units of 31st Escadre were originally equipped with B-26C-45-MO models, the last Marauder batch built at Omaha. French roundels were superimposed over US insignia although the white bars (see left wing and fuselage) were not removed.

Right: The French Marauder training unit used 'war wearies' from the US groups. This B-26C previously served with 319th BG and still carries that organisation's white fuselage band. French trainers had their rudders painted in blue, white and red stripes. /P. Gardiller

Below right: The differing low speed flight attitude of 'twisted wing' and other models is well illustrated by this formation of GB II/20. No 33 is a B-26C and has a pronounced nose-up sit compared with the other three aircraft, all B-26Gs.

Bottom right: A B-26C, 42-107786, and B-26G of GB II/52, 34th Escadre. All equipment was as in MTO US Marauders and similar unit identification markings were adopted. 34th Escadre had green bands and battle numbers while 31st Escadre used dark blue. Propeller spinners of all French aircraft were red, indicating their 1st TAF assignment.

169

La Grande Geste

Extensive, low-lying cloud was usually welcomed by German troops on the Western front during the final months of hostilities; for inclement weather offered some respite from incessant Allied air attacks. Sunday, 4 February 1945 was such a day with the prospect that bombers would be unable to continue attempts to destroy the one major bridge over the Rhine still open to Alsace, where the Wehrmacht was fighting a stubborn withdrawal action. Over a hundred guns, including many '88s', were dispersed around this vital link at Chalampé-Neuenburg to deal out deadly punishment to any Allied formation that ventured to attack.

The cloud and mists thinned a little at mid-morning but the overcast with a 1,000 to 1,500 feet base persisted. Banks of grey stratus at lower altitudes added to the gloom over the Rhine valley as the day wore on. At approximately 1630 gun crews were brought to alert by the sound of aircraft engines. Perhaps a sneak fighter-bomber attack hugging the tree-lined slopes? Raid spotters strained their eyes to spot the intruders emerging from the murk. Then between the broken stratus a lone twin-engine aircraft was seen. It turned, and began a dive towards the bridge apparently intending to attack along its length. Cannon and light arms fire opened up as the aircraft swept down just above the trees, bomb doors extended. Four bombs released, exploding against the target and sending up great columns of water after the aircraft had started to climb away in a right hand turn which quickly took it back into the safety of the clouds. As it passed low over the bridge some gunners saw blue, white and red cockades on the fuselage and wings. Others were surprised to recognise a Martin Marauder, a medium bomber normally encountered bombing from 3,000 to 4,000 metres. They would have been even more surprised had they known that the bomber contained only one occupant.

The grand gesture of a brave, frustrated Frenchman resulted in what must have been the most extraordinary combat sortie ever flown with a Marauder. Commandant Michaud had formed the fifth Marauder Groupe de Bombardement, II/63, and led them into battle from Sardinia in September 1944. The subsequent move to beloved France had brought the unit considerable action until the atrocious weather of winter 1944-1945 set in and severely retarded operations. The French units having no pathfinders could only bomb successfully on fine days, and these were few and far between. Aborted missions brought frustration which aggressive men like Michaud found difficult to endure. On 4 February the low cloud over Lyon-Bron had twice caused the cancellation of a mission in the morning and finally operations were called off for the day.

But Commander Michaud had other ideas. Telling an enquirer he was going 'for a walk', Michaud climbed up into his B-26G – '30 Vert' – still loaded with four 1,000lb bombs – and settled himself in the pilot's seat. Minutes later the airfield tower cleared what they thought was a local weather flight as Michaud's Marauder disappeared into the mists. Flying by instruments he set course northeast and an hour later broke out of the overcast near Mulhouse, 180 miles of near spot-on DR navigation despite the constant attention to cockpit checks. Recognising landmarks, Michaud turned east, dodging around patches of lower cloud until he picked out the vital bridge.

If his mission was partly unsuccessful, for although severely damaged the bridge still stood, he was able to make good his escape from the flak and navigate back to Lyon-Bron through the clouds. The Marauder displayed a few bullet holes but had escaped serious damage.

The authorities did not condone this one man raid for reasons of military discipline. Whatever Michaud's purpose; he had taken a B-26 through appalling weather, attacked a heavily defended objective and returned safely to base, all single-handed. Here once again was proof, if more was needed, that the Marauder was no problem for a good pilot.

Mangled Marauders

Above: An 88mm flak burst made a mess of B-26C, 42-107740 of 391st BG on 20 May 1944. Repaired, this aircraft went on to fly 96 missions./*USAAF*

Left: On 2 December 1944, B-26G, 43-34165, T6:H of 391st BG took a direct 88mm hit in the fuselage which killed the top turret gunner and isolated the tail and waist gunners in the rear of the aircraft. Although pilot Lt Edmund P. Dunn had been wounded by another flak burst, he and co-pilot 2/Lt Edwin Armstrong managed to fly the aircraft back to friendly territory and make a successful belly landing – which enlarged the gaping hole./*USAAF*

Above far left: A 20mm cannon shell was responsible for the hole in the rudder of *Idiot's Delight II*. Frank Remmele was captain of this B-26B when attacked by fighters on 27 August 1943. /USAAF

Above left: Apart from this damage – including loss of the complete right elevator – 397th BG's *Patty Kaye IV* also had the right engine put out of action by flak on 25 February 1945. Lt Richard Crumett was able to bring the aircraft safely back to base./USAF

Left: A hole through the wing big enough for a man to stand in and a shattered nacelle were the results of a brush with an Me262 jet on 5 April 1945. Lt Gregg was the captain of this 387th BG B-26G, 43-34190, KX:N. /W. Nieznalski

Above: Debris from another Marauder which exploded after a flak hit did this damage to a 17th BG B-26B-40-MA. Two cylinders were smashed./USAF

Right: Pulling up the undercarriage too quickly on take-off caused the right prop' of this 387th BG Marauder to strike the runway. The pilot managed to keep the aircraft in the air and later make a safe landing. /Via A. Crouchman

Left: There were other dangers apart from flak, fighters, and other Marauders. This shattered plexiglass resulted from meeting a flock of geese while returning to base. Bird strikes were, in fact, quite common./USAAF

Below far left: The astrodome of this 322nd BG B-26B broke loose and embedded itself in the fin. The astrodome was hinged to the top of the radio room and could be swung into position when the circular hatch was swung down. As heads were frequently banged, astrodomes were removed from most combat aircraft flying daylight missions./Via T. Allen

Below left: A 105mm shell passed right through the rear fuselage of the 397th's 42-96125, 9F:L on 17 August 1944, the first known occasion that a B-26 had been hit by such a large calibre shell and survived./R. Ward

Right: Before emergency lowering gear was available, many Marauders landed wheels-up due to battle damage. A single bullet that hit the nose wheel actuating cylinder caused the demise of *Black Fury.* (323rd BG)./USAAF

Below: Time and again men walked away little hurt from a Marauder that was involved in a violent crash-landing. The 319th BG's *Little Salvo* went down on take-off, 28 January 1944, with a full load of bombs and fuel. Some of the 500lb bombs broke lose and two can be seen in front of the aircraft. The Pilot, Lt.Mayben, was praised for his skill in handling this situation. /Via E. Oyster

What's in a Name?

Left and below left: The original pilot usually chose a nickname. The ancestry of Lt D Klimovich (386th BG) and Lt A. G. Van Antwerp (323rd BG) is reflected in these./*A. Van Antwerp*

Bottom left: When *Goatee Hell* had its tail wrecked after 51 missions and *Weary Willie* suffered a broken nose in an accident, 42nd Service Group Engineering decided to join the two 322nd BG aircraft together. M/Sgt Curtis D. Foster was overseer to the job and the obvious nickname was applied. *Half and Half* was unique in that the rear end had flown 160 missions and the front 134 by the war's end./*USAF*

Below: Radio call letter used by this B-26C was Q-Queen and led to *Twin Engine Queenie*. The artwork was extremely popular with men of the 319th BG. Ashley Woolridge (r) and Bill 'Jabbo' Craddock. /*Ashley Woolridge*

Left: Old Iron Sides was the first B-26 B-30-MA received by the 432nd BS, 17th BG and was so named because this model introduced the steel armour plate bolted to the side of the nose for pilot protection (above M/Sgt Frank Davitt, Flight Chief). *Old Iron Sides* had 164 missions to its credit by May 1945. Crew chief was T/Sgt Falstick./*F. Davitt*

Below: Tondelayo survived IJmuiden, 14 May 1943, and a later nasty situation. That was the excuse for the double meaning *Mister Period Twice./USAAF*

Left: The first two letters of each surname of the six crew members made up this one in 387th BG. Later another crew renamed it *Eaglet./R. Allen*

Top: The critical pronouncements of the Truman Committee on the B-26 led to some critical observations on Harry Truman expressed in nose art. The dunce's hat character was not approved of in April 1945 when he became president but by that time *Truman's Folly* had proved the point by completing 171 combat missions./*J. Perlinski*

The Ginnie Gee's **progress**

Above and left: Many US Marauders were named after wives or sweethearts, using the lady's first name and the initial of her surname. *The Ginnie Gee* was an extension of this practice. When the camera was pointed at this aircraft on 14 August 1943 she had 50 missions. On 25 November, 70, and by April 1945 130. Robert L. Saunders was crew chief./*R. Saunders*

Right: The 323rd BG were fortunate in enlisting a pretty WAC from IX BC to paint nose art. PFC Barbara O'Brien touches up *Jolly Roger* which would survive 130 missions./*USAAF*

Below: Rear gunners often added a comment on their end of the aircraft. The rear gunner of *Ticklish Percy*, Sgt Bell, applied the familiar crap term. Sgt Dusty Esquidel made use of his unofficial title./*Via T. Allen*

Below right: There was nothing like being patriotic by giving your 'plane the same name as the President's dog. Lt Bill Kahley also had a Roosevelt dog mascot carried in the B-26C-6 for good luck./*USAAF*

Last Laugh

When a formation of 323rd Group Marauders attacked a bridge a few miles from St Vith on Sunday, 15 January 1945, the weight of bombs dropped by 9th Air Force B-26s since medium operations began in Europe reached 100,000 US tons. This effort had entailed over 80,000 sorties for some 300 aircraft lost. Although enemy defences had taken a bigger toll of medium bombers since D-Day, the Marauders' operational performance was still better than that of any day bombing contemporaries.

Command pilot of the 323rd on 15 January was Colonel Wilson Wood, who had been a flight leader on the first ETO medium altitude operation back in July 1943. This, like practically all other 9th Air Division Marauder raids despatched during the final months of the war had a pathfinder guide on hand. During the winter two-thirds of the attacks were by pathfinder aid and every effort was made to improve this technique. Wherever possible, pathfinder crews operated with the same groups to establish mutual relationships,

while the establishment of the 1st Pathfinder Squadron was built up to 40 aircraft to ensure adequate replacements. Reliability of Oboe was becoming so good that of all abortive raids by pathfinders, only 20 per cent were due to equipment failures.

While 9th Air Division could reach most cloud-obscured targets with Oboe, this facility was not available to the 1st TAF Marauders which were continually frustrated by weather. When the Marauders of 42nd Bomb Wing had moved up from Corsica, General Anderson had hoped that they might eventually join his B-26s under central operational control. Although this made sense during the final months of hostilities when all were flying in the same theatre and from nearby bases, USAAF command politics apparently mitigated against such a move and the two B-26 forces continued to operate separately until the end of the war. 1st TAF Marauders later overcame some of the weather restrictions by the introduction of Shoran, an American development of Gee, the radar navigation device. Like Gee it required two ground stations and had a range of 250 miles. The equipment was installed on the left of the B-26's rear bomb-bay room, housed in a big black box weighing 290lb with accessories. The 320th Group using this aid initially trained two pilot-bombardier crews in each squadron. The first apparatus was received at the end of January 1945, but the 320th had only two B-26s so equipped at the time two trial 36-plane missions were run on 10 and 11 March. The same two 320th aircraft led the 17th Group on its first BAT mission (Blind Approach Technique – code name for Shoran) two days later. The accuracy of many BAT attacks was extraordinary (99.20 per cent of bombs in target area in one) but on a few a complete failure. Overall Shoran gave nearly as good results as visual bombings. In the first five weeks of use the

Bottom: The sun fails to make much impression on *Wabash Cannonball's* white mantle but spreads a strange shadow on Beaumont-sur-Oise. This B-26B served with 386th BG throughout its use of the B-26./*R. Denison*

Below: Dead astern view of another frozen 386th veteran, *Bomb Boogie.* Open bomb-bay doors and extended flank hatch wind deflectors give an indication of the drag they caused in flight. /*R. Denison*

Above left: Dark Stranger. An all black B-26G, 43-34205, used by 8th AF's 25th BG for night reconnaissance over the Continent.

Left: Ground crew removing packed snow from a 323rd B-26G at Loan/Athies, France. The B-26G was the first production Marauder to have full emergency gear for lowering the undercarriage if hydraulics failed, and it also introduced a 'blast blanket' between nose wheel and bomb-bay to give more protection to the vulnerable hydraulic lines in that area. This particular aircraft was wrecked a few days after the photograph was taken./*USAF*

average bombing accuracy for an equal number of visual and Shoran missions was 59.73 and 51.19 per cent respectively. A mission begun as a Shoran attack was always carried through, even if good visual conditions were found at a target. This equipment was also being used by two 9th Air Division A-26 groups; there were, however, no plans to install Shoran in the Division's B-26s and the 1st Pathfinder Squadron continued to use only Oboe.

Two 9th Air Force A-20 Havoc groups had converted to A-26s by the end of 1944. Conversion of the third was delayed because all B-26 production was scheduled to finish in March 1945 and, with the likelihood of a shortage, it would be necessary to convert a B-26 group to A-26s. When early in February the 386th Group was informed it had been chosen for the change, it was resented by the personnel. They had many veteran Marauders, including a dozen flying since mid-1943. One 386th aircraft, *Bar Fly,* had for a long time held the record for the B-26 with most missions, until an engine failed on take-off on its 176th mission, New Year's Day. Lt Altenburger's crew escaped without injury, but *Bar Fly* was too badly damaged for repair. When the 386th flew their last B-26 mission that February, their most prized veteran, *Rat Poison,* with 164

missions, was retained and converted for use as a group transport. The 391st was the only other B-26 group to convert to A-26s before the end of hostilities, becoming operational with them in April. Like the Marauders of the 319th, those of the 386th and 391st that were in good condition were checked over at depots and later passed to other groups as replacements.

The durability of the B-26 was such that

Above: Guard squats behind stacked bombs to lessen the icy blast across Beauvais/Tille. The 322nd BG Marauder is the last B-26G-10-MA made, the block which introduced the tail shell case collector as a factory fitting. /*A. Bennett*

replacements were not a problem during the last months of the war. Losses continued to be low, but flak persisted in keeping the sheet metal men busy on every Marauder field; an unscarred machine was the exception. Some B-26s had collected a prodigious number of patches in their time and occasionally had whole panels replaced. The appropriately named *Flak Bait* of the 322nd was said to have been hit by over 700 splinters by the time she reached her 180th mission in March.

After the debacle on 23 December, very little was seen of the German fighters for many weeks. On St Valentine's Day, when the 9th Air Division, making the most of good weather, despatched nearly 860 sorties to communication and ordnance targets in eastern Germany, the Luftwaffe responded with one of its occasional shows of strength. In a number of aggressive actions, where Me109s and FW190s were able to avoid the fighter escort, a total of 11 Marauders were shot down. The following week Marauders began to experience interceptions by Me262 jet fighters. Now that the mediums were operating almost entirely over Germany they evoked more fighter opposition.

In an effort to cause massive and widely spread devastation to Germany's already badly disrupted road and rail network, Allied air forces attacked with unprecedented intensity on 21 and 22 February. The Marauder groups, briefed for bombing rail targets from 8,000 feet, were to descend and strafe certain marshalling yards and stations, flak permitting. This was the first planned use of package guns for almost two years. Some 14,000 rounds were expended during these raids. Only one B-26 failed to return – hit by ground fire on its strafing run. As the package

guns had hitherto been unnecessary in the medium altitude operations in which Marauders were normally involved, the 12th Air Force groups had removed these on their aircraft while based in Sardinia, to save weight and so add speed. Thus the 17th and 320th groups could not take part in this low level activity.

Prior to the Allied spring offensive much effort was expended by the 1st TAF Marauders in bombing enemy defensive positions on the eastern side of the Rhine ahead of the army group they supported. On 15 March, while bombing strong points in the Zweibrucken area of the Siegfried Line, the 320th Group alone flew six missions and 113 sorties for an all-time record effort by a B-26 group, only to better it next day with 114 sorties. One mission on the 15th was the 320th's 500th. Also notable on this day was the occasion of the Group CO, Colonel Ashley Woolridge, flying his 100th sortie in Marauders. Woolridge had been a member of the original 319th Group that staged through England to Africa and suffered grievously in the early days; transferring to the 320th when the 319th went back to the States. Woolridge was also the first US airman to complete 100 bomber missions in the war against Germany – and this in the aircraft said to be unfit to fly in, let alone fight in. There were other B-26 airmen with lengthy operational records. On the last day of March, Lt Col Joe Perrin, Group Bombardier of the 17th, completed his 100th B-26 mission. Perrin had started with the 320th, been transferred to the 17th to improve its performance, and then to England to fly a few missions with groups there before returning to the 17th.

Below: Most 9th Air Division missions during the winter of 1944-1945 were on a Pathfinder lead as in this instance as *Helen Highwater III* unloads 500lb bombs into the clouds. Yellow diagonal strip on tail identifies 397th BG./*USAAF*

While the airman who had ventured into combat 100 times was a celebrity, by the early spring of 1945 nearly 350 Marauders had passed this mark, almost half the 9th Air Division force; more than 40 had completed 150. Still way out ahead was *Flak Bait* of the 322nd which had a 20 mission lead over any other Marauder in France. By early April in the closing stages of the war, this old B-26B-26 approached the 200 mission mark. Fortune was kind and on 18 April *Flak Bait* took off from Le Culot in Belgium to lead the 'Annihilators' to Magdeburg. Halfway to the target the bombardier discovered a failure in his equipment so the lead position had to be relinquished to the deputy. Not one puff of flak was seen and *Flak Bait* came home without need for patches to add to repair work that had covered over 900 previous shell fragment and bullet holes. *Flak Bait* went on to fly two more missions, her 202nd being on the 322nd's last raid of the war when 1/Lt Warren Langar piloted the distinguished old warplane across an overcast to an oil depot at Schrobenhausen.

Following the crossing of the Rhine in late March, the Allied Front moved rapidly east and for the B-26 groups range became an increasingly critical issue. In an effort to extend range the Marauders did not circle to gain height over their bases, but achieved this by a direct line of flight towards a target while over friendly territory. By late April the targets could not be reached and it was left to the A-26s to carry out operations until the German surrender.

The average bombing accuracy of 9th Air Division was superior to that of any other force attacking targets in Germany during the final month of the war. The 387th

Top: Viewed through a shattered wall, a result of Allied bombing when Beaumont was occupied by the Luftwaffe, *Rat Poison*, the 164 mission B-26B retained by 386th BG after conversion to the A-26. /*USAF*

Above: Cpt William E. Smith put in 88 missions as a bombardier, 61 leading the 386th Group. The hole to the left of the Norden in *Rat Poison* was made by a 'close shave' flak splinter that scattered plexiglass fragments in the bombardier's face./*USAAF*

Left: A 32nd BG B-26G using package guns to strafe a factory at Montabaur, Germany on 22 February 1945. First rounds smash up the tree tops!/*USAF*

183

Right: The *Draggin Lady* of 394th BG rides over Haltean flak, 22 March 1945. The Group identity marking was a white diagonal band but on this B-26G a new 'silver' fin and rudder have been installed and the marking signified by two black lines. /USAAF

Below: Flak and fighters gave Marauders a hard time on St Valentines Day, 1945. This 323rd BG aircraft (42-107613, YU:S) appears doomed as flames stream back from fuel tanks but miraculously the fire burned out. /USAAF

Below right: A direct hit in the aft bomb-bay killed the turret gunner and cut *Vosne Ramanee* in two over the Karlsruhe area, 14 February 1945. Three men parachuted from the tail half, and the co-pilot from the front section. The bombardier and Commandant Roland of GB I/32, the pilot, were unable to escape. /USAAF

Group's average accuracy of nearly 90 per cent within 2,000 feet of the aiming point and 85 per cent within 1,000 feet far exceeded that of any other B-26 group, upholding Colonel Grover Brown's exacting measures.

During the last few missions flown Me262 jets made several attempts to intercept Marauders; successfully on 20 April when about 15 shot down three 323rd Group aircraft, caused another to be written off and slightly damaged ten. Group gunners claimed two of the Me262s. It was the 323rd, together with the 344th, that flew the last 9th Air Division bombing sorties on 25 April. Again jets attempted to attack but were driven off by the escort. On the following day the Marauders of 1st TAF flew their last missions against German targets. The 17th Group,

oldest of all B-26 groups, on its 598th mission, was briefed to hit Lechfeld, an Me262 base. The jets, however, were not all on the ground, and at Staffel strength attacked the 17th while still some ten minutes from their target. In the ensuing fight three B-26s were shot down, the last US B-26s lost by enemy action, and another was badly damaged. For the 17th Group, 'Daddy of Them All', as they dubbed themselves, the final days of combat brought the heaviest losses for some time. Only two days before, two of three B-26s forming a screening force had been shot down by Me262s. The missions of 26 April also saw the 320th Group's deputy commander, Lt Col Lawrence J. Hayward, become the third Marauder man to complete 100 missions. He had flown all his missions

184

Left centre: Colonel Ashley Woolridge after becoming the first man to fly 100 bombing missions in a Marauder, 15 March 1945. This aircraft 43-34257, '10', was the first fitted with Shoran in 320th BG, and after this mission was named *Clearfield*, Woolridge's home town. Badge is insignia of 441st BS./*A. Woolridge*

Left: Lt Col Joe Perrin, bombardier extraordinary, struts out after flying his 100th mission. By the end of the war Perrin had completed 101 combat missions and seven coastal patrols in B-26's. His A-2 jacket badge is that of 17th BG./*USAAF*

with the same group during two operational tours extending from Africa to Germany. At the end of hostilities Col Ashley Woolridge had completed 106 operations over enemy territory and Lt Col Joe Perrin 101.

The last Marauder missions of the war were undertaken on 30 April and 1 May 1945 to the Ile d'Oléron, an island guarding the approaches to Bordeaux where a German garrison was still holding out. The missions, to 'soften' defences prior to an assault by French ground forces were flown by the 17th 320th Groups using Shoran and achieving extreme accuracy. French B-26s of 1st TAF having no Shoran guidance were unable to participate.

With peace some Marauder groups moved into Germany; the three youngest, 344th, 394th and 397th, were designated part of the occupational forces, the rest hopefully to await orders to return to the USA. With production completed and phasing out commenced, there was no point in flying B-26s back to America as with most other multi-engine types. Many of the best were bestowed on the French, others went to the three occupational groups and the rest to storage or to be broken up for salvage. It appears the USAAF could not get rid of the Marauder quickly enough and before the end of 1945 the last surviving units were withdrawn, the B-26s being ferried into the Landsburg storage depot in Germany. Here the most ironic twist in the story of the Marauder was enacted. Some 'useful' equipment was removed, an explosive charge put in the fuselage and then detonated by US Army engineers.

German salvage gangs then broke up the remains and carted it away as scrap to revitalise German industry – which a few months before the Marauders helped to destroy. By February 1946 there were no active US Marauder units in Europe and by the end of the year it had all but been struck off the USAAF inventory. The French Force was reduced to two escadre in 1946, and soon afterwards the B-26 was discarded altogether. The final snub to the Martin Marauder came when some unfeeling bureaucrat in Washington decided to redesignate the A-26 as B-26.

Yet the record of the Marauder was outstanding; its bombing accuracy in Europe and the Mediterranean was overall the most accurate achieved by medium or high-altitude bombing; its longevity and durability gave Uncle Sam as good a value as he got from any of his World War II warplanes.

The Marauder, the most maligned aircraft of its day, would still have the last laugh on the scene. Not all the combat Marauders were blown to pieces on the airfields of their crews' former enemy. At the end of hostilities the makers of the plane managed to arrange with the USAAF for the veteran *Flak Bait* to be dissembled and shipped back to the United States. Subsequently it was placed in the Smithsonian Museum collection at Washington DC. So it happens that the only surviving representative of the USAAF's vast bomber fleets with an extended combat record is a Martin Marauder! A fitting representative too, for no other individual Allied medium or heavy bomber flying in the dangerous sky over Europe completed so many operations.

Left: Chipped and scarred, old *Flak Bait* flies her 200th mission; piloted by Cpt William G. Fort (85 missions) with Col John S. Samuel (71 missions), 322nd BG CO as co-pilot. Despatched as leadship, no nose gun was installed to give bombardier more room./*USAF*

Right: 17th BG unloads over Ile D'Oleron during Shoran led mission of 2 May 1945. This was Group's 600th mission. The 600 operations entailed 57,000 combat flying hours, 12,700 individual aircraft sorties, and 18,000 tons of bombs./*USAF*

Champions

Above: Scoreboard of Marauder believed to have the most missions with 17th BG. A 95th BS aircraft, it flew 167./*S. Wherry*

Above right: Mean Young 'Un, a B-26B-10-MA of 443rd BG, was top 320th BG Marauder with 163 missions. (*O'Riley's Daughter* had more, 165, but only 56 were flown with 320th BG). /*J. Johnston*

Left: The famous *Flak Bait* and crew at Le Culot, Belgium, April 1945./*Via P. Dole*

Right: Five By Five and T/Sgt George Corwin who sent her on 188 sorties without once incurring a turnback for mechanical reasons. Believed runner-up to *Flak Bait* as B-26 with most missions, this B-26B was named by Roger Ray, its original pilot./*Via A. Crouchman*

Slaughter At Landsberg

Left: Hundreds of unwanted Marauders await their fate on German soil./*USAF*

Centre left: A few miles from the prison where 'the joker who started it all' conceived 'Mein Kampf', *Heaven Can Wait*, ex-344th BG, stands primed with 20lb of TNT, her waiting nearly over./*USAF*

Below: Framed between two deceased kin, the bomber – that had cost $212,932 to build – is blasted to scrap./*USAF*

Right: A US Army fireman hoses down flames in the wreckage and soon German salvage teams will move in to carry off the remains. *Heaven Can Wait* survived 99 bombing raids./*USAF*

Below right: Like so many squashed flies, the corpses of the aircraft once called *Baltimore Whore, Flying Prostitute, Widowmaker, Winged Coffin, Marter Murderer, One-Way Ticket*, and the like. Yet the painted record on their noses bore witness to their remarkable record. In terms of operational achievement and endurance the Marauder probably gave the USAAF better value than any other bomber./*USAF*

Marauder Index

Individual Marauders featured in this book with call number (serial), battle letters or numbers (where applicable), units of assignment (where applicable), and page number.

Slightly Dangerous	134941,RG:D	552BS,386BG	110
Smokey	131667,RU:N	554BS,386BG	64
SNAFU	117751	439BS,319BG	31
Son of Satan	131613,YA:Y	555BS,386BG	65
Sourpuss	05213	19BS,22BG	17, 25
Stinky	131686,FW:B	556BS,387BG	111
SUSFU	117754	439BS,319BG	31
Suzy Q		69BS,38 BG	27
Swamp Chicken	135000,YU:R	455BS,323BG	85, 86, 87
Sweet Sue	118201,88	432BS,17BG	93
Tail End Charlie	48654		14
Terre Haute Tornado	295906,71:H	497BS,344BG	118, 190
Teton Special	2107563,45	438BS,319BG	95
Texas Tarantula	118284,RU:M	554BS,387BG	64, 65 ,71
Thunder	117869	34BS,17BG	32
Ticklish Percy	134727,VT:O	453BS,323BG	59, 119
Tondalayo	117995,DR:T	452BS,322BG	49, 177
Too Much of Texas	117985,DR:Q	452BS,322BG	48, 49
The Trail Blazer	131903,IH:T	1st PFS	75
Truman Committee	131788,PN:A	449BS,322BG	79, 106, 110
Truman's Folly	131983,VT:D	453BS,323BG	178
Twenty Niner	131580, 29	438BS,319BG	101
Twin Engine Queenie	134895, 76	440BS,319BG	176
Two Way Ticket	131602,AN:T	553BS,386BG	63, 65
Vosne Romanee	62	GB 1/32	184
Wabash Cannonball	131610,AN:P	553BS,386BG	180
Weary Willie		322BG	176
Winnie	131617,RG:A	552BS,386BG	65
The Wolf	131597,AN:V	553BS,386BG	65, 66
Wolf Pack II	134865,VT:X	453BS,323BG	82
Ye Olde Crocke	131755,RU:F	554BS,386BG	110
Zero Four	134868, 04	437BS,319BG	97

Marauder Men

191

Right: O'Riley's Daughter sets out on one of her first raids after transfer from the 319th to 320th BG. At the end of hostilities this Marauder had completed 165 missions. Togglier can be seen in the nose with plenty of flak vests spread in front of him. Barometric pressure instrument protrudes through nose flap – just forward of dark circular patch (painted out 437th BS insignia). Of the three other aircraft visible, a B-26G retains one set of package guns while the other aircraft have none./B. *West*